SOLDIER

OF THE

YEAR

SOLDIER
OF THE
YEAR

JOSÉ ZUNIGA

POCKET BOOKS
New York   London   Toronto   Sydney   Tokyo   Singapore

The author gratefully acknowledges the following sources for use of these photographs: 1. Raquel V. Zuniga; 2. collection of José Zuniga; 3. Salvador Zuniga; 4. Salvador Zuniga; 5. Salvador Zuniga; 6. collection of José Zuniga; 7. Raquel V. Zuniga; 8. collection of José Zuniga; 9. collection of José Zuniga; 10. collection of José Zuniga; 11. Jeff Philips; 12. collection of José Zuniga; 13.photo by José Zuniga; 14. Dave Falik; 15. Laurie Falik; 16. Dave Falik; 17. Dave Falik; 18. Laurie Falik; 19. Dave Falik; 20. Dave Falik; 21. Dave Falik; 22. Laurie Falik; 23. Dave Falik; 24. Joëlle Charlot; 25. Dave Falik; 26. Dave Falik; 27. Laurie Falik; 28. Hilary Nichols; 29. collection of José Zuniga; 30. Laurie Falik; 31. collection of José Zuniga

POCKET BOOKS, a division of Simon & Schuster Inc.
1230 Avenue of the Americas, New York, NY 10020

Library of Congress Cataloging-in-Publication Number: 94-67227

ISBN: 0-671-88814-5   *95 - 111*

First Pocket Books hardcover printing October 1994

10   9   8   7   6   5   4   3   2   1

POCKET and colophon are registered trademarks of
Simon & Schuster Inc.

Printed in the U.S.A.

To my gay brothers and sisters, who from morning to night have the vim and the will and the courage to fight—the courage to love and to learn, to hope and to live

ACKNOWLEDGMENTS

WITH GRATEFUL ACKNOWLEDGMENT, I LIST THE NAMES OF those—loved ones and friends, strangers as well as enemies—who have enabled me to discover who I am and thus inspired me to write this book. I thank my parents, Salvador and Raquel Zuniga, to whom I owe more than my existence; my longtime companions Dave and Laurie Falik, who fortified me against the dissolution of myself; Dave's parents, Louis and Marilynn Falik, who covered me with a mantle of family warmth when, unfortunately, my own parents could not; my agent, George Greenfield, whose guidance in matters foreign to me was indispensable; and, finally, my editor at Pocket Books, Thomas Miller, whose confidence in and support for a neophyte author I hope he deems well rewarded.

At the risk of neglecting a name, my gratitude to the following: Elizabeth Birch, Robert Bray, Margarethe Cammermeyer, President Bill Clinton, Deena Davenport, Tanya Domi, David Drake, Zoe Dunning, Barney Frank, Barry Goldwater, Steve Gunderson, the Reverend Jesse Jackson, James Kennedy, David Kilgore, Bradley Kleger, Glynn C. Mallory Jr., Keith Meinhold, David Mixner, Carol Ness, Lee Nichols, Sam Nunn, Torie Osborn, Michael Petrelis, Colin Powell, Tom Rielly, Allen Schindler, Randy Shilts, Eli Smith, Joseph Steffan, Shawn Stuart, Gerry Studds, Tracy Thorne, President Harry S Truman, Stanley Yantis, and my canine companion in times of loneliness, Teardrop.

Supreme Court Justice Felix Frankfurter once wrote a dissenting opinion in which he used the phrase "one word more remains to be said"—and then went on to write twenty more pages, plus a sixty-two-page appendix. In my case, one name more remains to be mentioned here: God.

FOREWORD

DAWN CAME FROZEN AND HUSHED THIS LATE-WINTER DAY, BUT IT was a good warmth that filled the '73 Dodge Charger. Three of my Army buddies and I were driving south down a familiar stretch of Texas Interstate-35, our stereo belting out George Michael's "Freedom."

"Why are you bitching, Zuniga?" Eleanor ripped. "I'll be in the field Monday, you'll be in San Francisco." She was right, of course: I had no right to complain. My transfer from Texas to San Francisco, an assignment I had requested instead of field time in Alaska, had been approved. So why was I so scared?

A final blowout at the Bonham Exchange, the gay dance club in San Antonio that had been our sanctuary for the last two years, would settle my nerves. Eleanor, Mitch, Patrick, and I counted ourselves among the few and the proud who just happened to be gay or lesbian. In the safety of the bar, behind its peephole at the door and changing password, we could unbolt the closet doors kept locked when we were in uniform.

This weekend would be my last with these friends. Was that why I was so afraid? We had shared plenty of good times as the four of us climbed the career ladder. There had also been the difficult times, times we mourned the loss of a friend purged in a Gestapo-like sweep or stolen by the AIDS pandemic. But there was hope for us, at least with regard to the military's fifty-year-old ban, Eleanor said as she spoke of Arkansas governor Bill Clinton's presidential candidacy. "He's going to lift the ban!" she announced one day in a telephone call to my office after watching the noon news.

I scoffed at her political naïveté. A staunch Republican, I listened to the Arkansas governor's words suspiciously. Besides, I was used to my life. Although I was sometimes ashamed of its duplicity, I was proud of my accomplishments and felt I could continue living a lie if I had to. But now Clinton had brought to the debate the possibility of abolishing that requirement. His position became the topic officers and enlisted men discussed over the water cooler and at social gatherings at San Francisco's Presidio.

Gradually, every media mention grated on me. The military had been good to me, and I to it. But then the freedom to be myself, especially now that I would be living in San Francisco, was overwhelming. I was a sergeant in the U.S. Army. But I was also a gay man. My life had become a love-hate response to both of those realities.

In March 1993, a three-star general named me Sixth U.S. Army Soldier of the Year. I began to sense that my story could have an impact on the debate. I was proud of my accomplishments, and I knew that my military record could make for the type of headlines needed to dispel pernicious stereotypes and reach undecided Americans who felt they did not personally know anyone who was gay.

But I also wondered if my sacrifice might not be required, since several other gay and lesbian service members were already waging battles against the ban. Other people's names, faces, and stories would reach Middle America and save the day.

My resolve gradually solidified as I watched the Senate Armed Services Committee's bungled efforts. The tide seemed to be turning, and by sitting there in denial, I was helping to bury the best chance yet to advance the cause of equality under the law for gays, lesbians, and bisexuals. With the help of a close circle of friends, strategists, and lawyers, I began to devise a battle plan, with my military career as the weapon.

On the night of April 24, 1993, four months after President Clinton reiterated his promise to lift the ban in his first postinaugural press conference, I came out of the closet, denouncing government-sanctioned discrimination in the guise of Department of Defense policy. Buying into Bill Clinton's promise to "stand with [us] in the struggle for equality for all Americans, including gay men and lesbians," I stood before America in full dress uniform that night. By uttering three honest words—"*I am gay*"— I joined my community in its battle against bigotry and homophobia.

My status as an active-duty soldier, Persian Gulf War veteran, and 1992 Sixth U.S. Army Soldier of the Year drew the media attention I was hoping for. Headlines screamed across newsprint: '93 SOLDIER OF THE YEAR: I'M GAY. The lighted newsreel in New York City's Times Square flashed: ARMY DISCHARGES SOLDIER OF THE YEAR BECAUSE HE'S GAY. How obvious was the bigotry in this matter and the justice required to reverse it, I thought. I had joined the combat that was well underway.

The following weeks seemed endless, as print and broadcast journalists from across the country and abroad lined up for interviews. The questions and answers eventually became routine, but the pace was always grinding.

When the question was finally asked "Have you ever engaged in sexual intercourse with a man?" I found myself in the dilemma of having to choose between denying my past or handing myself over for unjustly harsh punishment under the Uniform Code of Military Justice. All the cases that had dominated the headlines up to this time were *status*, not *conduct*, cases. Would I admit to and accept punishment—including possibly prison—for the crime of loving a man? With a one-word answer—no—I set an uncontrollable chain reaction into motion. I had tried to keep my personal life private, to focus solely on the contradiction inherent in the Army's discharge of one of its best. But gradually, one personality feature after another focused on my *virginity* as a gay man instead of the issue for which I had come out.

THE LONELIEST SOLDIER, read a headline introducing an eighty-inch *Washington Post* feature, JOSÉ ZUNIGA, GAY VIRGIN, DRUMMED OUT OF THE ARMY. YOU FIGURE IT OUT. JUST AS SOON AS HE DOES. Never slept with a man but sacrificing a banner career on principle, the writer trumpeted.

I had lied. I *had* slept with a man. False words once uttered, when any other answer would lead to punishment obscenely disproportionate to the alleged crime, took on a life of their own. Months later, news accounts continued to report the myth as fact, assuming that it was still the case, even if it never had been. To the best of my knowledge, not one reporter used my answer to point out the distinction between status and conduct cases.

A number of people have asked me why I am writing my life story at such a young age. I respond that mine is simply one of the many unfinished stories illustrating a decades-long quest for gay equal rights. History means nothing without human drama to compel people to listen. I have also written this book out of regret, which some have attributed to my Catholic upbringing, that I may still not have done enough in this battle. Writing this book has been—perhaps the most selfish reason of all—a combination of catharsis and confession. I urgently felt the need to step out from behind the shadow of the Soldier of the Year award and live my life, without tabloid drama, as a gay man. To recount with pride a complex love story painfully kept hidden in simplistic newspaper headlines.

The war is not yet over, despite having lost a battle to a Congress under siege and a presidency crippled by cowardice. The last pillar of our democracy, the judicial system, will make momentous decisions in the coming years. If early cases don't bring complete legal success, then the great struggle and loss that have marked the issue of gays in the military will sow the seeds for an eventual full victory. My hope is that, in the twilight of my life, I never regret that future generations of gay men, lesbians, and bisexuals might have lived lives free of the oppression our generation has endured for so long had I only tried harder.

PART 1

DAMNED PROUD
TO SERVE

IN MARCH 1993, LIEUTENANT GENERAL GLYNN C. MALLORY, JR., the Sixth U.S. Army and Presidio of San Francisco's commanding general, sat with several colleagues and me in the conference room of the public affairs office. General Mallory's keen memory, remembering not only our names but our backgrounds as well, allowed him to sit and chat with us as individuals. His greatest characteristic was an almost palpable respect for our work as journalists and acceptance of us as soldiers, something few commanders feel, much less communicate.

The general's eyes darted abruptly to one of the six television screens left on all day to monitor breaking stories. A CNN special report about gays in the military, I surmised, as a portrait of Navy Petty Officer Keith Meinhold, his signature American-flag jacket draped over his lanky body, flashed on the screen. Keith had become a national poster boy for the cause of gays in the military after he'd courageously announced on national television that he was gay. Through a combination of luck, location, and lawyering, *Meinhold* v. *U.S. Department of Defense* had become one of the most prominent cases challenging the military ban. Meinhold was stationed in the Bay Area, and I saw him on screen, in print, or on the streets of the Castro district almost daily.

Talking heads had been debating the issue of gays in the military well before October 1991, when candidate Bill Clinton had staked

3

out his position during an appearance at Harvard University's Kennedy School of Government. The media kept the topic alive, working with little but speculation. This changed as gay-rights groups, religious right-wing organizations, politicians, and the military's top brass breathed life into the issue, creating a discordant undertone for a fledgling administration.

A defiant Meinhold sound bite followed. *Not now, Keith, the general is watching* . . . As footage of a Clinton press conference replaced Meinhold's image, the general flung his arms in the air.

"Fags," he told the air, which seemed to be listening, "don't belong in this man's Army!" His caustic words reflected the attitude of most senior military service members. *Bill Clinton dodged the draft, then tried to lie about it! He tried to get high once, but he didn't even inhale! Was the U.S. military to remain silent while Bill Clinton systematically tried to dismantle it?* The answer was simple, General Mallory hinted; no debate was necessary. I went flush, then felt a chill. Had an alien entity heard the general's fierce protests, no doubt it might have thought Clinton was opening the ranks to Satanists, anarchists, or convicted felons.

I said nothing.

A week later, the general and I were the only two in the massive hall of the Presidio's Golden Gate Club. I remembered when I too had spewed such venom in order to preserve my career. The difference was that General Mallory meant it and I did not. Now I tried to concentrate on the more than two hundred soldiers and civilians who were expected here this drizzly day in March to honor the 1992 Sixth U.S. Army Soldier of the Year. Aside from General Mallory, I had invited three guests, including retired Colonel Salvador Salazar Zuniga, my father, who I thought might want to fly from Texas to witness his son's crowning military achievement. My mother was dead.

Just a week ago the colonel had called excitedly to announce his plans to be there for me—a benefit of retirement, he added. I'd believed him, just as I had believed I would see him at my high-school graduation, basic-training graduation, three promotions—every important date in my life. This time, too, he canceled at the last minute with an apologetic telephone call. No reason given. No reason needed, sir. I should have known better; yet deep inside, despite my years of training, my hopes had been raised. The wound that's never healed remains tender.

Dave and Laurie, a married couple who had fast become my closest civilian friends in San Francisco, would be my only invited guests. Although seating arrangements had not been made, General Mallory insisted that my friends sit at the table reserved for the Presidio's top brass, yes-men one and all. Sitting at the dais with the general and his wife Lynda, I secretly wished I were somewhere else. Glancing in the direction of Dave and Laurie's table, I wondered what they could be chatting about with men who, with their silver hair and wrinkled countenances, didn't understand anything that didn't involve strong handshakes and well-polished schmooze techniques.

I waxed nostalgic at the good fortune that seemed always to have been my lot. Outside, behind a diaphanous curtain of rain, a majestic Golden Gate Bridge rose above a fleet of small sails drifting ethereally across the waters of San Francisco Bay. Every sunrise and sunset here served as a poignant reminder of why this two-hundred-year-old garrison was the Army's premier assignment. Presumably without irony, President John F. Kennedy had once told a mother lamenting her son's impending transfer to Korea: "Some boys go to San Francisco, some boys go to Korea." Life isn't always fair. South Korea was my next assignment.

The bespectacled man with the three stars sewn on his collar (no doubt he anticipated a fourth before retiring) had been one of the Pentagon's star tacticians during the Persian Gulf War. He now commanded the Sixth U.S. Army on active duty, as well as U.S. Army Reserve and National Guard units stationed here and spread out across the twelve western states. Standing in his presence provoked a slight tremor in me for the martial splendor in a man. What strong reactions I had to the names of generals Robert E. Lee, George S. Patton, or H. Norman Schwarzkopf. Respect. Admiration for any soldier who earns the right to append the title *general* to his name. Deference to the mantle of ability, achievement, reliability, dedication, and patriotism.

The general looked up at me periodically from a set of pale blue index cards on which my military career had been abbreviated to a couple of run-on sentences. An imposing figure, despite his stoop-shouldered, below-average height, General Mallory had been my role model years before my transfer to the Sixth U.S. Army. At Fort Hood, Texas, he had commanded one of two heavy-armor units, the 2nd Armored Division. I had been with the 1st Cavalry Division, his rival on the opposite side of the post.

"We won't hold that against you," General Mallory promised me every time the 1st Cavalry Division combat patch I wore on my uniform reminded him of my days with "that other unit." He swore he'd make up for any deficits incurred with a good dose of 2nd Armored training.

Covering change-of-command and retirement ceremonies for the Fort Hood newspaper, I had listened to and admired his many speeches on the qualities of a soldier: honor, loyalty, resolve, physical and ethical fitness. To hear this general expound on self-sacrifice while relating a simple story, like that of an infantry soldier in Vietnam who threw himself over a grenade to shield his buddies from shrapnel, made me twinge with patriotism. I knew that this man would have mirrored the actions of that mythical soldier. I must confess that on these occasions the fingers of a military journalist traipsing across a keyboard are tempted to type "how great thou art" stories. These times truly tested the objectivity of the journalistic ethic. But such was the power of his rhetoric.

Today, an officer I admired as a stalwart American hero was about to reward me as an exemplar of the qualities I had emulated in my boyhood heroes, in my father, and in him.

Once the lunch plates were cleared from the dais, the general and I walked to our pre-assigned positions in the center of the hall. He stood not more than three feet away from me. Instinctively, I froze at attention, standing stock-still at center stage. As the three-star general began an eloquent history of a twenty-three-year-old Army sergeant's accomplishments, the hall hushed to listen to impressive-sounding bullet points of a résumé well known to me. He spoke without a microphone, his resonant voice daring the listener to try to avoid hearing it.

"You can be justifiably proud of this distinction, and I know that you will continue to serve with the same dedication which prompted your selection as the Soldier of the Year." The general's voice boomed in my direction though he faced the audience. He pinned a fifth Army Commendation Medal on my freshly pressed uniform. Pride was replaced with fulfillment as he said in a stage whisper, the way a father might have, "I'm damned proud to serve with you, son."

As I basked in the admiration of my peers, regret that my father, the man in whose name I had accomplished so much in so little time, was not here began to seep through my soul. In his place, General Mallory praised me and honored me by calling me "son." Yet with his words also came the sickening realization that the soldier with whom he claimed to be so proud to serve, the 1992 Sixth U.S. Army's Soldier of the Year, was also, by the letter of a ludicrous policy that governed the military, unfit for service. The scenery blurred, despite my conscious efforts not to be distracted, into a kind of slow motion.

"Fags don't belong. . . ."

"Fags don't belong in this man's Army!"

"They don't, it's that simple. No fags . . . no debate!"

Those words of protest, not the ceremonious tribute he lavished on me today, rang in my ears as he shook my hand and handed me the Soldier of the Year plaque.

Last week, I had kept my mouth shut in that conference room. His acerbic gaze had quickly darted between me and the images on the screen. I had probably even reverently nodded my head in seeming approval of his opinion. After all, he wore three stars and I wore three stripes. Would I have slapped my knee and laughed too had he done so? I had laughed at and even initiated jokes in the field to deflect suspicions of my own gayness. But then I was only thinking of survival. I loved the Army, and I would have done anything to stay in it, including making fun of my own. But then, I had rationalized, they weren't anything like me. The drag queens, the flaming queers, the child molesters . . . to hell with them! And what about my gay buddies caught up in the witch-hunts? Sorry to lose them, but once they were out they fell off the face of the earth. Why should I care? Then, I didn't.

I did now.

"Good job," my company commander said as he took his turn shaking my hand. I was in a trance, my mind registering something halfway between panic and bliss.

What would happen if I revealed my secret here and now? If I revealed to everyone gathered in this hall that Sergeant Zuniga, the combat veteran with whom General Mallory had established an almost paternal relationship, was a closeted homosexual? What picture would form or be shattered in their minds?

I shook more and more hands like an automaton, the answer to the questions floating in my mind starting to become clear. To continue my military career would mean to continue compromising my honor and integrity, the very principles upon which the military was founded and for which countless thousands of men and women in uniform had laid down their lives. I was tiring of the facade, the code words, the constant urge to look over my shoulder at a café in my off-hours.

I began to visualize my opportunity to make a difference. Would I be happy living a lie? Would I have to stand at the back of the bus the rest of my life, the way African-American people did before Rosa Parks? Or would I add my name to the roster of Davids fighting the Goliath that was the military institution? Was I strong enough to challenge the rules regardless of the consequences, even if it meant being thrown off the bus and arrested?

The answer to the questions that whirled through my mind like a symphony gone mad was yet another question: Could I live with the absolute knowledge that I could have helped in the struggle for gay rights but was paralyzed out of fear or a selfish desire to continue my career? I had kept my mouth shut for so long and achieved so much.

The audience delivered a minute-long standing ovation. The 1992 Sixth U.S. Army Soldier of the Year stood frozen at attention. Such discipline, I imagined sergeants major extolling. No wonder he won the competition. The fag in possession of my mind was screaming within. I soon realized my mouth was not uttering a word beyond the obligatory "thank you."

Only a handful of people knew my secret. My two guests, Dave and Laurie, both of whom were fairly active in gay politics, had just the day before joked about using this event to launch a public-relations blitz to blow the lid off the Department of Defense policy. Imagine Mr. and Mrs. Normal in Middle America trying to reconcile the fact that someone just named soldier of the year could also be considered unfit for service. Was the military wrong in selecting him, or did his selection prove the policy wrong? Our joking had never crossed over into serious discussion. But at this moment I struggled.

My dream of coming out began to take shape. Local press would be required if my kamikaze mission were to have value. National press coverage would make it easier to stomach the loss of my career (though as a journalist, I knew full well the media's power either to smother or catapult a story). I would take a stand—as one of my boyhood heroes, Colonel William Barrett Travis, had done at the Alamo—but only if it made a difference.

The ceremony ended. I would make a difference some other day. Today I would bask in the glory that was rightly mine, accepting the congratulations of friends and colleagues.

"Sergeant Zuniga, phone call," the office receptionist chirped the next morning. Anger quickly trumped my pride as I answered a congratulatory telephone call from the chief of public affairs at the Pentagon. Ten minutes of banter, and I slammed the telephone receiver in its cradle.

Who was I angry at most? The Army for placing me in this predicament? General Mallory for making his hatred of homosexuals known to me? Or myself for not acting like my childhood heroes?

My Only Living Hero

I FONDLY REMEMBER MY LAZY BOYHOOD SUMMER DAYS WHEN ALL I did was sprawl out on the living-room carpet in the morning and into the afternoon, my eyes glued to the television set's black-and-white images of ruggedly handsome U.S. Marines storming a Normandy beach front, or the early colorized images of Colonel George Armstrong Custer leading a futile cavalry charge against an Indian force triple the size of his own. The remote control makes it easy to skip past these classics now, but for a boy, the smoke and mirrors of Hollywood, the drama of men sacrificing all for little or no reward, was enthralling. Honor, duty, country: a far cry from the sagas of six-guns, shot glasses, and Miss Kitty's garter belt.

I loved watching John Wayne or Audie Murphy trudge onto enemy shores from the safety of their amphibious vehicles. As they dodged enemy fire or jumped over a dead buddy, they knew that the outcome would be black or white, win or lose, live or die. They kept going forward anyway. These "real men" were my heroes, even if the neighborhood kids thought it weird not to admire caped crusaders. Even if they were only reciting words from a script, my childhood heroes were teaching me some of the most valuable lessons of my life through their valiant actions.

When I was of an age to comprehend the difference between reality and Hollywood, I was introduced to the heroes whose real-life stories did not require props for impact. The Zuniga (paternal side) and Vaca (maternal side) lineages were filled with stories of two great Spanish families, each with its own proud heritage.

On May 7, 1969, while the city of Cincinnati, Ohio, was alive with carnival bunting, the scent of cotton candy, and the shouts of children winning stuffed giraffes, a particularly sharp kick convinced my mother that the hour was at hand. My parents had driven here from Indiana to visit friends left behind in a previous assignment. They were greeted fortuitously with news of a two-day citywide celebration to coincide with the May 8 birthday of President Harry S Truman. Despite my mother's premonition, it was my father's desire to open a savings account that morning in Cincinnati for his yet-to-be-born son, and Father always got his way.

She would never let him forget the price she paid for his stubborn streak, from the minute they climbed into the elevator going up to the new accounts department. It wasn't really his fault that I decided to announce my imminent arrival between the eighth and ninth floors of the twelve-story building. After realizing that my mother's water had broken, he rushed her to Christ Hospital. I took my first gasp of air at 4:32 A.M. the next day—she had extended her agony, she quipped, just long enough so that I would share a birthday with President Truman. At the age of forty-four, she gave my father a healthy, eight-and-a-half-pound baby boy, José Manuel Zuniga— Pepé, as Mother called me—the son he had dreamed of and whose life he had already started planning.

With all the modern pop-psychology debate about the effects of differing approaches to parenthood and child-rearing, I have to note that whatever mistakes my parents may have made, my twenty-four-year-old sister, Sandra, and I are who and where we are today because of their good intentions. Ours was as typical an upbringing as that of most soldiers' children. Moving cross-country, often cross-continent, in the course of a year (if we were lucky enough to stay in one place that long) seemed as normal a part of growing up as cavities. It wasn't until my teens that I discovered otherwise.

From the age of six or seven, we were used to packing our few toys—educational toys and books, never Barbie dolls or Tonka trucks—into boxes twice our height. Everything got packed away at least ten times in my life. Everything but Lucky, our German Shepherd, and my treehouse, twice vacated in the last year, got packed. I once packed a friend—with his permission and cooperation, of course—into a wardrobe box in preparation for our next move. At least that is what my mother told me I did years later as we reminisced about our gypsy childhood. All of this upheaval to drive, bus, or fly to a new beginning. A new place of duty. A new campsite for the colonel to pitch his tent.

If history lessons were not enough to establish that my father was the son and grandson of military heroes, his parenting made clear he was their progeny. Heredity had molded this overpowering six-foot-tall man into the stereotypical military father, replete with the genetic pattern needed of a leader of men—and, to his way of thinking, a leader of his family. In this fiefdom, the colonel was lord of the manor. Democracy, he said, had no place in the Army. It served only to undermine good order when allowed to run rampant through the ranks, he threw in for good measure. Give-and-take played no role in his leadership style and even less in his home life. It was made crystal clear from the day we developed our oral skills that if we were to camp out under his tent, we would abide by his rules and regulations or cut short our stay.

If I had to compare my life then to anything I've lived to date, boot camp is the closest analogy. "Blocks of instruction" dealing with the proper way of making a bed—with or without military corners—were repeated until the lesson became so ingrained in our young minds that they became instinctive motor functions. A sharp-looking bed was part of keeping an inspection-ready room; each toy was arranged by height, shoelaces were tucked into shoes neatly aligned and free of dust.

Some would consider my father the incarnation of tyranny; I considered him at the time a normal father asking nothing out of the ordinary.

Why rebel? Back then it was a matter of course; there was no question this was the way things were done. Most of my friends had it worse—at least I was confident I was loved. Even if my father didn't express himself emotionally, I somehow knew, or rationalized, that his stern approach to child-rearing was his way of expressing love.

My mother could be a controlling and, yes, domineering woman sometimes, though she set my spirit soaring. Raquel Vaca Zuniga exacted control over every aspect of her life, and she wielded the reins well. Hers was an unending need to ensure we did not stray from the right path, hoping that, through her diligence, the mistakes she or my father had made in their own lifetimes would be averted. Unlike millions of other women her age, she relished the role of traditional housewife and mother, sacrificing a career in fashion design to rear her husband's two children and care for their well-being. My mother's greatest legacy, she was convinced, would be her children. To that end, from crib to college dorm, she dedicated her life to us.

From the sandbox to the treehouse, I was following along right on schedule my father's energetic master plan to rush a boy into manhood, never mind how many steps he missed. Despite the military-style strictness of my home life and the Golden Rules taught by the nuns and priests in school, the salient features of my formative years were those of the average American boy. From almost burning down the garage in a science fair experiment to Atari, I had a life closely parallel to that of most of my friends.

Our days were generally peaceful. We knew early on what the rules were, and they were fairly simple to follow. Few were the times we incurred our parents' wrath. When we did dare break the rules, I was usually the one who hid as my sister's fragile voice filled the house with shrieks of terror. The usually beguiling six-year-old sought cover from the interrogations of the prosecutor, judge, and jury of one who, regardless of the facts, would usually find me guilty as charged.

I guess it was at this young age that a rift developed between Sandra and me. She was only a year younger than I, but there seemed to be decades separating us. We were opposites. She was fragile—her asthma made her so. I was healthy. She could do no wrong; girls were incapable of it. Boys were meant to be wicked. With a barrier between us, we grew apart under the same roof.

Sandra and I attended parochial schools because my parents disapproved of the public-school system and because religion, despite my father's protests (I imagine he must have reviled its "blessed are the meek" ideologies), was the cornerstone of our education. I became an altar boy at age eight, waking up at five o'clock for Sunday morning services and forsaking childhood games for the Church's unabashedly prodigious rituals. Donning vestments the color of burnished skulls, I was responsible for preparing the altar cloth with the crossed pair of palm fronds, the chalice, paten, and golden candle flames—all the ceremonial icons that symbolized the consecrations of Catholicism. Helping the priest-celebrant, a pale relic intoning Latin prayers, with the "Divine Sacrament of the Eucharist" was a testament to my devotion to God and His Church. Whether real or not, I enjoyed the closeness I felt with God. Or at least I enjoyed my active role in this ancient ritual.

My goal was to serve God; I bought into the mystical fear of a higher being. Attending a Mass, mouthing from memory the Latin Mass as the priest struggled to remember the words, I wanted to raise the Eucharist to heaven and for a magical second have the hand of God touch a wafer, touch my soul.

Catholicism played as pivotal a role in our mother's lesson plan for child development as discipline and order did in my father's. From the time I was very young, no matter where we lived, my mother walked with us to church without fail. Filling out the individually addressed tithing envelopes the morning of Mass, stuffing a crisp dollar bill out of our weekly allowance into it: this was as much a part of my spiritual upbringing as was human contrition uttered with each breath.

How portentous the epigrammatic words sounded to an impressionable ten-year-old: *Sin*. Benevolence. *Satan*. Saint Francis of Assisi. *Burn*. Resurrection. *Sinful*. Repentant. *Forever*. Amen.

When I sat in the pews as a member of the congregation and not up on stage, throwing my envelope into the collection basket to feed a starving child brought the hope that a good deed—benevolence, tithing—might cancel out at least one of the infinite number of sins a boy committed all week. What I can now say only as a bit of buffoonery, laughing at its deceit, was true then as I sat in the magnificence of the church where thousand-year-old idols seemed at home in the pomp, majesty, and solemnity: I wanted to be a priest.

Of course, my dream of being a man of the cloth was scoffed at by a military man who rejected the very notion of spirituality. A priest in a family of warriors? No son of his would end the tradition of soldier-statesman.

He bought me my first pistol the day after I announced my intention. An archery set followed the next week. The thrill of marksmanship eventually replaced the piety of song and prayer. I started to dream of being an officer.

My recollection of my elementary-school years is fuzzy, but I'll never forget the cruel wooden rulers the nuns were always ready to use to bruise a little boy's knuckles. In particular, Sister Marie Jésus. Although her face was lined, her hair white, and her low voice somewhat shaky, Sister Marie Jésus was still strong, and she disciplined for the fun of hearing boys yelp or catching sight of a tear or two.

My report cards described me as quiet and pleasant; little foil stars and glossy smiling faces hammered the point home. "José is a studious boy who shows outstanding potential, especially in writing. He has a vivid imagination," my third-grade teacher, sister-in-training Lynda Wojack, scribbled in the comments box, setting the standard by which I thought I would be judged all my life. I know she did not sit behind her desk and diabolically plan with every lick and paste of a red foil star a clash with my father's plans for me. I don't think she was capable of intending such harm.

My lunch hours were spent in her reading club, a motley group of twelve "outstanding" students, not all of whom were that outstanding. We passed our lunch hours reading the prohibited classics: *Paradise Lost, Pilgrim's Progress, The Scarlet Letter*. It was with this woman that I shared my deepest, darkest secrets at the end of the hour, a ritual begun the day she begged to know why a child's eyes seemed so full of sorrow and fear.

"I didn't wipe my shoes clean this morning," I confessed. "My father will be upset," I added, to emphasize the gravity of my offense.

We never missed a day of school. To do so ran counter to the colonel's unshakable philosophy that, regardless of health, there was no excuse for failing the mission. *Take two aspirin, dress warmly, and carry on, troop!* was one of the few mantras I adopted as my own from the colonel. (I later took this to the extreme shortly after the Persian Gulf War, when I reported to work after spending four days in the hospital with amoebic dysentery. My body felt the pain, but my mind felt the need to continue working, and there was nothing but my commander's direct order to go home and eventually an ambulance driver strapping me onto a gurney and driving me to the emergency room that could stop me.) My father instilled in me self-sufficiency: If I skinned a knee on the asphalt playground during a rough-and-tumble, I should care for it myself and not expect anyone else to come to my rescue. "You should never depend on anyone," he said all to often. I internalized his words. When one of us got hurt, he would respond in flying rages. We thought he was mad because we hurt ourselves. It wasn't until years later that he explained his anger was at whatever malign power had caused us to get hurt.

I was eight years old when the colonel passed on his tattered and dye-stained shoeshine box; a pair of scuffed military low quarters, the standard-issue military formal shoes, followed days later. It was the first time I had ever shined shoes. I had watched him in the past. He would sit in his toolroom, a quarter of which was reserved exclusively for shoe maintenance, and spin out his parables while he buffed.

José Salazar Zuniga's murder did not make front-page news in *El Diario de Monterey*. If it had, the story would tell of a traveling immigrant who worked back-breaking jobs in America to support his wife and six children in Mexico. A man who, at age twenty-two, had commanded a battalion of men in a revolution that awarded him a chestful of gold medallions for bravery but left him penniless. In his twilight, he lived a life of quiet decency and honor, the li-

onesque warrior's glory eclipsed in a country trying to forget its
war-ravaged history. He was a man who, at least once a month,
would pay half his wages on a sliding-scale fare (usually in the con-
ductor's favor), forsaking material needs to make an eighteen-hour
pilgrimage by train to his family's small provincial home outside
Monterey.

It was early morning on one of those days that the former military
officer approached his family's home and a gunman accosted him.
Ten-year-old Ismael, the oldest of his six children, was hanging out
the window that morning, as he often did in summer instead of
pulling his weight in chores. He saw his father stagger and fall dead
from the bullet that pierced his heart. Absurdly, Colonel José Salazar
Zuniga was killed for a cheap American pocket watch he had brought
back as a birthday present for one of his sons. The thief unwrapped
the gift on the spot, unceremoniously discarding the foil as he
slipped back into the shadows of an alleyway.

This left my grandmother a widow with six children, fifteen
months to eight years old, to support and little money to splurge
on the niceties of life. Creditors' demands seemed so cruel. Had
they no mercy?

From that day on, my father endured hardscrabble times until he
was old enough to do something about it. Devoid of education,
pulled out of school almost immediately after my grandfather's
death, he learned on the streets the harsh lessons life sometimes
doles out to its most innocent victims. Theirs was a meager existence, not only because they lacked the niceties but because they
often went without the necessities of life. Like other Americans
whose values were shaped by the Great Depression, my father was
shaped by his economic situation.

I used to ask him if, like Abraham Lincoln, he was self-educated.
In these moments he fell silent. I already knew that as an eight year
old he had shined shoes in Monterey's public gardens and plazas.
Having visited Mexico almost every summer of my life, my heart is
filled with great sadness at the sight of six-year-old boys buffing
grown men's shoes to make enough money for a loaf of bread, a
schoolbook, or, I suspect today, drug money. I can't help remembering his stories, and I see him in the children God and society have

forgotten, trying to make a peso. Yes, he would say without further explanation, there was plenty of self-learning.

It was when my father recalled his upbringing—the days when he and his brothers collected shoeboxes, put cardboard wheels on them, and used them as toy cars—that we saw in him the vulnerable human being behind the walls erected by time and self-preserving instincts. As he relived a distant past from the comfort of his retirement home in San Antonio, a tear welled up not very often, but often enough to tear down his stone-hearted facade. His dark eyes would brighten and then become misty as quickly as he switched from anger to sadness and back. So it was always with some modicum of gratitude, which replaced the initial bristling at lecture time, that we listened to and memorized his stories. Years later, as I shared them with friends, they questioned the detail I repeated, saying it was the stuff from which rags-to-riches movies were made, not reality. But I never questioned its veracity, because he could not feign the suffering that covered his age-worn face like a veil.

He made sure I understood his point as he officially yet unceremoniously passed down this box. It was part of an important lesson in life. He said, "Look, I could go out and buy patent-leather shoes and never have to do anything but wipe them down. I require my men to look sharp and walk around in spit-shined shoes. They can't afford the patent leather I could wear, and I must set the example."

He explained how, with his shoeshine box as a prop, he had taught his men the secrets of proper shoe maintenance. As much as I reviled having to shine his shoes, I learned that it was important for me to understand and appreciate the mundane, because only then could I advance to the greater tasks in life. At least that was what my father said.

Regardless of my station in life, I will always remember what it felt like to be an average Joe, shining shoes in a garage somewhere. After a while I started to rebel; before the lesson was learned, I went so far as to take sandpaper to a pair.

By the time I was ten, my mother's overprotective zeal in walking us to and from school became a source of great distress. Every afternoon, as we took our usual route home, kids taunted us. One day I heard cries of "faggot" and "sissy." Ignore them, my mother said. My hurt quickly grew into anger. I blurted out to my mother feelings I had suppressed for so long: Either desist or walk a block behind me! "Stop treating me like a baby!" I screamed at the top of my lungs, the words betraying what the kids were calling me.

There was hurt and a glint of compassion in her eyes, but she refused my request. The next day, however, with my father's help, I began walking a few steps ahead of her, and she let up on the reins just enough for me to do that. She realized I was not going to be that little boy she had to—or could—dote over much longer. As terrified as I was of the school bullies, I walked with my head held high, showing off my budding manhood. To the limited extent I could, I tasted freedom that day.

Bishop Noll Institute in East Chicago was the epitome of the rich, white Catholic boys' schools. Girls had been reluctantly admitted less than two years before my freshman year, but it was still largely a male-dominated institution. Middle-school classes were held in the same building as high-school classes. Moving to this school brought me, wide-eyed, into contact with older boys in the hallways and the lunchroom. This was the first opportunity for me to interrelate with nonmilitary brats, children of baby boomers who studied Pavlovian conditioning in Psych 101 and were raised under the mantra of positive reinforcement. The stories of their home lives left me aghast at my own isolation. Or was I so naive that they were pulling my leg?

I asked question after question about parents, homelife, curfews, eating habits. With every answer my subconscious resentment grew. As I described my childhood, they cringed and laughed. "Eight o'clock curfew? No house key? Why don't you say something, man? Why don't you teach them a lesson? Hey, let's get you stoned and then you can lay down the law with your old man! Show him you're not a baby no more."

To say I was nonathletic is an understatement. I detested sports. Although I was never that quintessential lonely "geek" standing alone on the sidelines, both teams unwilling to pick him because he cannot run, bat, catch, throw or dribble (whenever I locked 99 percent of an artist's soul in my gym locker and used the testosterone-engorged 1 percent required to wage battle on the court or the field, I made baskets, hit homers, and ran relays well), I shared the self-loathing that comes with that predicament.

Explain battleball to me, I asked my father defensively after he'd chewed me out over a gym teacher's phone call to snitch on my "lack of interest" in the game (a gross understatement). "What sense is there in standing against a wall and dodging incoming rubber balls that hurt if they hit you?" I asked.

"That *is* the point," he said exasperatingly. "Dodge the ball or you're out. The warrior ethic is central to the game." Dodge the *bullet* or you *die*, I translated. This is middle school, sir, not Vietnam, I thought.

There was no logical reason why I should invest the time and energy—or, worse, subject myself to unwarranted physical punishment. What glory was there in hobbling back to a locker room? In contusions and broken noses, spattered with mucus and blood? Talk to me about literature, the arts, music—these were the basics on which civilizations flourished, which, unbeknownst to my father, uplifted my soul and truly made me happy.

I suppose my mother taught me fairly early what it meant to live a duplicitous life. She loved art. Her favorite painter was Matisse, although she quietly confessed a weakness to a certain Léger or a Liechtenstein. Raquel Zuniga felt perfectly at home around a group of Braques, comfortably conversant in the history and language of art, as she held her children's tiny hands, explaining detail as reverently as she would say a prayer. More than anything else, Mother had a penchant for music. Irving Berlin's "The Song is Ended," Rodgers and Hammerstein's "South Pacific"—she knew all the words, in English and Spanish. It was rare to hear silence in our home—her soft hum or warbling voice echoed through the house. Sometimes while ironing, washing, or cooking, she forgetfully transposed lyrics from one language to the other, just as my sister and I would often go back and forth from English to Spanish with Mother (Father only "understood" English).

Mother had fallen in love with the stage as a young girl, in the years before her life was so complicated, before she was married.

Her marriage contract "obligated" her, in word and deed, to renounce her passionate love affair with the arts in return for the security that marriage offered. As much as Father loved order and discipline, he detested the arts, even the rigid and structured ones, because they bred imagination and daring. He would not, and most likely could not, understand how amorphous red and yellow "splodges" on a canvas could be titled *Receding Anger*.

Mother could not sever her ties to the freer world. So she didn't. She simply went undercover. When my father was away, my mother was a changed woman, buoyant, even effervescent. She never passed up an opportunity to expose us to her world, one so different from my father's that I now wonder if she wasn't perhaps schizophrenic or just a martyr to the law-and-order man. When he was home, he wielded a machete, severing our lifeline to art. I suppose I should thank or blame them both for my romanticism. Their inability to share love with me forced me to connect strong feelings to song and art, to develop a strong romantic sense of love before reaching puberty.

In retrospect, I think my mother regretted surrendering her dreams in exchange for the security of marriage. In her youth, her family had attempted to dissuade her from nonconformist pursuits. Her dream was to not be a Victorian daughter. She'd envisaged a life of literary pursuits and works of belle lettres: history, poetry, essays. Her destiny was to be a wife and mother, to marry and bear many children so that the bloodline did not end. To that end, the genteel culture, with its cozy world of lunches and teas, ancient lineage and society, enslaved her and trounced her dreams. She was fortunate to be allowed to educate herself, she admitted, where many girls in her time were excluded by society's patriarchal elite from pursuing literary ambitions, even if they were consummate artists. My grandparents' wish to cloister Mother in Mexico, to enslave her to a traditionalist role—which she never escaped in marrying my father—would one day force her to abandon her birth family and home.

My mother left for the United States while in her midtwenties, drawing her father's resentment. My grandmother, I remember, begged forgiveness years later for having collaborated in an attempt to suffocate her daughter's dreams, for not having stood up to my grandfather. Through no fault of her own, my mother had been born a woman in the last generation before some true freedom was won.

In the United States, until her marriage, my mother would forge her way without the strictures of tradition and the limitations Spanish-Mexican society imposed on its women. With an eye for fashion design, she quickly found employment in an East Chicago garment shop as a designer, struggling to make ends meet on fifty-two cents an hour. Mother succeeded, she claimed, because of the survival skills my grandparents had taught her. I believe she was destined to succeed. Her strong will and determination would have it no other way.

I remember the longing stares when her girlhood desires to write, dance, and sing were evoked in conversation as I helped her unweed shared boxwood-edge flowerbeds of begonias and golden iresine. Her dream had been to not only know the words, brushstrokes, or notes, but to master each art and create freely from each, indulging her imagination.

My first literary success came at age twelve when I won a public-broadcasting essay contest about space exploration. The essay was a class project, and the best essay was to be forwarded to Hammond's PBS affiliate for competition. I spent two nights working on this assignment, skipping the three hours of television I was allotted, reading and rereading the essay to anyone with ears who could tell me if I was way off base. When I won, shock gave way to elation, which then gave way to an ego whose birth I can accurately pinpoint on a calendar page in November of 1982. On that day, my love affair with the written word began.

Until then, I had always been shy and quiet, inexpressive even when I felt passionately about something. On the rare occasions I did express my thoughts verbally, I could not help feeling awkward when I said something above my classmates' heads and they would not listen, so I remained the shy boy in small, self-contained groups, relating to teachers and books more than classmates. Now, a pen and paper opened a channel of communication. Here I had written an essay about our government and its role in space exploration, an essay full of personal opinion, and my teachers weren't the only ones reading my work.

My English teacher hustled me into the newspaper sponsor's office that afternoon, my essay in hand. With minimal persuasion I was named editor of the *Charger Chatterbox*. Editing a middle-school newspaper, even if it was eight pages of mimeographed chatter, allowed me access to people otherwise beyond my reach, because they were the athletes, the Boy Scouts, the elite. I now had a soapbox, and an opportunity to impress with my newly beribboned writing skills. From the age of twelve, I never again had to open my heart or my mind to anyone and put myself at risk of rejection. My fear of face-to-face encounters was no more. Now I could compete with popular, student-body-president types. I jumped into writing with gusto, masking stunted development on other nonacademic fronts.

Middle school ended without much fanfare as my gypsy life continued. If my years in middle school had taught me the power of writing, high school with a Catholic twist taught me—unintentionally—the importance of questioning everything. My parochial school's goal was to mold children into productive, well-rounded, yet guilt-ridden Catholics. Theology classes delved into the whats, whens, and wheres. My mind began asking the whys behind what I was hearing—that abortion is wrong, homosexuality is an abomination, adultery is taboo. If it happens, though, ignore it and it will go away. Repent, then go forth and sin no more. As I remember, the doctrine continued, the universe is running out of energy and will one day run out completely. *That day all shall be judged. . . . Glory hallelujah!*

I questioned, yearning for knowledge in all its incarnations. The discovery of my dormant inquisitive self coincided with my weariness of those asking me to believe with blind faith. I was finding it hard to swallow that the final truth about life was to be found within the confines of religion. Why waste the remaining precious time celebrating a gloomy eventuality? Why live in the shadow of imminent extinction or salvation? No answers.

*   *   *

After years of cross-country moves, my mother began to resist the notion of transplanting her children as often as the military required. In the summer of my fourteenth year her adamant resistance to playing the gypsy role prompted my father's retirement and the end of yearly migrations. I suppose this marked the moment I finally realized that what had seemed a very normal ritual of burrowing out of a place we temporarily called home year after year really wasn't. Now that I could plant roots, maybe I could more easily develop a self-identity.

My father's life had been one of successful adventure; he had fought in foreign wars, led men, and was the object of commendations for his savvy and bravura. Now, after a glorious retirement ceremony in May 1983, the colonel's life was a memorial to days gone by punctuated by the occasional reunion or convention. I keenly felt his resentment toward us for having been the instruments my mother used to trump his continued achievement and self-worth. Reciprocating, my father must have known of my intense jealousy as he advised a young captain in a way he should have, but failed to, advise me. After his retirement, other retirees replaced the young officer who sat at the dining-room table with us, the center of attention lavished on him by a proud father figure. The usurper bragged about his girlfriend or about his softball game. My father beamed. I had no such stories to share, so I sat silently in dismay. Any similar aspects of my life were not the unqualified successes that evoked such pride from my father.

I was not terrified of my father resorting to violence to make himself heard. More than anything I was terrified of his screaming threats to throw us out of his house if we did not conform to his whims and desires. I would live in fear until I was seventeen years old, when there was nothing left to fear.

We lived in the middle of a neighborhood where old-time Mafiosi had built their Victorian mansions, and later Hispanic and black families found a supply of housing they could afford. The gentrification process continued, and now these mansions were the property of military retirees who, with their extra time and income, restored the houses to their Victorian splendor. In our house there were mahogany bookshelves, everything was warm, elegant, and hedonistic in a restrained way—a chaise longue looking its age, a big leather armchair, cluttered with issues of *Newsweek* and *Army Times*, a rich teal-colored love seat shoved over by a stained-glass window.

Whenever my father was home, war stories and visits by colleagues and friends occupied his time. His were always the units of soldiers full of spirit, willing to follow their commander into the mouth of hell if he asked them to, because he fostered in them a sense of loyalty and devotion. His old Army jokes, stale from years of repetition, still brought a surly smile to his face. I could not begrudge him this laughter, no matter how hollow. So I laughed. I had felt sympathy and leniency for my father since the day I began to judge him, as every child must eventually judge his parent and at that moment judge everything. Like most children, I had thought of my father as a larger-than-life figure, an image reinforced by a booming voice and his imposing frame. At some point I experienced a turning inward and found that fear and pity had supplanted wonder and awe.

The ubiquitous tour of the wall of fame in our home became his trademark. He had always professed the philosophy that personal discipline was far more important than achievement, yet his actions and our home belied that claim. An enormous lavender marlin, a good three feet longer than I was tall, hung prominently above the fireplace mantel, his awards and commendations stacked neatly on a wall in his den. In word and deed he glorified his past, memorializing it in simple frames.

In high school my bullheaded drive, once a source of great annoyance to almost everyone and especially my parents, became my signature. However much unhappiness and resistance this trait brought me, it also assured me success. And success was, I quickly discovered, what drew people in droves. Success became the linchpin to my sense of self, where all my demons were securely shackled behind an impenetrable emotional wall.

I detested what I saw as my old, shy self, so I set about creating a new and improved self. With my father's retirement to San Antonio in November 1983, I attended a public school for the first time in my life. An *A+* student most of the time, I busied myself in as many extracurricular activities as possible: newspaper, drama, and the U.S. Army Junior Reserve Officers' Training Corps. From the day I set foot in Wheatley High School until the day I graduated, I made sure I was among the "big men" on campus. There were possibly two organizations I was not a member of, the cheerleading squad and the Future Farmers of America. My net was cast wide, if not always deep, and I soon found myself filling in leadership positions.

However much I thrived on the control these positions offered, it was in journalism that I discovered my karma. Born to be a warrior, as my father all too often directed or reminded me, my only true ambition was to be a writer. And here I was given absolute free reign. My sophomore year I was awarded the position of editor despite the vocal and mean-spirited protests of students whose *rightful* place I was usurping, whose age and status in the school should have assured their right to the role. I had nothing to lose, since I had few peer relationships outside the professional ones. My soapbox was my column, and although people did not always agree with my stand, they at least respected my opinion and the fact that I was willing to voice it.

My teacher Callie Vassar was my greatest inspiration in high school. To her students she never showed her true self; she cultivated a hard exterior that masked a warm, giving personality. I loved her. She not only understood duplicity, she mastered it like a devout thespian and admired it in my writing. She was tough, and she demanded perfection. I was more than her student; I was her protégé.

For me, her most difficult assignment required us to step into our parents' shoes and write an essay about their life. We had to find a photo of our parents and attach it to our assignment. Digging through boxes of mementos and relics from my father's Army days was a revelation. A five-by-seven black-and-white of my parents at a Christmas party in the late 1960s caught my eye. My father wore civilian attire, not a uniform. A suit and tie looked so foreign on him; he now wore his double-knit suits only to weddings and funerals. Mother looked elegant in a strapless satin dress. This was Salvador and Raquel as I had never seen them before. They were still young and trim, and they were both blissfully happy. Where had that rapture gone?

LATE BLOOMER

IN HIGH SCHOOL, I BEGAN TO FEEL A BIZARRE FEELING—MORE A curiosity than an attraction. I had no clue about sexuality. I know some will either refuse to believe that fact or judge me the epitome of naïveté, but people who have experienced late comings-of-age will understand. For many people, at puberty romantic feelings become attached to sexual urges. For me, sex was only an awkward physical awakening. My romantic notions remained completely sex free.

I don't remember the onset of puberty. My first erection? "I couldn't even find the top of my zipper at age fifteen," I once heard a comedian joke about his late blooming. Of course I felt the curiosity most boys experience when thrown into a locker room full of other boys. Surely this isn't a sign or symptom of a budding queer. I know I wasn't the only one stealing glances at other guys' genitalia just to make sure all was right with my own. And I know I wasn't the only one to feel internal terror upon seeing the first uncircumcised cock, wondering if I were somehow cheated at birth or whether foreskins, as I later learned they were called, were a sign of maturation like facial hair and thickening vocal cords. Curiosity would eventually turn into fascination, frustration, and later, experimentation.

At age fifteen I was just beginning to discover the sensuality of my own body. One night my penis rubbed against the sheet a certain way. Unlike the millions of times before, my penis responded and my body began to writhe in pleasure. What was going on here? My blood-engorged penis scared me. Is this a boner—what my friend Matt was kidding about the other day in class? What do I do now?

27

Nothing; try ignoring it. But the next night I sinfully cupped a hand around it, stroked it, and felt it explode seconds later. What's that? Should I ask my father?

I knew I enjoyed what I was doing. But I had no clue what it meant, much less its proper name. I didn't dare ask anyone for fear I'd be considered a prude. After all, when the guys joked about getting laid, I was always in on the joke. I always knew exactly what they were talking about. "Yeah, sure, I've done it. Haven't you?" Jacking off. Spanking the monkey. It was as if the veil of everyday perception was lifted away, and suddenly I saw things as they were. I was a sexual being. What a revelation!

The ensuing curiosity was more than I could bear at times. Okay, I had a penis. I knew what the other guys were allegedly doing with theirs. It didn't make sense to me. Maybe they were wrong. But there was only one way to find out. My curiosity engulfed every synapse.

I masturbated, but I never connected the act with the concept of sex, romance, or relations with others. It was a private act, disconnected from the rest of the world. Matt said he jacked off to *Penthouse*. I tried but to no avail. So I jacked off to myself. Was I a narcissist? Aren't we all? As much as friends joked about getting laid, I was, at least at that time, satisfied to relieve the pressure that graduated in intensity with each experience. Exploring my body, running my hand across my chest, discovering the sensitivity of a nipple . . . I didn't need anyone else to help me feel the ardor of my newly discovered sex.

At first I didn't consciously make the connection that this was one of the abominations against God I was supposed to avoid. When I later discovered my grave sin, I made a conscious decision to look the other way. I hadn't gone blind, and God knows I should have been struck blind a hundred times over after the first week. The curiosity most boys my age had to explore their sexuality plagued my mind constantly. But I had to compromise: I would continue this one minor transgression in lieu of violating the moral strictures prohibiting me from quenching the bigger curiosity. I would not desecrate my body or anyone else's because it would be too great a sin. Reading the classic love stories in school would be as far as I'd go, dreaming without daring to touch reality. No kisses, although I longed to put my lips against another's—girl or boy. No touching, although I craved the contact I witnessed daily between my friends and the objects of their affection. No sex, although my body ached to experience the act so expertly censored in the *Romeo and Juliet* video we watched in British literature class.

Claudio, one of my closest friends, provided the perfect rationalization for not indulging, one I now figure we must have both been desperate to accept. An outcast in most social circles, he refused the invitation to join a disparate clique whose sole common characteristic seemed at times a profound desire never to be wrong. He had been wrong once, but all those hallucinogens had not yet completely fried his synapses, he often joked. High-school graduation day was a month away for him.

Despite my fear of guilt by association, Claudio had become my confidant. He wore black, as if to say he believed in death, isolation, and meaninglessness. His eyes, huge dark orbs planted in a moon-shaped face, added to the illusion. Yet he was the more vibrant of two Catholic boys sharing a special friendship.

"Remember that biology class on the preying mantis?" he asked rhetorically. "That's the way I look at sex. Think of yourself as a mantid's boyfriend.... Get her riled up and she'll devour any closeby moving thing—even you."

Of course I remembered that class. Who could forget the corresponding video graphically depicting a female mantid annihilating her naive gallant during the sexual act? ("Sinking her teeth and leg spikes first into his back, then his neck, she promptly decapitates her suitor," the narrator states matter-of-factly. "His copulatory movements continue, for the ganglia controlling his muscles are located in the body, not the head—providing a singular case of sex not rearing its ugly head.")

I had to admit that Claudio's rationalization was impressive. It quenched my curiosity, at least for now. It wasn't until well after college that I even dared integrate any aspect of sexuality into my conscious life. Then I learned that the curiosity I had felt about my male friends had graduated to lust. I learned, too, how much harm sexual repression and hypocrisy had caused. I felt awkward, like a toddler on the brink of slamming butt-first on a hard floor after taking its first tentative step.

I didn't know what homosexuality was at that age. Heterosexuality, much less homosexuality, was never mentioned in our home. My parents neglected to explain the birds and the bees. Biology classes glossed over the facts in a scientific overview. It was in literature that I learned the definition of love (read *sex*). Literature described a state of emotions unlike any I had ever experienced: the kiss, the caress, the lovemaking . . .

For a myriad of reasons, displays of affection were not a part of our family life. I saw my parents kiss only twice: during their twenty-fifth wedding anniversary, when my mother planted an unexpected kiss on my father's lips, for which she was reprimanded the next day; and in a Texas intensive-care unit years later.

I had been prohibited from showing affection toward my father at age seven. After having kissed him good night my entire life, Father one night equated such behavior with that of excessively sentimental girls. My self-image was so fragile that one reprimand erected awe-inspiring walls in my head to protect against another. I never questioned the boundaries of my newly circumscribed self. I only played on my strengths; my weaknesses were hidden behind the wall, never to be shown in public.

Where today I see a push toward educating America's youth about sexuality on sitcoms like *Cosby* and *Roseanne*, a forum in which sexuality is talked about in the same tone of voice as dinner fare, in our family sexuality did not exist, and I don't remember hearing about it on television.

In many more ways than my status as a late bloomer, I was unlike the majority of my male teenage friends who were full of raging hormones and primed to party the second dad turned his back. I never took the family car, never battled over the size of my allowance, and never showed the judgment of a gnat when dealing with my elders.

Through my teenage years, I had been desperate to please my father. Eventually, his lack of respect for my accomplishments forced me to give up trying to please him. Good grades were never enough: a B+ in an A+ lineup was enough to arouse his disapproval. A plethora of leadership positions in school organizations could never be enough, since none were in sports. Above-average scores on college admission tests were not enough. Even the glowing letters of acceptance and full scholarship offers to every college I applied to were not enough.

By my senior year of high school I had one more chance and proceeded with what I thought to be my life plan. Opening a white, government-franked envelope one afternoon, I thought I had finally achieved something worthy of approval from Colonel Zuniga; this had to be in the plan he had formulated seventeen years prior. The letter notified me that Representative Henry B. Gonzalez (D-Tex.) had nominated me to the U.S. Military Academy at West Point. One of two childhood dreams had come true. Now I had the chance to continue the Zuniga-Vaca military tradition while training at the best military school in the world. Not even this great honor elicited overt praise or pride from my father. Perhaps it was the least he expected, another step in his grand plan. At my request, he drove me to Fort Sam Houston for appointee physical exams. An hour-long interview with a retired lieutenant colonel and professor of military science at Trinity University in San Antonio went without a hitch. I passed the Army's physical fitness test with an above-average score. It seemed certain my dream of becoming a military officer like so many of my ancestors was within reach. "You're going to West Point," the interviewer said glowingly.

But it was not to be, and I harbor no regrets.

I will never again ridicule those who swear that the strange coincidences and juxtapositions of life always come with a silver lining.

Coming home from school early one afternoon in May 1987, I found the colonel cradling my mother's head in a blatant display of affection never before witnessed in our home. Whenever there was bad news, my family gave it the best spin. I remembered the day some years before my mother had sat Sandra and me in her bedroom to tell us of our father's need for triple-bypass surgery. She helped soften the blow then. Not now.

I sat on the ottoman, a dazed look on my face. The silence was broken as my mother, thin black lines for eyes, tending toward teariness now, whispered her diagnosis: terminal gastric cancer. The colonel's mouth was limp, as if in the wake of some extreme grief.

"Pepé, I don't want you to change your plans," she said, tears streaming down her face. This was the face of the woman who had read my work, scissored between her fingers, expressionless, her hazel eyes training slowly across the pages before them.

In denial, I bounced back, "You'll be fine, Mama."

She shook her head slowly. A sense of defeat in her eyes temporarily replaced the gleam of her extraordinary fervor for life. My father sat back in his easy chair, as if escaping from the here-and-now, his mind *terra incognita* to all but himself.

What else could I say? I walked away, locked myself in my bedroom, thought of losing her, and cried. My mother seemed already to have given up. I pictured her sitting at home, staring at arthritic hands like lame animals in her lap. I couldn't go away to West Point. I would settle for Texas A&M.

THREE HOURS
FROM HOME

My ACADEMIC CAREER AT TEXAS A&M UNIVERSITY, A SPRAWLING complex located a three-hour drive from San Antonio, started not as a student of a 42,000-plus university but as a cadet in the 2,200-member Aggie Corps of Cadets. A highly regimented institution, the corps commissioned hundreds of officers in every branch of the service each year through the Reserve Officers' Training Corps. In organization, the college ROTC program was much like the program I had commanded in high school.

As a senior in high school, I had attended San Antonio College and during the summer the University of Texas, at Austin—referred to as **Texas University** by Aggies (to correct the notion that this particular university is not *the* university of Texas, as it is so frequently referred to by the uneducated or those who claim it as an alma mater.) Texas A&M University was not West Point, I knew, but it was the closest I would come to intense officer-candidate training while going to school near home. I had ignored my mother's plea for me to go ahead to West Point despite her bout with cancer. Rationalization helped me accept the sacrifice I had willingly made to be near her. Besides, Texas A&M offered nothing less than what the U.S. Military Academy offered: hazing, camaraderie, and full scholarships. And when I graduated from Texas A&M, my commission as a second lieutenant in the U.S. Army would look just as formidable as any West Pointer's. The butter-bar rank insignia of a second lieutenant pinned on my uniform would shine just as bright—if not a little more so, to hide an irrational inferiority complex.

I had scored high enough in college placement tests and had taken basic college courses while still in high school, so by the time I arrived at Texas A&M seeking a bachelor's degree in political science, I was three-quarters of the way through with my degree requirements. Unfortunately, as most Aggies know all to well, some misguided cadets have been known to major in the corps (not an accredited degree program) and minor in their original major, eventually finding themselves five- or six-year residents of Bryant-College Station, a university town in the heart of Texas. For a cadet, the Quadrangle (a plot of real estate around which beautiful brick buildings framed college life) was an oasis. I was drawn to my new surroundings.

The corps handled training much like the Army's basic-training doctrine, except it had a little more respect for a cadet's mental acuity. The tactics were all the same: Mind games. Hard work. Long nights. Inspections. Deep decorum. Even the occasional fraternitylike hazing that made corps life fun (we made a pact never to divulge our nefarious deeds). With these demands alone, some cadets found themselves overwhelmed by duty versus studies.

For those lacking in self-discipline or spoiled by their first taste of freedom, there was the added dynamic of booze. There were the Flying Tomato's daily keg parties and quarts of whiskey waiting for gaunt and pallid drunkards to "put them away." How cruel the bar owners seemed, closing the pubs at half-past ten, thus salvaging a few careers. The fact remained, though, that, hangover or not, even a degreed chemist has to study to pass Chemistry 101 exams.

After my plebe year in the corps (*flashback:* **Animal-A! The best damned outfit on the campus! Whoop!**), I knew that if I wanted to graduate before developing arthritic hands (a disadvantage in the journalism field), I must abandon the corps. Of course, that news did not fare well with my father, who didn't understand my reasoning. I was quitting the corps because it was too damp a place to shine; where there is no oxygen, the fire will not light, I explained.

My father all but demanded I change my mind or he'd cut me

off. My mother reminded him I was on scholarship. Good for you, Mom! She was pleased to hear I'd be finishing my degree requirements at Texas A&M and taking electives at San Antonio College. As for my father, she advised that I ignore his temper tantrum and concentrate on my writing.

"They haven't brainwashed you yet, have they?" she joked, to my father's chagrin.

Since I'd left for college, time seemed to stagnate in my parents' home. My mother continued the chemotherapy treatments her doctors (hopefully) predicted would prolong her life so long as the cancer remained in remission. Father continued his frantic busybody schedule. "He misses you," my mother confided. And Sandra—well, she remained the quiet sister with whom I shared nothing in common, destined to be pushed in a perambulator by my parents for as long as they had life.

I started to love football. Amazingly, I had grown to love not only the testosterone feast in the bleachers, but the excitement of the game itself. Athletic rituals and lunacies have a way of intriguing even the most ambivalent observer who manages to survive the pandemonium. This, of course, came as a great relief to my father, who until now, had secretly considered me a geek.

After a year in the corps—most of which time blurred into a day or two of the same regimentation of my home life, only with much more beer, gin, and Jim Beam—college suddenly became a fascinating adventure. No longer a cadet, and outside of the Quad's creative restraint, I now felt like a guest at a gigantic, eclectic intellectual banquet. No, I didn't read every book in Irving Library either in alphabetical order or by call number, but I was edging closer to my true calling.

Floundering in a state of hyper-receptivity, I found it impossible to ignore even the most nebulous of ideas. The first translation of the hieroglyphic texts inscribed on the four gold-encrusted shrines that enclosed the sarcophagus of Tutankhamen ... C. G. Jung's last work detailing the problems of philosophical alchemy and the synthesis of opposites ... The first full-length biography of William Butler Yeats ... Each left an indelible mark.

I had a couple of outstanding professors, one or two. A phlegmatic Frenchman with majestic common sense, after taking nostalgic ego trips each morning, taught the importance of triviality while lecturing zealously to hundreds of rapt students about mathematics. Why a partial derivative? Why a derivative at all? Why not an integral, or a cosine, or perhaps a logarithm? Stuck on the proof of a lemma, he groped on the blackboard for less than two minutes, consulted his notes, and read aloud the relevant entry. It was "The proof of this lemma is trivial." Move on, he said smugly. Clearly a planned lesson. *Superbe!*

"The hermeneutics of tragic modulates by imperceptible degrees into the hermeneutics of post-tragic joy, at the creative freedom of the interpreter . . ."

I started writing—for myself—what would four years later become a novella. This time for me was not all peace and discovery. There was grim poverty here, and congestion and unemployment and small crime. And here the confusion and loneliness of my high-school days in San Antonio revisited my spirit. While most who had opened the same door to enlightenment seemed content with a life so ostensibly devoid of disturbance, for me there was a sedulous fascination for quality of life, which was frequently exasperating.

The quirks of the mind are unexplainable, the means of acquiring knowledge are equally so. For some it means capturing the atmosphere of a sunset in a poem or converting a sunrise into splashes of words on the canvas of a computer monitor. And for others it means capturing the pageantry of nature, the songs of birds, the fragrance of flowers, the October twilight, the playfulness of a kitten, or the relaxed attitude of a cat stretched out in the sun, its paws serving as bookmarks in texts about murky skies and polluted rivers.

As great an adventure as these musings were to me, I could not overlook the dreary realization that drugs, AIDS and the sexual revolution, violent videos and raunchy rap music, rising suicide rates, peer pressure, an epidemic of guns and knives in schools, and declining test scores, the threats that allegedly replaced our parents' age-old fears of cholera and influenza—all of which were theoretically a product of inner cities—were here too. In the small college town of

Bryant-College Station, population 42,000 in fall or spring, 8,000 on the break, homicides weren't unheard of. Three corpsmen fell victim to gun-inflicted deaths; one was a suicide. This was my wake-up call. The blinders fell off. Guns are everywhere. In the headlines, on the streets, and, most tragically, in the hands of kids who should be packing brown-bag lunches rather than semiautomatics.

Before moving to San Antonio in 1983, I didn't know that children were sidetracked by the temptations of the street, where personal achievement takes a backseat to drugs and gangs. My parents sheltered me from the reality that five-year-olds died in drive-by shootings.

The vacant windows in abandoned buildings on each block across from my school were outnumbered only by the vacant eyes of people devoid of aspirations and hope. A lost generation of people my age whose baggy flared jeans and white ribbed T-shirts were less a political statement than a social statement of kids unwilling even to try overcoming the exigencies of their hardscrabble lives.

Journalist Donald Marquis wrote that the great desideratum of human education is to make all people aware that they are gods in the making, and that they can walk on water if they will. My mother believed this, and I was the beneficiary of her belief. Like many young people I felt immortal.

Along with my greater social awakening came my first experiments with alcohol (an acquired taste), cigarettes (couldn't finish one), and the required chewing tobacco (threw up the first two times; "must never swallow juices," I chanted to remember).

One weekend some buddies and I spent a Sunday night in San Antonio. I called my parents from Dallas the evening before to gloat about the Aggies' triumph over the Fighting Irish of Notre Dame University in the Cotton Bowl, and I warned them I might drop by.

I checked my breath with a cupped hand before ringing the doorbell. I prayed that the Clorets would cloak the Tanqueray Collins, beer and peppermint schnapps used to help celebrate our victory. But how could I suppress my drunken boisterousness? I'd been rumored to say some weird things when intoxicated. Although I was not quite legally drunk that night, out of respect for the sanctity of my parents' home, I have to admit I was buzzing on cloud nine. Just as happy as a clam, my mother later joked.

I thought sure I had behaved well until I was asked outside by my father the following morning. "Come outside for a minute, son," he said, no trace of a negative tone in his voice.

Time for The Talk, I thought, with dread building.

"I don't have a problem with you drinking," he said, much to my surprise. I awaited the ever-lingering *but*. "But you were a little loud there last night. . . . A little foul-mouthed, too. What'd you drink, Jim Beam?" A sly smile. Approval?

This was taking on more the air of a pat-on-the-back session than a lecture for misbehavior. It seemed I had finally done something to make my father proud. He liked to drink, and drinking had made me a man. It had been that easy all along. I almost kicked myself for not having gotten it earlier.

As summer approached, I registered for a media law and ethics course at San Antonio College and started working part-time at the *San Antonio Express-News*, the leading newspaper in circulation of southwest Texas. I moved back home, which made my mother happy. I helped my father with the multiplicity of chores and projects he seemed to invent daily, which made him happy. I spent time with Sandra, which made her happy; we rarely saw each other during the school year, our academic schedules always conflicting.

But I was not happy. I had discovered in college that one does not study journalism, one *does* it. A stint at the *Express-News* might improve my mood.

Working for a major metropolitan daily was not all it had been made out to be. At the *Express-News*, tight deadlines and a frantic pace were a part of everyday life. Tough deadlines, I had learned in college, come in handy when you're forcing words from atrophied brain tissues. But I was a twenty-one-year-old "snotnose wannabe journalist," as my college journalism professor referred to me (a term of endearment, he claimed), and my career seemed to me to be going nowhere fast.

Sitting at the city desk, scanning the AP wire, watching golf on a television set meant to tune into CNN, avoiding the billows of tobacco smoke rising from the longtime journalists by hiding behind air fresheners—that was my nine-to-five life. Gossip around the water fountains, vending machines full of junk food, and the morgue (library) enlivened my days but did not make the boredom any more tolerable.

Very quickly I made acquaintances with every soul in the newsroom, pumping each for information on the system. There were all kinds in this business, from the sixty-year-old assistant city editor who sat in her chair applying lipstick or smoking a Virginia Slim with every turn of a phrase, or the two queers sitting in a corner of the newsroom enthralled in always animated conversations.

Rumors abounded about those two. I will never forget how uncomfortable I felt during an impromptu briefing by the office snitch: "Yeah, we have two *fags* on staff. Watch your back, man. I do." Even before his warning, my nascent "gaydar" (an intuitive sixth sense gay men and lesbians use to find "family members," no matter how concealed or invisible) had detected their presence. But they never approached me. Theirs was always a silent awareness.

I looked to elder journalists who had worked there at least three years and had yet to be promoted. What were *my* chances at promotion? In middle school I edited my first newspaper (mimeographed). In high school I was the editor of a biweekly newspaper and a biannual newsmagazine. Just a semester before I was the managing editor of my college paper and editor of its literary magazine. All these cradles of journalism had garnered national awards; I was seasoned beyond my years, aspiring to be a young Woodward or Bernstein. My graying temples (which would return to dark at the earliest opportunity, thanks to Miss Clairol) should prove my seasoning if my twenty-one years of life didn't, I thought. Guess again!

My first news brief was edited twice—one time too many, the city editor snarled. I graduated to obituaries two months later. My first published obit was a shadow of its former self in the next morning's paper. Too much feature, little news, mumbled my editor. My cocky attitude was checked. I had to learn to accept harsh editing, even if I disagreed. Where I used to defend my writing tooth and nail, forcing professors to admit that my approach was an acceptable "alternative style," here my instinct told me to question nothing.

A journalist entering the mass media, I learned through patient observation what lay in wait for the unwary. Editors swearing at their computer screens, tearing up copy, hacking up smoke from abused lungs in between phone calls to the copy desk. I swore I would never envy their positions, much less emulate their style. Their lives were in pathetic disarray, the spice of life checked at the door. They were chained to their desks and rewrote copy out of vengeance, making changes for change's sake to satisfy their hungry egos while crushing others'. I would not be fodder for these literary piranhas.

Each new obituary became a challenge, a way to prove myself worthy of serious notice. As easy as it may sound to write an obituary, it is one of the most demanding assignments imaginable. One has to call survivors for quotes, verify and reverify facts, check the spelling on a name, all the while terrified of the offense an error could cause.

After a while, I was sure I had successfully enterprised, tackling every assignment with the fervor of the new kid on the block, wanting to make my first real step into the professional world a solid one.

Months later I was still an obit writer.

Having discussed my frustration with the city editor and his deputy, I was left with the impression that my time had not yet come. They told me clearly that many veterans of the business would kill to do what I was doing. There was no better job than obit writing, they asserted; it was not considered a rite of passage or a hoop to be jumped through. Besides, everyone read the obit section in a retirement town. What a great way to make a byline.

I wanted much more than this enviable job.

My journalism professor urged patience. But I was twenty-one years old and getting grayer by the minute—or so I thought. My life until now had been one of continuous upward mobility. No pauses or hiccups. I could not afford them. Father, although he disapproved of my career as a whole, would not accept them. Perhaps I could find a way around the wait, a detour that could get me where I felt I deserved to be.

PART 2

RUSSELL

EARLY ONE EVENING IN MAY 1993, CAROL NESS, A *SAN FRANCISCO Examiner* reporter, and I were connected by the marvel of portable-telephone technology. Her voice sounded strained and preoccupied; there was no semblance of her usual upbeat self. Paul, a friend and former colleague, had called her to obtain my address in San Francisco. During their conversation, Paul had mentioned a mutual friend.

"Paul said Russell was your lover," Carol said, more questioning than playing back his words.

My heart skipped a beat. There were three days left before my discharge from the Army. The story of my so-called virginity had spread from front page to front page like a virus, and I was sure everyone was aware of it. I knew why she was asking, but to what end was my answer important to her? Didn't she understand the difference between conduct and status cases? Hadn't she uncovered in her research that a charge of fraudulent enlistment would likely propel my case, and my "virgin" ass, to Fort Leavenworth, Kansas, for a prison term of no less than five years? Had she seen through the unquestioning reports on the valiant stand taken by the gay virgin? Should I expect a *National Enquirer*–type exposé tomorrow? My head was spinning as I realized what she must be feeling, what she might well consider her professional obligation to the truth.

"Russell was a great friend from my days in San Antonio," I started tentatively.

"Is he gay?" she interrupted.

"Yes. We were friends," I insisted, praying she would deem my hedging response something far short of news. I had felt a bond develop with Carol during our first interview, late in the evening before my announcement in Washington, D.C. After numerous interviews, squeezing in one more reporter seemed a chore. But this reporter, unlike the many before her, had shown a compassion and understanding that came from covering San Francisco's gay and lesbian beat for years, and also from her own empathy.

I was getting nowhere with my explanation, which ended short of a full denial. The guilt of betrayal flooded my heart. I had come out to stand for honor and integrity, my soul screamed out. The myth of my virginity was something for which I did not feel responsible.

She asked another question. I barely heard it over the pounding in my ears. I asked her to hold, pressed the mute button, and ran downstairs to seek advice from the three lawyers assembled in the bedroom watching C-SPAN coverage of the Senate Armed Services Committee hearings.

"Try to discuss the gradual process that coming to terms with one's sexuality is," Dave said, emphasizing "gradual" with a slow sweep of his hand.

"Focus on the issue of denial and self-hate," Laurie added.

"Don't say anything specific about any relationship. Beg for privacy," my attorney, James Kennedy, concluded.

My voice quavered with nervousness as it never before had. I pressed the mute button and blithered a semicoherent answer similar to what I had been advised. My head was about to explode.

Carol gave me no hint whether she understood the parade of excuses or even if she would accept them without investigation. This statement was all I could give her. I felt wrung out as I replaced the receiver. If I have trouble constructing an answer now, I thought, how miserably I would have failed in the initial interviews to explain the true nature and significance of my first gay relationship.

The apostle Simon's threefold denial of Jesus, who had been arrested in the courtyard of the Sanhedrin, had been a central doctrine drilled into the pliable minds of Catholic children on the Sunday mornings dedicated to theological study. As far a stretch as it might seem, my conscience had applied this doctrine to my quandary with Russell. Just as Sister Marie Jésus interpreted the Scripture to say Simon's denial had been a morally neutral and prudent act, so too I came to consider my denial.

I met Russell in the media section of the San Antonio College library the summer after my graduation. My life still had no clear direction. For a year, the Corps of Cadets had stepped in to replace the strict regimentation that my home life had provided. Later, good study habits replaced the corps' rules. Now my job at the *Express-News* from at least nine to at best five, and living distinctly out of place in my parents' home, provided structure. Friends had been few, my acquaintances many. My circle of friends in college was limited to my colleagues at the newspaper. Fellow corpsmen were buddies I conveniently kept at arm's length. It was easier that way.

Life at home had not changed much to accommodate the changing circumstances of my life. In almost every respect, in my twenty-first year of life, my father's house, and my place in it, remained unchanged. I still had no house key—I cannot explain why—and the curfew was still enforced, albeit with some give-and-take in hours. Retired, my father had immersed himself in house projects: gutters, cement, painting, electrical work—there was always something that could be singled out as not quite perfect. He kept the same hours he had observed in his military days, reveille at 0530 and retreat at 2200. I couldn't help feeling, on some level, that my sister and I had become the two-person company he was assigned to lead until we moved out or he died.

Meeting Russell resurrected some life in me. The twenty-six-year-old hotel room-service waiter was strikingly beautiful—he was Mexican-American with exotic Aztec features—and by no means effeminate. Russell had been a halfback in high school until the Texas legislature passed a "no pass no play" education bill that side-lined him from the game he loved because of borderline failing grades that would someday sideline him from high school altogether. Although he possessed little if anything in common with me, he had a magnetism that tore down wall after wall constructed in my teens

45

to hide my repressed sexuality. At the age of twenty-one I learned the intensity of a kiss, a caress, and holding a hard yet gentle, vulnerable human body next to mine.

I gradually grew weary of reliving my childhood life and retreated more and more to a duplicitous life with Russell, spending every free moment with him. My fear of the street weakened with time and through experience.

When my father reached for the door handle one night and reiterated that if I wished to live under his roof again I would have to live by his rules—his outburst spurred by my 9 o'clock arrival from a birthday party instead of by the 8 P.M. curfew set on my fifteenth birthday—I walked out. I had tasted unconditional freedom in college and I did not wish to submit to my father's rules ever again.

But the bolstered ego of my college days had given way to feelings of burden and self-hate. I thought I was trading my father's rules and emotional coldness for freedom and the warmth of someone who wanted to make a new home with me. Soon after we met—exactly two weeks after—Russell lost his job. I supported him financially, and he kept house for me. Given the environment in which I was reared, this arrangement quickly felt like home. But behind the nurturing he ostensibly provided, a deeply dysfunctional game was at play. That we were novices at this type of relationship made our problems all the more destructive.

From the beginning, Russell was passive-aggressive. My self-image was his to manipulate, and I was particularly vulnerable without the regimentation of school, corps, and family. Now stress was destroying my stomach, along with my self-esteem. I started guzzling Maalox by the bottleful. With my Roman Catholic upbringing firmly blocking my mind from making the connections that would cause further emotional turmoil, the fact that I was in a relationship with a man did not even enter the picture. As the sexual element was banished, the relationship seemed akin to that I shared with my parents, only without *any* semblance of love or respect.

The plethora of problems associated with my newly acquired freedom were compounded by our social set. I came to the relationship with few friends and no gay role models. Many of Russell's friends were like me. Lane was a seventy-three-year-old World War II veteran and a registered Republican. He was self-hating, and he never self-identified as gay. And he was just one of many who formed this gaggle of repressed queens. As if the depths of their closets weren't enough, each of these men seemed ashamed to show any emotion. For the number of months in which Russell's apartment was my home, repression and denial, rather than self-discovery, were the order of the day.

I lived with Russell in a one-bedroom apartment, enjoying the feeling of coming home to a prepared meal, a clean home, and someone with whom to share the rest of my day. In retrospect, ours was a domestic life more idyllic than that of the Cleavers. Yet it was warped in many ways. I sought the mother and maid most straight men seek in their mates because they have been trained never to sever the apron strings. He was the first person of either sex with whom I had ever experienced the pleasures I had denied myself. But what, exactly, our relationship meant, I surely did not know then and I can hardly figure it out now, even with the help of a psychiatrist. Although we lived together for almost a year, Russell and I shared a physical relationship spanning less than a few weeks.

Russell reveled in the knowledge that he was delivering me from the repressed state in which I'd lived since adolescence. Yet just as abruptly as he had given me carnal knowledge, Russell ended our physical relationship, preferring, I thought, emotional closeness. This was, after all, I rationalized, what love was all about. Feeling the beat of a human heart, hearing "I love you," and caring for each other. Unfortunately, his concept of love was fathoms away from mine. I wanted romance and commitment; he didn't.

"Sorry, Joe, this is not me. Don't expect much from me," Russell said one night after dinner at a restaurant.

"I know it's wrong," I answered after taking a sip from an almost empty wineglass, the fifth of the night. "Who cares, though?"

"I'm not a fag! We can't be lovers, or whatever it is you fags call each other." He got up from the table and took a cab home.

I sat alone, not knowing whether to cry or not. Had he used me?

47

Why was I so stupid? Of course he was right. And damn him, I wasn't a fag either!

"I'll show you," I slurred, then left two twenties on the table and hailed a cab. I closed my heart to love that night. I closeted the lust. Never again would I act on it until the demon spawned in my body was expelled. But I remained in limbo, expecting some resolution. Does developing self-hate qualify as resolution?

"I'm no fag either!"

Were we ever lovers, as he recounted to reporters five years later when my name made local headlines? Perhaps in Russell's tormented, guilt-ridden mind; perhaps, sometimes, in mine too over the last few years. Perhaps we each wished that something deeper and more mature had come of our time together, but our youth and self-hatred forbade it.

There was love. The *L*-word was used, but what did it mean if we couldn't own up to being able to love each other with passion and affection because we were of the same sex? In order not to hate Russell now, I have to believe that there was some love between us. It is clear to me now that our love took the confused shape common to some early relationships between people who do not or cannot identify with themselves, much less with another human being. There were times I reveled in this arrangement—times of intense bliss, emotion, and tenderness. There were many more times that I abhorred it. But neither regret nor hatred forced my denial of our life together. I owed Russell an explanation.

It wasn't until well into my public trial that I wrote him a brief letter.

May 20, 1993

Russell,

Five years ago, I ran away from myself and from you because, although I couldn't pinpoint it at the time, I was growing to hate both of us. You provided me with a feeling of home and a world in which to assimilate. I hope for your sake that you have been able to develop a sense of self to replace the gnawing doubt that festered within us. My journey to self-discovery has been long and painful. I pray yours has been or will someday be less so.

As hard as it was for you to hear the edited version of my life played over and over by the media, as painful as it was to hear your very existence denied as Simon denied Jesus in the hours before His crucifixion, the pain also tore at me. I know that rational explanations—even those grounded in the prospect of prison—do little to assuage your resentment. But please know that the price I have paid for the celebrity status you claim I possess has been enormous. Believe me when I say you have been spared some agony by being left out until now, when I can tell the story in my words, without intermediaries or headlines.

Forgive me for hurting you, both then, and possibly again now. You demanded that our story be told, and now that I am able, I do so. You retain a place in my heart. . . .

Joe

ESCAPE

I promised my mother I wouldn't miss her famous lasagna dinner for the world that night, so I drove straight home from the *Express-News*. It had been ages since my last meal at home. A few extra pounds gained since college, testament to a bad diet and not enough exercise. Instinctively, I scanned through the last two weeks' worth of mail.

"Your father should be home any minute," Mother yelled to me over the clamor of metal scraping the grill and Evita Perón—by way of Andrew Lloyd Webber—straining her tonsils from a worn record. Father's monthly checkup had taken longer than scheduled.

Unless he had miraculously learned to respect and appreciate the medical profession since his heart attack, his would be a foul mood I would have avoided on any other day by asking for a to-go box before his arrival. But I was craving a healthy, home-cooked meal, so I stayed put.

My father made his arrival known by hurling his jacket on the ottoman and joining us in the kitchen. "How about a cheese omelet?" he asked, adding a side order of potatoes and an ice-cold beer to round out his meal. In short, give him everything the doctor forbade. Ever faithful to the superman persona that was Army standard issue, he would ignore a diet sternly recommended for a man suffering from arteriosclerosis.

After fifty-two years of life, his waking hours and routines were consistent day in day out. Up at 0530 daily, he read the morning papers and watched CNN. Until his triple-bypass surgery more than five years before, there was silence, save the sound of the frying pan, sizzling as high-fat meats hit its Teflon bottom. Eggs and bacon. Eggs and sausage. Eggs and potatoes. Breakfast was incomplete without eggs, he still swore, although more often than not he followed doctors' orders to regulate his cholesterol. Thanks to the lasagna already sitting in the oven, we were spared the epicurean delight of the omelet and bacon my father was having for dinner. Inhaling my meal to avoid witnessing his blatant act of self-destruction, I excused myself from the table and made my escape to the living room. A shaft of sunlight cleaved the dark room, falling on the dingy slipcover that hid the love seat and spilling onto the once gray shag carpeting. My father has not suffered a second heart attack yet, but his habits and attitude keep him on that path, and I don't believe he is going to turn off any time soon.

"Good evening, I'm Dan Rather," the "CBS Evening News" anchor said, then segued into a special report on the American economy. Wouldn't mind having Dan's job, I thought. I watched intently as he anchored five minutes of breaking news, then cut to a commercial.

The whirl of helicopter blades captured my attention. An Army recruiting commercial propagated the images of glory behind the slick ad slogan to *Be All You Can Be*. I had ignored this commercial at least a hundred dozen times before, but tonight I was engaged. Adventure, opportunity, change.

Here was a chance to fulfill a goal on the life plan my father had drafted for me twenty years ago while escaping my involvement with Russell and what I was becoming because I feared it. A chance to continue the Zuniga military legacy I had been purposefully eluding.

My mind slowed my usual quick pace as I walked the few blocks home from the U.S. Army recruiting station. I told no one where I was going, much less why. The evening of July 27, 1989, without my parents' knowledge but assuming their consent, I signed a contract with the U.S. Army for a six-year enlistment. I did so with some trepidation, but also with a sense of relief. The ambling was over. The lack of direction was over. Life with Russell was over.

As a bonus, in satisfying my needs I would again acquiesce to the colonel's life plan. He would consider the news a victory, that I was finally doing something right with my life. I was born a warrior, he never tired saying.

Mother would lament my decision. She had given up her dream and would think I was now giving up on mine. If he didn't wisely applaud my decision to end our destructive relationship, Russell would see this as the end of his meal ticket. All Sandra had to say was that now she could call me G.I. Joe.

In my youth I had promised myself never to regret any decision I made. But looking in my mother's teary eyes, I could tell she felt that with my signature on the enlistment contract, I had thrown water on the torch she had passed on to me.

No journalist slots were available now.

You trumped our dream . . .

I had agreed to enlist as a combat medical specialist—a Florence Nightingale fantasy, a friend once joked. More like F. Scott Fitzgerald, I rationalized.

A college degree meant I could have been an officer, my father needlessly reminded me.

Should I confess to the colonel that I had chosen to enlist as a private because I valued the grit of the soldiers who formed the Army's backbone, as opposed to the politics of officer status? I think he knew.

The two months between signing the enlistment contract and shipping out to basic training were forgettable, at best. Family life remained much the same. Old habits die hard. Russell had said nothing except goodbye when I announced my action over the telephone the following morning. And work at the *Express-News* was business as usual. My last day at work was uneventful, except for a final review and hefty final paycheck, bloated by the addition of accumulated vacation a cub reporter was given but could not take. There were no real goodbyes in a world of type and art that somehow melds minds with computer terminals—an incredible communion, as reporters and their editors labor over cathode-ray tubes. There were no emotional farewells from my few friends because when one escapes, one does so with stealth.

My mother predicted I would never again live in San Antonio, a city she thought of as a mecca surpassed in its grandeur only by the edenized Mexico of a childhood to which she could never return. She was right. Although she did not know the life I was leaving, she knew I was fleeing.

My recruiter, a Samoan who had joined the military to escape the rut of poverty, commuted the thirty-five minutes to our place at 0400, September 29, 1989, to deliver me in his Saab to the military enlisted processing station ten minutes from home. In the silent pause that precedes any goodbye, I looked around the house at the somber faces of a family unaccustomed to sharing its feelings, soaking it all in for memory. Four hours later, ten recruits and I boarded cabs to the San Antonio International Airport. An already delayed and overbooked United Airlines flight would deliver us to our custodians at the Fort Bliss basic combat-training course in El Paso.

I opened the sack lunch Mother had given me at the door. She detested airline food and insisted I eat some good home cooking before getting to El Paso. Looking around to ensure no one was spying, I opened the crushed bag I had stuffed into my carry-on bag. A note from my mother was wedged between two meatloaf sandwiches. Suddenly I wasn't very hungry anymore, just homesick.

September 29, 1989

Son,

I know I didn't make your time with us any more pleasant with my sad demeanor. Please understand that I am very proud of you and know you will do well in all of your endeavors. I just don't understand your decision to enlist, and as a medic of all things. You are a writer, you have been since you were a child. I suppose I am just afraid that your gift of writing will go to waste as mine did so long ago.

I am finishing this letter after a brief argument with your father about you. He, of course, thinks you have done the right thing. I disagree with him for his biased reasons. But I will not disagree with you if you believe in your heart that the path you have chosen will lead you to happiness. Follow your heart, *hijo*. God bless you now and always.

Your mother,
Raquel

BOOT CAMP

"GET THE HELL OFF MY BUS! COME ON, MOVE!" DRILL SERGEANT Tacdol screamed from the driver's seat in an unending string of insults. The forest-green Army bus came to a screeching halt in front of a row of dilapidated circa 1940s' wooden barracks, our home for the next two months.

Twenty nervous recruits tried clamoring off the bus through the narrow door two at a time. The twenty-five-minute drive from the El Paso Airport to Fort Bliss had featured stone silence. The driver seemed to enjoy our nervous energy. Before our eyes, though, this drill sergeant had metamorphosed from serene to maniacal, hurling insults left and right. We ran to keep up with his angry directions leading us through the quadrangle to Company Delta 1, 1st Battalion, 56th Air Defense Artillery Brigade's Basic Combat Skills Training Center.

Today would be my reintroduction to the U.S. Army, I convinced myself on the flight to El Paso. Not too long before, I had abandoned the Aggie Corps of Cadets and the prospect of a military career as an officer in my search for fame and fortune. My reasons for enlisting were selfish, but this was a *quid pro quo* arrangement: I would commit my life to the Army in return for an escape from a life that wasn't working. Instead of fixing the problems, I chose a new start. The Army was a beneficiary of my escapism. I was here because I did not want to belong to a group of people my age whose once-wiry bodies had sagged and swollen from an avalanche of fried food and Diet Cokes; nor did I want to belong to a group of people whose lives were adrift like the society twit Gloria in the movie

Auntie Mame. Outweighing all those selfish reasons, however, I am convinced that I was in El Paso that afternoon, tolerating tyrannical drill sergeants' orders, prepared for the hell of boot camp, because I could not escape the life plan that had been laid out for me by destiny.

Philosophical pondering ceased almost immediately as a group of at least twelve drill sergeants pored out of the barracks like a pride of lions about to stalk the fresh meat delivered to their doorstep. We flinched as they each took turns, or barked insults and slurs in chorus. Their vocal cords strained as they assaulted and shredded every vestige of pride and dignity a recruit possessed. They were desperately looking for rebellion to justify an increase in their tirade, but none was offered.

Implement Plan B.

A drill sergeant the size of a sumo wrestler, a gleam of unrelenting hunger in his magnetizing green eyes, glared at the exposed jugular of what looked to be a former high-school quarterback. Within minutes a two-hundred-pound giant squirmed like a mosquito on flypaper, twisting and turning, getting more stuck on his wounded dignity and bordering on the brink of tears. Drill Sergeant Lobue (recruits were never privy to a drill sergeant's first name) had presumably been elected to the office of super villain by his colleagues in a game of "good cop–bad cop," with no one assigned to play the good role. He was now in charge, dropping everyone for pushups.

"Looks like we've got ourselves a bunch of *pansies* here!" the platoon sergeant howled, a menacing glare never leaving his face nor those of the drill sergeants circling around us like vultures, trying to break our morale with veiled threats. "On your feet, scumbags!" he screamed, before a fit of manic laughter, becoming spastic, seized control of him. It dissipated just long enough for a gracious welcome to the U.S. Army, followed by a snarled introduction to "Lobue's Army," as if the two existed in a symbiotic relationship.

"I'm going to make men out of you little faggots!" he growled, seconds before dropping us for another set of pushups. "You little maggots aren't fit to spit-shine my boots!" He himself pumped out pushups in perfect form, a hell-bent skin pic of a tank displayed prominently on his bicep. "When I'm done with you mama's boys, you'll be *real* soldiers!"

Although the drill sergeant intended his message for the group as a whole, his barbs were clearly aimed at one recruit in particular. The recruit he targeted could not even begin to imagine the sheer hell in store for him. He had already started squirming in formation. His would be a hell endured in the name of unit cohesion.

Private Steve Clement was a pink-cheeked farm boy from Kansas. He wore his naïveté like a flashing neon sign on his forehead. Many of us would later joke that his recruiter must have been desperate to meet a quota the day he swore this one in. His innocence became the weakness on which the drill sergeant fed. The unit was, theoretically, going to grow stronger by feasting on the scraps left over.

"Come on, grandma!" the drill sergeant snarled repeatedly at the recruit, even though the young man often outperformed many of us. He was too flustered to see the lack of a basis in reality. The realization wouldn't have helped him anyway.

In every platoon formation, without an ounce of provocation, Private Clement was singled out due to some undefinable characteristic the drill sergeant usually attributed to homosexuality. Whether the recruit was in fact gay I do not know, nor did facts seem to matter much. The drill sergeant seized on Private Clement's weaknesses, real or imagined, as an opportunity to build esprit de corps. The rest of us dutifully focused our hatred and venom on the target. We would bond by purging one of our own, a lesson contrary to any I would learn as a leader in the real Army, where your unit is only as strong as your weakest link. According to accepted leadership doctrine, you strengthen that link; you do not excise it. Not so in whatever cruel manual governed basic training.

There was no consideration of the pain being collectively inflicted on our drill sergeant's human teaching aid. As our anger increased, fanned by a drill sergeant intent on making us strong by attacking this private, we memorized the Army's "No Fags Allowed!" doctrine. Private Clement's career was being extinguished in the process. Three weeks into training, the recruit was discharged for "failure to adapt." The strategy achieved its desired effect. And his dream of becoming an Army doctor, a goal he promised his parents he'd accomplish while serving his country, was dashed because he had been randomly selected to symbolize everything the Army sought to extinguish in the rest of us. He was the punching bag on which we—every last one of us, regardless of our individual levels of shame or disgust—developed our muscles. Private Clement crumbled. We simply redoubled our efforts, afraid of becoming weak links and, in turn, the next example.

I cannot measure what the impact of this taunting had on Private Clement. I can only offer a framework in which to measure the impact this training technique has in creating the type of monsters who could perpetuate hatred and misogyny without even noticing it. Strength in machismo. The lesson taught here was to associate perceived weakness with a species of "submales." For female soldiers this created double jeopardy. Either females were strong and masculine, and hence lesbians on the road to eventual discharge, or they were weak and an easy target for sexual harassment.

The Clement incident marked my first encounter with an inherent contradiction in military psychology. The Army requires fellow soldiers to form close bonds founded on caring and concern, yet it forbids them to care for one another too much. Thus a soldier's stripping, showering, and childishly chasing another naked soldier around the shower room to slap him on the butt with a wet towel is an acceptable gesture, only if a "fag" joke follows to defuse any note of sexual tension underlying the horseplay. From ass-grabbing to sexually laden double entendres, the aura of homoeroticism in the military is ever present, fostered but denied in the same breath. The confusion lies in the contradiction implicit in the crash course on homosexuality the Army offers its usually less than worldly recruits while labeling the homosexual *lifestyle* (whatever that is) as the military's nemesis. Even as the drill sergeants promote certain of what can only be called gay values—intimate male bonding—they teach recruits to hate elements of themselves and their new strengths.

The course never lost the momentum it gained on that first day, regardless of how long it took our bodies to adjust to the newness of a regimen that required every last ounce of mental and physical energy and then some. Wakeup at 0400, like everything else, eventually became routine. The daily dose of push-until-muscle-failure physical training, consisting primarily of pushups and situps, took longer to adjust to. But it was the twice-weekly three-mile runs in temperatures near freezing, the air so thin that simply breathing was painful, to which I would never adjust.

Meals heavy with carbohydrates, proteins, and fats helped keep ravenous enlistees alive, even if, while we were sitting at the long mess-hall tables struggling to keep our eyes open, we could not identify our power source—food and fear. We grew strong.

As if the physical challenges weren't enough, the mental strain of sitting through required hour-long classes jerked the rug out from under our feet at the end of each training day. We learned about first aid, land navigation, military courtesy and customs, and the dreaded sexually transmitted disease lecture, complete with gory slides for effect. All of this in preparation for field time, a taste of what the real army was all about, Drill Sergeant Lobue explained on one of his rare "love you guys'" days.

That night the temperature outside dropped to at least ten below. In twenty-four hours we would be sleeping in the New Mexico desert, which was at least five degrees colder. We listened intently as Drill Sergeant Lobue reviewed the survival skills course, something he claimed to do only for classes he liked. He punctuated the review with a flip through a 1950s-vintage medical picture book of cold-weather injuries. Black-and-white photographs of various appendages people failed to keep warm, sometimes still attached, drove the point home as no verbal warning could.

The next morning we boarded buses bound for White Sands Missile Range in full battle gear. The more lax treatment we had grown accustomed to during the last few days as recruits and drill sergeants had begun to bond suddenly ceased to exist. We were going to war! The grunt's language and actions began to reflect those of leaders concerned with accomplishing a mission. Nineteen recruits were supposedly ready to accomplish this mission, given the combat and survival skills absorbed in less than a month of intense training. Bottom line: We had been taught the skills necessary for the evolution from warrior to hero to imperialist invader to rude guest who doesn't know when the mission has been completed and it's time to leave.

"Let's say goodbye to Fort Bliss the right way," Drill Sergeant Beaudin suggested as the bus doors closed and the bus driver disengaged the parking brake. He had been the docile one throughout our training, though we feared the size of his biceps and the shoulders bulging underneath his battle dress uniform (BDUs). Make him mad, and he could run enlistees into the ground without breaking a sweat himself.

"Yeah!" every soul on the bus screamed in response, perhaps thinking he meant a smart wave of our hands or a solemn recitation of the second platoon motto. We quickly discovered how wrong we were as he filed us out of the bus, M16A1 rifles in hand, fifty-pound ruck sacks strapped to our backs.

"All the way up ..." Drill Sergeant Beaudin purposefully kept the cadence slow, "and all the way down. Get those dicks off the ground! All the way up ..."

These pushups seemed pointless as we were about to start a mission. Sadism in the name of bonding. It was sunset when we finally left Fort Bliss for a week in the desert surrounding the White Sands Missile Range.

New Mexico was beautiful, but not to be enjoyed. Our lips were chapped, our eyelids drooped from too many exhausting days, our hands callused from pushups on gravel and repeated clawing over the intractable obstacle course. However harsh life had seemed to us until now, we were in for a real surprise at the end of this nine-hour bus ride.

BOOM! BOOM! RATATAT!

The deafening noise of artillery blasts, machine-gun fire, and blaring sirens signaled the start of a confidence course that would test all the combat skills we knew in an almost surreal combat environment. More machine-gun fire, grenade blasts, and the screams of unrelenting drill sergeants watching nineteen other similarly frightened enlistees crawl through and around a maze of concertina wire laden with camouflaged booby traps. The wire was real, as were our fears.

Artillery simulators dropped one after another, each detonating with the whistle of an incoming round, followed by an earsplitting explosion. This forced many, including me at times, to freeze in place and contemplate quitting this man's army because of the nightmarish game of war the drill sergeants seemed to enjoy making as real as the sand we were eating.

"Halt!" a drill sergeant screamed, stomping off to chew out a recruit lagging far behind.

We wore full mission-oriented protective posture (MOPP) gear, including a protective mask that restricted oxygen flow and felt like it raised our body temperatures by at least a good ten degrees. What a welcome reprieve, for those of us not being chewed out, to lie in the sand and rest a minute while we waited for a signal to continue. Also time to reflect on the horrors of chemical warfare that Drill Sergeant Tacdol had graphically described. To think that this uncomfortable and suffocating gear could save our lives. The explosion of a booby trap forced us to gather up any remaining ounce of adrenaline and low-crawl toward the finish line.

Not more than three feet from the finish line, a tear-gas smoke canister popped off, creating a layer of ground haze that fanned past us. You knew who had not checked and sealed their masks correctly. It was clear from the collective coughing and choking barely audible over the blares of live ammo flashing over our heads, that that would be almost everyone. The drill sergeants darted around, screaming maniacally, firing blanks into the air from M60 machine guns they pulled off the mounts and balanced against their hips.

This sure felt like war. The object tonight was to push us to the limits of our endurance. The lesson, the drill sergeants would later review, was that soldiers driven to the limits of their endurance can withstand the rigors and horrors of combat if well trained and motivated.

"Let's go! Come on, grandmas!" Drill Sergeant Lobue screamed, popping off a practice grenade to accent his carefully chosen words.

Seconds later, the last man having crossed the finish line, the desert's silence enveloped us. There were no weak links in this platoon seemed to be the common thought as we beamed with pride, exhausted as we were. Each one of us deserved the pat on the back Drill Sergeant Beaudin would deliver around the campfire after a two-mile hike back to our encampment.

Our first night in the arid expanse of the New Mexico desert proved how easy it was to forget every lesson the drill sergeants taught us in preparation for the week-long bivouac. I cursed myself for falling asleep so many times during lectures and awaited the punishment I was sure would inevitably follow. Surprisingly, the anticipated barrage of derision never reared its face. I suppose the drill sergeants, who had pitched their tents and started a warm, roaring fire before we could even unpack our sleeping bags, felt that the feeling of utter cold and stupidity we collectively displayed in a pathetic slack-jawed expression was enough torture. They covertly checked on our progress to be sure that no forgotten lesson would, at least that night, lead to tragedy.

By midweek, we'd remembered or relearned enough that it seemed less odd each night to crawl into a frozen sleeping bag, and less uncomfortable to slide out of it at 0400 and sit in the cold for a minute, allowing the frigid air to evaporate the sweat before blundering out into the predawn darkness to piss.

"I want that piss clear as gin, and it better be a gusher," Drill Sergeant Lobue said, attaching an order for every soldier to drink at least two full canteens of water a day, warning that even in cold weather dehydration could kill a man. I saw a buddy pass out early in our training, clearly related to the dark yellow urine he had reported to the medic the day before. We learned our lesson fast. Although two canteens full of water were enough to make me puke, the risk of failing to carry out the order could be death.

When it came time to eat, we ate like gluttons. Lectures and hands-on training continued even in our subzero environment. Daily hikes without rucksacks were necessary to prepare Fort Bliss basic trainees to pass their rite of passage, a seven-mile foot march through the desert in full combat gear. Only then could we be called soldiers, the drill sergeants said, somewhat frivolously, also somewhat ominously.

A front breezed through the desert around midnight two nights before our rite of passage, and the desert turned from bitter cold to absolutely frigid. For a moment I stayed in my sleeping bag, debating whether to get up and tend to nature's call. When drinking quart upon quart of water, there's really not much choice. Ambling out into the billion-starred morning, I thought of my mother. I would feel this way again (*déjà vu*) some other morning in my life, and the same thought would warm my insides.

Sliding back into the sweat-soaked liner, I felt a piece of paper, a letter, caught between the cot and the sleeping bag. Fetching an iciclelike penlight out of my rucksack with one hand, I fumbled to open the envelope with the other. It was, as I suspected, a letter from Mother post-marked four days prior that had fortuitously arrived the night before my rite of passage, a calming force to quiet the self-doubts I was desperately trying to repress.

November 5, 1989

Dear Son,

I hope you're feeling better and that your cough has healed. I know it's a horrible time to catch a cold. Remember to bundle up as much as you can out there in the desert!

Your father and I are fine; as always, there are good days and then there are bad. The days I'm on chemotherapy are particularly bad, but I pray to the Virgin of Guadalupe that someday I will be cured of this disease.

Your father and I had hoped to drive down to El Paso for your graduation but we've incurred some major expenses around the house. Your father had to hire someone to replace twenty-two support posts under the house after the torrential rains of the last few weeks. Even had these expenses not arisen, we wouldn't know until the 10th whether your father could drive or I could travel that long a distance. You know I wish I could be there but, quite honestly, I don't think we can.

Sandra is doing well in school and your father, of course, continues to think up some new project to keep himself busy.

Please take good care of yourself. God will guide you through these tough times. Remember you are not alone. . . . I am always with you. Reach high, never lower your great expectations or make the mistakes of the past.

Your father says I should cut the letter short. They don't give you much time to read letters in basic training, he says. Let me know. God bless you, son. Receive the blessings of a mother who misses you like she would a piece of her heart,

Your mother,
Raquel

P.S. Pepé, don't forget to pray!

It was now morning and we were about to set out under a clear cold sky, toting rucksacks that now weighed upward of sixty pounds. "Cold" could not begin to describe the temperature. I dug a cathole, squatted and did my business. In less than a few seconds there were chills coursing through my veins. Burying my waste quickly with a clump of sand, I ran back into the tent to get warm before our departure. I beat my BDU cold-weather jacket against the sturdiest tent pole available, an unsuccessful attempt to get at least the sleeves to soften. Even then, I could not put it on without feeling I was stepping into a custom-built freezer.

The tactical foot march put to test every skill we had learned since that first day on the Fort Bliss quadrangle. Wedge formations. Fields of fire. Defensive perimeters. We were ambushed with a chemical attack on the seventh mile, and when the tear-gas mist blurred our vision, it was hard to discern whether we cried like little boys because our necks and shoulder blades were rubbed raw from the shoulder straps of the fifty-pound rucksacks, or because our brains were screaming that our bodies could go no farther. Thankfully, there was no farther to go. We had made it!

On graduation day a week later, the surviving members of Basic Combat Training Course 10-89 were lined up in alphabetical order behind the ramshackle auditorium that served as the training post's movie house and recreation center. We had been trained to rely on one another, to share close quarters with men we never imagined we could even communicate with, to consider ourselves brothers in arms. In combat it was on our shoulders that responsibility for our buddies' lives would rest; Drill Sergeant Lobue's words flowed like a textbook extract delivered in rote.

As I walked across the highly buffed hardwood stage floor, accepted my diploma, and shook each drill sergeant's hand, I could not help thinking of the lamb whose career we had sacrificed to learn our lessons. I had cleared the first hurdle in my quest for a successful military career, but at what price? What had happened to Private Steve Clement?

LIQUOR CLOSET

I WAS NERVOUS—QUITE HONESTLY, TERRIFIED. TO ANYONE ELSE who wasn't as paranoid as I was, a simple invitation to lunch at the post Burger King from a fellow Academy of Health Sciences student would be just that. For me, it rang every bell and set off every alarm. Corporal Juan Perez had *accidentally* bumped into and started up a conversation with me this morning in the mess hall. We agreed to do lunch that afternoon. A pharmacist specialist with "no idea why any sane person would want to be a combat medic," the twenty-four-year-old Puerto Rican started describing the *joie de vivre* in San Antonio.

He apologized if he seemed forward, but he felt we had much in common. True, we'd both been reared in traditional Hispanic, Roman Catholic families, but the similarities in our lives ended there. His home was squeezed between an empty warehouse and a graffiti-scrawled wall in Harlem's red-brick tenements. My home sat in San Antonio's King William District, an affluent historical annexation. He'd enlisted immediately after graduating from high school. I had a degree in journalism. He was on fire, not pretending to be something he wasn't. I could pass for straight. Perez said he'd *spotted* me in the breakfast line that morning. He insinuated that bumping into me was not as accidental as I had originally believed. I didn't much care after he allayed any fear I had that a Freudian slip, stereotypical trait, or gaping hole in my hetero disguise had betrayed my secret. I guess it takes one to know one.

"It was that *sashay*," he said jokingly after lunch. "Let's hang out."

I recognized that my view of homosexuality was narrow and

skewed. I had to discover firsthand what it meant to be gay, Perez said, because contrary to what I believed, this was not a phase and I was not alone. Like him a couple of years before, I had to find my place in the gay world, he said. What was more important, I had to answer the questions that were churning in my mind, questions that until today had remained moot. Did being gay mean that I had to be effeminate? What about fetishes?

Gays and lesbians in the military form a mutual, underground network of emotional support to weather the indignities and humiliations that sometimes seem too hard to bear. This was my first gay military friend, and he was determined to snap me out of the misconception I had about homosexuals. Sitting on a stool in this Austin gay bar, I looked around me at the number of bar patrons, many virile young men in telltale military haircuts, who all dressed like me, talked like me, and even looked as scared as I was. I was surprised. No one threw himself at me, as many of my homophobic friends had suggested when telling gay jokes.

I met several of Perez's friends, with whom I spent many of the few weekends the course allowed me to enjoy. However much fun we were having this evening, the experience came to a crashing halt when someone came running into the bar, screaming for all the military types to run into a back room.

Within seconds we were whisked into a stockroom, the slam of a heavy deadbolt and our breathing the only sounds echoing through the room. Probably military police coming to check if any military queers are here, Perez intimated. After a few minutes the deadbolt was unlocked. The coast was clear.

I struggled with the humiliation of having had to hide behind locked doors because the Army placed most gay bars off limits and the Criminal Investigation Division (CID) used Gestapo-type tactics to raid bars they suspected catered to a gay military clientele. This bar looked like any other bar in any other place, I insisted as Perez and his friends tried to calm me down. I could understand if this were a sex club. Can't people be allowed to unwind in their own time and let their guard down without fear of discovery? I wondered.

"There is no safe place in which the CID or military police can't reach us," Perez said squarely. "They're out there right now, taking down license-plate numbers."

If I had difficulty understanding what the closet meant before that night, it became startlingly clear after that scare. Having to hide in that liquor closet was identical in kind, just different in degree, to the life gay soldiers are forced to lead on a daily basis: always hiding because even the simplest conversation is a trap for the unwary. I was trying to commune with other gay and lesbian soldiers experiencing similar difficulties, trying to gather the strength necessary to deal with my closeted existence. But I found myself unable to do that without constantly having to look over my shoulder for Big Brother's probing eyes.

Driving home that night, I grew desperate to share my pain, the thoughts that were flooding my mind, with someone, anyone. I called home, but there was no answer except the answering machine.

"Please leave your name, number, and a brief message."

"Hi, this is Joe. Umm, sorry to call so late. . . . Hope everyone is okay." *Click.*

Friday night. I could have been out celebrating with fellow course graduates at the Fort Sam Houston Enlisted Club until 0200. After all, graduating from this particular course, infamous for its high attrition rate (fifty-fifty odds said you became either a medic or a cook), was no small feat. Three months of intensive life-saving skills training, complete with an experimental phase to see if Army medics could master the National Emergency Medical Technician Registry Test, had followed directly on the heels of the hell of basic training at Fort Bliss. With this morning's graduation ceremony behind me, I was now a combat medic with orders to report to the 21st Adjutant Replacement Detachment at Fort Hood, Texas.

Not having bonded with any of my classmates as the competitiveness of the course all but prohibited the time or inclination to develop friendships, I felt no real urge to spend any more time than necessary with CMS Course 1-90. I could have spent the night celebrating with Perez and my hometown twenty-something party-boy crowd. On a Friday night, they would undoubtedly want to party.

Instead, I drove up Interstate-35, a sliver of a moon bathing the monotonous plains of central Texas in an awkward bluish haze. At my father's suggestion, I was making this three-hour road trip to my new assignment four days before my report date. I demanded to live off-post to make up for the six months worth of privacy the army had snatched away from me since basic training. I packed my Dodge Charger with all my earthly possessions, drove up to Fort Hood, and spent my leave getting settled—still escaping from myself.

THE FIRST TEAM

MY EYELIDS DROOPED AND I ALMOST MISSED THE GIANT ROAD SIGN, illuminated by what seemed a megawatt bulb equally suited for use in a coastal lighthouse, directing me to veer off Interstate 35 and onto a backhills road. If the map and my terrain association skills agreed, the road began at the Stop 'N' Go conveniently located off the exit ramp and ended in "Killeen—Home of Fort Hood." During the last hour, I had lost reception of all but a buckaroo country-western station and static and been required to muster every last ounce of resourcefulness (short of using toothpicks to keep my eyelids propped open) to stave off an unrelenting sleep.

Time for a break, I thought, pulling into the Stop 'N' Go to take a quick pit stop, pick up a caffeine jolt, and ask the clerk how much longer Texas planned to extend the misery of driving to Fort Hood.

"*Oh*, it's just about an hour *yonder*," the cashier sang in a perky, trumpet-timbered voice. My reaction to her overly animated round face and bare arms, shockingly pale under the fluorescent lighting, as disguised as it was, didn't seem to please her much as she handed me my change. Either I desperately needed sleep, or I had developed overnight an almost intolerable sensitivity toward convenience-store clerks.

Taking a swig of the Diet Pepsi in the safety of my car, I decided it must be the latter and I should get to Fort Hood ASAP before experiencing any other manifestations of my tired delirium.

Much worse than any form of jet lag, what I felt was the shock of coming from cosmopolitan America and realizing that small-town America was the only America available to me now. The disappointment I felt in looking out the window of the twelve-dollar motel room I rented right outside Fort Hood was like getting identical sweaters for Christmas when you didn't like them the first time you saw them at the post exchange. My frustration that assignment orders to this cowtown had been issued with my name on them increased when, with every blink of an eye, the scenery did not magically vanish. This was the core of the Texas Bible Belt, a well-planned mix of boring suburban neighborhoods and bucolic farmland. Father warned me that Killeen, Texas, had nothing to offer but pawnshops, liquor stores, and strip joints. A drive through town proved he had again spared the hyperbole. "Don't spend *too* much time in any of them," he added with a sheepish grin.

A quick scan of Killeen's *Green Sheet*, a local rag available everywhere published for soldiers seeking off-post housing, proved more productive than I had imagined. In marathon style, within less than an hour, I inspected three apartments in a small, staid burb next to the post, put down a $150 security deposit, and walked away with the keys to 110 A Street, a duplex located between downtown Killeen and Fort Hood's front gate.

For $125 a month, fully furnished and all utilities paid, I had secured my privacy. Never mind the crimson-colored curtains, the burnt-orange shag carpet, or the kitschy furniture (faux Sealy PosturePedic included) that recalled the era in which this set of duplexes had probably been constructed. I bet it hadn't been refurnished in the interim.

In start contrast to the Lalique vases and Art Nouveau tables in my parents' house and the art-deco look of my apartment with Russell, this one-bedroom apartment was home, a place where I could live my life without the constant threat of Big Brother's prying eyes and ears—this homogenous community was where soldiers fled by the arkload to escape him.

I spent the two remaining days of my leave cleaning the apartment and adjusting to the community's slower pace of life. One afternoon I ventured to Belton Lake's military recreation area for some peace and relaxation, the first such luxury in more than six months.

*   *   *

71

Monday morning, 0850. I ran out of the apartment in a starched uniform, hopped in the Charger, and drove nervously to where my orders indicated I should be at 0900. That hateful, ugly plastic box some manufacturer dared call an alarm clock and swore could withstand even the most hostile morning swat had failed miserably to rouse me this morning at the appointed time. I was way behind schedule. "Prior Planning Prevents Piss Poor Performance," I repeated my father's advice over and over again to myself as I frantically readied myself for duty. Not having reconned the route, I could only pray I wasn't counted AWOL at 0901.

The 21st Adjutant Replacement Detachment was a warehouse-type distribution center where arriving soldiers, treated like new merchandise, were routed to units short of or needing soldiers with a particular occupational skill. It was 0856 when the in-processing clerk took my leave papers and instructed me to take a seat in the lobby. If I hadn't picked the right clock, I could at least rest easy that I had picked a nearby apartment.

"That lobby is your first duty assignment," said the sergeant behind the desk, stamping my paperwork and moving on to the next set.

I sat in that lobby for three days, whiling away the time by making idle chatter with a strikingly sensual, green-eyed corporal fresh off the plane from Germany. But even that diversion could not deflect the sheer boredom that deflated my morale. My mind scarcely wandered from the approved path. An hour off for lunch, dismissed for the day at 1700, with orders to report the next morning for reveille. Others had been sitting here for more than a week before anyone touched their paperwork. At least I had hand-delivered my paperwork to one of the cogs in the system. It took three days, but my name was finally called and assignment orders issued:

PRIVATE FIRST CLASS ZUNIGA, José M., Ambulance Driver, Company F, 27th Main Support Battalion, Division Support Command, 1st Cavalry Division

Whether driving or running the two miles from home to work down Motor Pool Road, I could not help feeling a sense of awe and then

72

pride at the military might parked in the hundreds of motor pools that, when combined, occupied less than one percent of Fort Hood's 217,000-acre expanse. This was the home of III (U.S.) Corps, World War II's Phantom Corps, and headquarters to a three-star general under whose command two tradition-steeped, heavy-armor divisions with more than 13,000 soldiers assigned to each worked, trained, and lived. Each division was commanded by a two-star general.

Luck was on my side the day the orders assigning me to the 1st Cavalry Division were printed, approved, and signed by the replacement detachment's adjutant general. The division, its history steeped in rough-riding traditions, had been formed in September 1921 at Fort Bliss. The 1st, 7th, 8th, and 10th cavalry regiments, each bringing with them rich traditions forged in Civil War battles, formed the core of the fledgling unit. The division's mission then had been to patrol the harsh deserts of western Texas and the Mexican border.

Technology eventually rendered the horse obsolete. The cav dismounted in February 1943 and its troops were ordered to the Pacific as infantrymen. A year later, the division stormed the beaches of the Admiralty Islands, at the tip of the Bismarck Archipelago. Making good on General Douglas MacArthur's pledge to return to Leyte Gulf, the division fought through 1944 to take the Philippines back from the Japanese. But it was the cav's victory in Manila a year later, the first American unit to enter the capital, that earned the division its nickname, the First Team. The division next served occupation duties in Japan, its soldiers the first U.S. troops in Tokyo. In 1950, First Team troops were dispatched to combat again, even if an Orwellian government refused to refer to it as "war" and instead called it a "conflict." The division landed inside the Pusan perimeter in South Korea, fighting north to take the enemy capital of Pyongyang. The paralyzing cold of winter and a flood of Chinese Communist troops into North Korea forced an Allied retreat in December 1951. The First Team returned to Japan. The mid-1960s pressed the division back to duty with a transfer to Fort Benning, Georgia, for retraining. Combat soon followed. The First Team was deployed as the Army's first air-mobile division in Vietnam and Cambodia. Twenty-eight years later, the division returned to Texas, its birthplace. One of the most decorated and battle-hardened divisions in the army, the 1st Cavalry Division made Fort Hood its home.

The pride First Team soldiers carried with them like a badge of honor, inherited from generations of cavalrymen, would assure them success in the division's next crisis, we all felt. I adopted that pride quickly. To this day, with the benefit of experience and hindsight, above all other assignments, I am still proudest of my service as a cavalryman.

I respected the division on the wrong side of post, the 2nd Armored Division, affectionately known as the Hell on Wheels division; it was a unit equally tempered in the heat of battles past. The First Team would be fortunate to inherit a Hell on Wheels brigade shortly before the Persian Gulf War. But a knot still forms in my throat when I think back to my days with the 1st Cavalry Division. I was a proud heir to its cavalry heritage and like cavalrymen of old thought I would die to preserve it.

I made sure to allot plenty of time to report to my new assignment, not wanting to start off on the wrong foot and establish a negative impression. Fox-Trot Company, 27th Main Support Battalion's head-quarters, was no more than a five-minute drive from home if the fifteen or more traffic lights on Hood Road allowed you clear passage; it was ten minutes when the signal lights chose to be rebellious and strand you at an intersection listening to the sound systems on wheels (as they could no longer reasonably be classified cars) that seemed to defy every sound ordinance on post.

Both the company commander and his executive officer were out for the day, I was advised by a pasty-faced, lank-mustached company clerk. Taking my paperwork to verify I was supposed to be here, the staff sergeant jumped on the phone and announced my arrival to some unknown person, presumably the first sergeant, on the other end of the line. Within seconds, the first sergeant had appeared from behind a floor-to-ceiling set of olive-drab file cabinets. Handsome in a lean, ropy, high-cheekboned way, First Sergeant Richard Gramm looked my paperwork over with what almost appeared to be rheumy eyes.

"Great! I've been needing an ambulance driver for a year now," the tall black powerfully built first sergeant concluded with a grin that revealed a gold tooth. He gave me the once-over too, his eyes wounded yet shifty, never still, the gaze of a creature on constant patrol for any threat. It made me nervous. "Come to my office for a sec, PFC Z . . . Zin . . ."

"Zuniga, First Sergeant." I was used to people butchering my last name.

More than a sec of welcome to the real army (loosely translated into My Army) followed behind closed doors in an office the size of a closet in my apartment. A drill sergeant had once advised me to never talk about my father. I ignored his advice that day, and as my words began to cast a pall on our conversation, I soon realized I might have to pay a hefty price for my indiscreet confession.

"How come you're not an officer?" asked the first sergeant in a slightly pedantic manner, slowing his speech, in obvious haughtiness, from the quick, fluid staccato of the last half hour. Having finished his prepared speech, he was no longer worried there might not be enough time to finish a thought.

"Because I want to get my hands dirty, First Sergeant," I answered in a show of bravado, unsure that my answer would convince him I was no coddled brat riding on my father's coattails.

Somehow, by panache or dumb luck, this was not seen as a smart-ass answer, and it won his favor. Dashing out and then back into his office, giving instructions in a pleasantly soft but slightly petulant way to the sergeant scanning through a copy of *Road & Track*, the first sergeant grabbed his cap. My mind raced as I thought of how easy it would be for this soldier with a Special Forces tab on his uniform to rip the puny rank off my collar.

"I like you, PFC Zinuga," he said out of the blue, pointing to the door. "Come on, let's go get your hands dirty."

A blistering sun seemed to concentrate its heat exclusively on Fox-Trot Company's motor pool, a phenomenon that seemed to occur about this time every afternoon. We had been authorized to take off our BDU shirts and work in T-shirts until retreat formation at the end of the day. The cotton T-shirt, less suffocating than the starched and tailored BDU shirt, made the temperature no more comfortable to work in. Like a sponge, my undershirt seemed to soak up all of my sweat and then make it hang sodden and clammy on the fabric against my skin.

This was my second week as an ambulance driver, and I had yet to drive an ambulance. I wondered if I could still lay claim to the F. Scott Fitzgerald image I wanted if I didn't soon find myself behind a wheel.

Full of expectations the day First Sergeant Gramm drove me to the motor pool and introduced me to his "company of medical professionals," by now I felt trapped in a job that required, if not rewarded, blind obedience to orders ranging from checking tire pressures to sorting a hundred different sizes of nuts and bolts.

Menial tasks made me cringe, my desire for dirty hands notwithstanding. Feeling trapped was but one of a deluge of emotions dashing my spirit. *Follow the leader, question not, make suggestions only when asked to . . .* Never. It was a shame to see the defeat in the eyes of those whose initiative and drive to excel, those who either knew better or merely exercised their common sense, was squashed because it lacked the weight of rank or West Point seals.

First Sergeant Gramm was not horrible simply because he was such a fervent yes-man; he was horrible because he was an ordinary, petit bourgeois functionary who promoted mediocrity by insisting on strict adherence to "the book." All the while, he seemed to view his meager results as better than the Army deserved. As much as I thought my hatred of his inflexible ways was obvious to him, I was shocked the day he pulled me out of the motor pool and assigned me to publish a company newsletter.

"Morale is a little low," he explained, whispering the word *low* as hushed as so many people whisper *cancer* or *AIDS*. "People need a pat on the back." He paused to take a drag of the Marlboro that always seemed to burn in his ashtray, then revealed the true impetus behind this assignment. He was asking a private first class for help. I knew the words were being ripped out of his craw. "The battalion commander wants it out by close of business Monday, so get to it."

I'd originally asked to be a military journalist but was thwarted at enlistment. Since the F. Scott Fitzgerald rationalization was going nowhere fast, I would happily abandon it no matter the deadline. Marching orders in hand, I hopped in my car and drove to the motor pool.

The interviews I got were either dull or maudlin. No matter, I would somehow make the stories seem interesting. The next day I concentrated on photos, begging soldiers not to smile into the camera or pose for what should look like candid, action shots.

By Friday, my task complete, I waltzed into First Sergeant Gramm's office with a proof copy of the *Fox-Trot Foxhole*.

"Volume one, number one . . ." His voice faded into a murmur as he read each story, caption, and blurb intently. This was my baby, and I had not been forced to compromise my style for the sake of an editor's overdeveloped ego. The layout and headlines, usually beyond the control of a reporter, were exactly as I wanted them. Given that much freedom, I could almost forgive him for the newspaper's name, his idea. A minute-long scan of the twelfth and last page was followed by an audible sigh. I could not help imitating his sigh, if only internally. "Good job! This oughta make the Old Man happy."

Thus began my glorious military journalism career.

Tormented
Journalist

The source of the evil agonizing my already throbbing head was a painfully pure, high-yield neon flash echoing the technopop beat of Erasure's "Blue Savannah." I stood nervously in a corner of the club with the rest of our clique, the dim lights illuminating us as we downed Miller Lites and tequila shots almost as fast as the bartender poured them. I didn't care much that first call was at 0430 for a five-miler around post. Getting smashed on a Monday night had been a rare but refreshing college ritual, a change of pace from the exacting course load I chose to maintain. In the Army—or, more precisely, my new assignment—any night of the week spent imbibing legal, over-the-counter cerebral relaxants was relief for a young soldier trapped in an ass-backwards Texas military town and a going-nowhere-fast job.

Eleanor, a Darnall Army Hospital medical supply clerk, brought me here to City Lights tonight. I expressed my discomfort at placing ourselves at risk so near to post. She equated my nervousness with timidness. She had forgotten—or, worse, the tequila had erased her memory—that I was from San Antonio, where you could relax in a gay dance club without worrying you might end up flat on your back in the middle of a beer-drenched pit, getting the shit kicked out of you by some redneck gay basher. I didn't bother to correct her. Moving away from the raucous group, I cursed myself for having agreed to come to this purportedly clandestine gay dance club. Although it was outfitted with a peephole at the entrance and required a code word for admission, it was no more than a fifteen-minute drive from the Fort Hood military police station.

This is Eleanor's first-year anniversary with her partner, I reminded myself. Pretend you're having fun.

The selflessness of that thought surprised the part of me praying for deliverance from this potential trap. What if this turned out to be a repeat of the Austin raid? Could I handle another "encounter" with the military police? How much prayer was not enough?

Finding closeted gays at Fort Hood, especially in the medical service corps, did not require going to the harrowing extremes I had initially anticipated. For weeks I traipsed between playing it safe and risking exposure. Playing it safe required maintaining a cover and driving to sanctuary in San Antonio or Dallas every weekend for emotional release among my queer friends in those two cities. The riskier option was to meet discrete closeted soldiers stationed at Fort Hood. The irony of developing my first functional friendships with gay men and lesbians only after enlisting in the Army—and the self-worth it fostered—was not lost on me. A new sense of self was developing, even if it was one whose sexual implications I could continue to squelch—if not completely, at least around other soldiers.

"Hi, my name's Mitch," a usually quiet and reserved member of my squad introduced himself while we formed up for our ritual, end-of-week company "fun run." I came to take advantage of these runs early on to vent my many frustrations.

Sergeant Mitch Taylor had the reputation of being a snob, a character flaw many in the company attributed to someone who considered himself ontologically superior. This facade and his Opie-of-Mayberry looks had fortunately not slowed his rapid ascension. At age twenty, he was the youngest sergeant in the brigade.

"Heading to San Antonio this weekend," he either said or asked. I could not tell. His speech was that frustrating type whose tones repeatedly rise in a way that makes each statement seem a question and each question seem a statement. Making matters worse, his demeanor seldom shed light on the mystery. "The Bonham Exchange," he added. This was no question.

Mitch must have read my face like a cheap novel, I thought. Flustered, I could think of no adequate response, so I delivered a cordial, patronizing smile. I didn't even dare look at his face.

"Maybe I'll see you there? I saw you there last weekend, but I didn't want to scare you." His words came slowly and carefully now. They were understood and appreciated nonetheless.

Mitch had taken a great risk, but only because sighting me at the Bonham Exchange confirmed that I was guilty of the same crimes. My silent acknowledgment instead of any denial placed me at risk too. The Machiavellian nature of the military's infamous witch-hunts was not well known to me—but Mitch had witnessed and survived a few in his two years of service.

"A claim of entrapment is without merit once you let your orientation be known," Mitch warned me.

Now my search for a kindred spirit was over. His mission, he confessed, was to add weight to my sense of place and belonging at Fort Hood. That he did. Ours was not only a friendship; we were more like the brothers we had each wished for in our youth but never had. Mitch gave me a map and the code words required for admission into the large underground fraternity of gay, lesbian, and bisexual service members at every military installation around the globe.

As I came to know, respect, and find role models among their ranks, I also found myself.

Captain Jeffrey Phillips, the division's incoming public-affairs officer, leaned back in his chair and collected my speech like a pool of water. I had come here to ask for a job—I wanted to be a journalist again, not a medic. A man I would later discover could switch from personal encomium to philosophical analysis at the drop of a hat, Captain Phillips understood my plight but was unsure what role he could play in relieving my suffering. My writing samples had impressed him. My plea had struck a chord. He professed to feel empathy for the tormented creative types in danger of being consumed by the bureaucratic machine.

Major Gary Hovatter, the public-affairs officer, rushed out of his office and stood briefly in the hallway. For an unknown reason, he circled back immediately.

"You know, there's a twelve-step program for your type," the major mumbled almost incoherently, winking mischievously at his successor. "I think a transfer here could help fulfill your artistic impulses, while still managing to maintain that emotional balance you seem to be losing rather quickly."

I began stammering something like an apology; I didn't understand why he was on my side.

"Hold on there, Joe." The major cut me off. "Now, repeat after me: 'My name is Private First Class Joe Zuniga and I am a tormented journalist.'"

I obediently, confusedly repeated his dictated words. They playfully answered in unison, "Hi, Joe," as if this were a three-member Alcoholics Anonymous meeting.

Coming here today had been a stupid and potentially disastrous stunt for a private first class to pull. I ignored warnings against setting foot in the 1st Cavalry Division's headquarters. Unit commanders placed the building off-limits, dreading calls from overzealous, venom-spitting officers, bitching about grunts scuffing the glass-finish shine on a piece of hallway floor or failing to render a salute in accordance with Army regulations. In speaking to my squad leader and my company commander, I had found no support. By talking to Major Hovatter and Captain Phillips, I was jumping the chain of command, setting the stage for a vicious fight pitting First Sergeant Gramm against Major Hovatter, Captain Phillips, and a major general, who was lending support with the power of his two silver stars. Predictably, we won what was reduced to a skirmish.

Furious, First Sergeant Gramm called my action mutiny. I called it survival. In less than a day I sat in my office at division headquarters, finally flexing the full range of journalism skills I had been forced to pack away for more than a year. I was now a military journalist, having left behind, at least for now, the medical corps. More important, I left behind an enemy who could have destroyed me had victory swayed his way.

WAITING FOR MARCHING ORDERS

*The Security Council condemns the Iraqi invasion of Kuwait; demands
that Iraq withdraw immediately and unconditionally all its forces to the
positions in which they were located on 1 August 1990; calls upon Iraq
and Kuwait to begin immediately intensive negotiations for the resolution
of their differences and supports all efforts in this regard and especially
those of the League of Arab States. . . .*
                              —United Nations Resolution 660

THE SUMMER OF 1990 WAS SHAPING UP TO BE A REPEAT OF THE
summer before. Mornings provided the only solace. Seventy-five degree
air greeted me as I stepped into my car and drove on post. By midday,
the temperature had soared to 110°. By now I knew that the best tactic
for escaping this hellish environment, or at least the giddy pervasive
August sun that seemed to focus its attention over Killeen, was to
go home to San Antonio where at least under the shade of a tree
you felt safe from ultraviolet rays. In central Texas the sun makes
you feel like an insect under a cruel child's magnifying glass.

This weekend had been one of wanton debauchery. The usual
posse had packed into three cars and driven south, stopping in Austin
for a scan of Sixth Street and a six-pack of Miller Lites. Patrick,
Mitch, and Eleanor rode with me, singing along to a George Michael song that seemed to never end.

"Freedom! Freedom!" we echoed in voices that would never make
a record label, as we made what had become an almost weekly pilgrimage down Interstate-35, away from the strictures of army life

and toward the freedom of San Antonio. There we were free not to hide who we really were. My visits home added a sense of schizophrenia to the trips—the censure of home versus the hedonism of the clubs. I remember this particular weekend fondly, though, because it was our last together in the revelry of freedom for more than a year.

Mitch and I danced at the Bonham Exchange, San Antonio's premier gay dance club, into the wee hours of the night, sucking on the nightlife. Although we were both physically attracted to one another, we feared that anything more than the bond we now shared would ruin a brotherly love. That fear, and the vow of celibacy I took upon enlisting, limited our physical contact to a hug, a playful peck on the cheek, or holding hands as we led each other to the dance floor.

Eleanor called us over to a corner of the dance floor to introduce us to yet another friend. "This is Tina," Eleanor attempted to say quietly over the rumble of Madonna exhorting us to express ourselves. She tried again, this time loud enough for us to hear. "She just graduated and is heading to Fort Hood tomorrow!"

We each playfully delivered individual condolences, in the next breath welcoming her to the underground community of closeted 1st Cav soldiers. Madonna's continued demands that we submit to her exhortations, and Tina's thirst for a refill, split us up for the night.

"Remember, we head home tomorrow at noon," I warned Eleanor before she followed Tina to one of the dozen minibars in each corner of the club.

"Relax!" she answered, her way of acknowledging the drudgery of work that awaited us at 0500 Monday. Until then we would enjoy the autonomy of our world.

Until this weekend, life had been business as usual for the 1st Cavalry Division. The 1st "Ironhorse" Brigade was recovering and licking its wounds after a month-long training exercise that had pitted them against an opposing Warsaw Pact–like force in the cruel world of the National Training Center (NTC) at Fort Irwin, California. The sandbox training center was the Army's classroom for armor maneuver combat, the closest thing to combat without bullets I had ever experienced. The 2nd "Blackjack" Brigade was frantically prepping for their turn in the Mojave Desert, eager to one-up their rival brigade.

As editor of *Cav Country*, the division's newspaper, I enjoyed walking into the tactical operations center and watching the mock NTC battles unfold on paper maps, where tactical pins plotted maneuvers and left behind holes where paper had once belonged but had fallen to the floor.

With both brigades home, there was little if any training going on. The wet, steambathlike temperature limited rigorous outdoor activities, a safety measure to avoid heat injuries. So the public-affairs team, like the rest of the First Team, unknowingly recharged its batteries.

The public-affairs team was made up of a motley crew of seven soldiers, only three of whom were official Army-trained journalists. Its mission was entrusted to two career soldiers at odds over everything from religion to politics, Army doctrine to work ethic. Captain Phillips, an armor-branch officer, had only recently taken over the office and managed to alienate most with his tanker mentality. "Work is more important than life," Katherine Mansfield once confided to her journal as she was dying of tuberculosis. That was my take on this young, ambitious officer.

As for Master Sergeant Tom Fuller, the public-affairs supervisor, every day spent in his presence I expected to hear him ask "Do I dare to eat a peach?"

Sergeant Britt Toalson was one of three remaining refrigerator repairmen in the Army, a specialty deleted from the military's roster of odd jobs. He also happened to be, along with Specialist Zak Hocum, one of the Army's superlative unofficial photojournalists. Known to speak his mind, which was typically one step out of the gutter, Britt and I would bond only when 10,000 miles away from the leering T&A world of Killeen, Texas.

Britt's sidekick, Zak, was an eighteen-year-old with grungy prettiness. Bullnecked and built like a fireplug, Zak was a tow-gunner on permanent loan from an infantry company in the 1st Brigade.

Specialist Dean Welch, "the voice of the First Team," was an

Army-trained broadcaster. Dean was the stereotypical gruff New Yorker, complete with Bowery Boy accent, feisty physical presence, and, I learned on my first day in this assignment, an aggressive way of dealing with outsiders.

"A medic?" he questioned. "Someone must have fucked up here." He kept his guard up for a few water-testing minutes as I told my story. What an asshole, I thought.

"Oh, okay. Welcome aboard then." A caught-in-the-act grin crossed his face.

Rounding out the team was Private First Class Robyn Gregory, a brash and impulsive tomboyish beauty. An official Army journalist, Robyn's emotional dramas du jour and snappy-tongued advice made life in the office a stage play. Her speech was a delicate blend of philosophical babble, which would trail off as she realized nobody knew what she was talking about.

We weren't a fractious team, but we had miles to go before we could ride into Kuwait and take care of unruly Iraqis who couldn't seem to keep their guns in their holsters.

Meanwhile, a world away, Saddam Hussein's Iraqi army had mobilized and within forty-eight hours penetrated a defenseless Kuwaiti border, boldly annexing the tiny country. Saddam claimed Kuwait as Iraq's nineteenth province.

The world condemned this blatant act of aggression. On August 6, the United Nations imposed economic sanctions on Iraq and asked for an unconditional withdrawal of troops. That day, at the behest of Saudi Arabia's King Fahd, President George Bush ordered U.S. troops to the Persian Gulf. Our immediate mission was to defend the Saudi sovereignty from potential Iraqi aggression against the oil-rich country. The next day, a deployment order tentatively called Operation Desert Shield, including the 1st Cavalry Division in the Southwest Asian operation, was issued. The 1st Cavalry Division was placed on alert. A one-page order irrevocably altered the predictability of a lazy Fort Hood summer.

Workdays were extended to fourteen, sixteen, and even twenty-four hours, and eventually the work week extended into seven seamless days. The days became progressively longer as we were saddled with project after project, all of which were piled on top of training and packing. Captain Phillips's stress level skyrocketed with every hour, and our feverish pace echoed his stress level.

Before long, the hours I spent in the office began to blur with the minutes I seemed to lie on my bed at home. I was not scared. I was tired. I closed my eyelids long enough to recharge close-to-dead batteries, sleeping whenever my mind could shut out the thud of practice artillery nightfire rattling windows, then threw on a uniform and reported to work.

The division's plan called for a muster date of September 15, an unrealistic goal for an Army whose last deployment had been more than twenty years before. While waiting, the tankers and Bradley crews fired crew-level gunneries in the blazing heat of a progressively hotter summer and early into the morning hours. If not on the ranges, they sat in simulators until their battalion could fire on the overcrowded gunnery tables.

Soldiers walked, marched, and ran in chemical protective gear, preparing for the very real possibility of chemical warfare. Saddam's army had once unleashed its biological arsenal against enemies. Trips to the gas chambers reminded First Team soldiers, including me, that if tear gas was awful, the chemicals used by an enemy might do more than just make us cry. Besides training came the intensive and time-consuming task of preparing the division's equipment for combat. Ten thousand pieces of equipment, dark green in a Cold War salute to Germany's emerald hill-studded terrain, required light tan paint to match the monotonous hues of the desert.

Brigadier General John H. Tilelli was a soldier's general. Wearing chemical gear, he visited troops as they trained for chemical warfare. He fired his Beretta alongside sergeants on the firing range. On-the-spot inspections of equipment were frequent and more often than not conducted by him personally. When he noted some slip in maintenance that could get his men killed, his wickedly hard ass-chewings were painful. There was no fuzzy objective here, General Tilelli scowled, no blurred standards. Soldiers needed to think of their equipment as extensions of themselves or they would die, he concluded.

Captain Phillips idolized the man, having spent hours with him during the last few weeks. A military history buff, Captain Phillips couldn't help feeling that this general, unlike others he had served with in his career, met the idealized image of the fifth century B.C. Chinese military code *Ping Fa*, which prescribed: "a general first in the toils and fatigues of the army, unwilling to spread his parasol in the heat of summer, dismounting from his regal horse and walking alongside his men . . ."

I interviewed the general for a feature story the week before the division's September 15 deployment deadline. Besides wanting to relay his perspective of the division's state of readiness as we prepared to go to war, my thrust was to present a portrait of a leader who had just inherited the First Team's reins. Many of his soldiers, except for seeing him on the ranges, had no idea what was behind the solitary star he wore on his uniform. Most knew, though, that the star hadn't been on the uniform long enough to leave a shadow if it were removed, even with the Texas sun.

Newly promoted, he had been given the task of mobilizing a proud, tradition-steeped outfit overweight from the laxity of the post–Cold War era. I sensed his nervousness and apprehension. After all, as most veterans know, the common joke in the military about brigadiers is about their coffee-making skills. But this joke is often cloaked in hushed, reverent tones because brigadiers eventually get that second star.

What struck me as this one-star sat at my desk—he had requested we meet here and not in his office upstairs—was that, contrary to the interpretation of the cynics in the field who saw General Tilelli's field visits as meddling or micromanagement, was a man who, as Sun Tzu expressed in *The Art of War*, treated his men as if they were his own sons. He left the ivory tower of his plush, air-conditioned office because he had to ensure that the men who would fight with him, and might even die with him, were ready. When he said without hesitation that the 1st Cavalry Division was ready, I believed him. General Tilelli knew because he made sure of it personally.

A week later, Captain Phillips ran downstairs after a meeting with the chief of staff, waving a copy of *Cav Country*, my feature article on General Tilelli circled ten times over in a blood-red marker.

"The Old Man loved it!" he announced, raising his hand in a high-five motion. I felt like reminding him he had originally poo-pooed the idea, but I didn't.

I was happy that the Old Man (another sign of how the chain of command embodies a paternalistic approach) approved. More than anything, I hoped my fellow soldiers could feel the soothing sense of self-confidence I absorbed from General Tilelli's words during our hour-long interview. Military journalism has multiple purposes, and chief in my mind was troop morale as we prepared to deploy. Making the troops feel more at ease, even if they couldn't pinpoint why, was my goal. That the Old Man was happy with the article was a bonus.

My father parked his Suburban, a U-Haul trailer hitched to its back, in a no-parking zone and came around the side. I viewed him as a stranger for the first time in my life, laconic, gray-maned, in a blue sweatshirt and running shoes. He looked haggard. The last couple of months had been trying for us all. Mother was slipping away from us. I recalled our emotional parting yesterday, every inflection, every feature in her face: cheeks whose flesh was sinking beneath the bones, eyes whose defiant stare predicted a brave fight. Now their only son was going to war.

Father and Paul, his buddy from the Veterans of Foreign Wars post, drove up this Sunday morning to pick up my furniture and semi-out-of-commission car for storage in San Antonio. The Charger's manifold had cracked months earlier, setting ablaze anything flammable under the hood of the car, ruining a rare weekend off in Austin, and costing me a paycheck. My father promised to have it fixed by the time I got back. He could not veil the pained look of a perplexed child who has sensed some grave change.

Nothing but wooden statements filled the silent moments between breaks and the arduous task of packing my life possessions into the U-Haul. We Zunigas glossed over our emotions, in this case the pain of saying goodbye for what might be a final time.

He lit a cigarette as I loaded one last box into the Suburban's passenger seat. I didn't bother protesting his disregard of doctors' orders. I knew he hadn't smoked for years now, and that this was likely a nervous tick. Unlike the hundred times before in the last twenty years, today we would not need to read one another's minds. His eyes were as sad and wistful as one who longs for something he cannot remember.

"I've always been proud of you," he whispered, blowing cigarette smoke through pursed lips. A second-longer-than-usual hug followed an "I love you, son."

I love you. I'd never heard that as a child. It was a sacred statement. Zunigas only said it at times of death. How should I respond? In kind? He climbed behind the wheel of his truck before I could formulate a proper response.

"Good luck, Son,'" he said and drove away. Paul waved goodbye as he followed closely in my Charger, hoping it would make the three-hour road trip.

Thanks, Dad.

"Kill a Fucking A-rab for Me"

THE BARRACKS WERE DESERTED ON MY FIRST NIGHT LIVING IN Government quarters since basic training. Dean had suggested getting wasted tonight, but the idea had never fully developed, and as we sat in my new room chatting about the back-breaking work that lay ahead, each seemed to agree that a good night's sleep might serve us better. No less than fifteen minutes later, realizing how short our time was in the States, Dean, Zak, and I changed our minds, throwing worry to the wind.

Private Alex McKinnon, a radio technician on loan to us from Fort Huachuca, Arizona, stumbled out of his room across the hall. Fresh out of basic and advance training, this was technically his first assignment, which was scary enough. I can just imagine what the prospect of going to war must have felt like. In reality, our positions weren't very different, but I wore my nine months with a cocky swagger.

From the day we met at physical training formation, the blond six-foot two-inch former high-school basketball player and I had become fast friends—rare because outside my office friends and closeted circle of queer friends, I shied away from military acquaintances. Perhaps it was his desire for someone to guide him into his new life that fostered our friendship. Or maybe it was his soulful blue eyes admitting a hidden reservoir of torments, foibles, and passions. In any event, he joined us and spent the night with us at a shit-kicking bar five miles away in Belton. Why not? What soldier could resist fifty-cent pitchers of beer?

"Kill a fucking A-rab for me," the bartender screamed over the tired screech of a Reba MacIntyre CD played at least a dozen times tonight. I'd seen him in tears earlier, bourbon on his breath as he toasted our safe return. "I'm going to miss you boys."

Although I had made it a point not to set foot in straight bars, tonight was an exception as the four of us emptied pitcher after pitcher of brew with fellow cavalrymen. We talked up a storm of bullshit cementing our camaraderie. It was a veritable testosterone feast. Never mind that the cement floor was gritty with sawdust and a carpet of cigarette butts—as long as more beer, iced down in Texas-size steel coolers and served up by beefy retirees ready to slug a drunk soldier just because they can, kept coming our way we were happy.

Dean, Zak, and I, the three amigos of the public-affairs office, had developed a bond that only twenty-four-hour-a-day, seven-days-a-week exposure to each other could feed. It was a reminder of Drill Sergeant Lobue's words in basic training when Zak, slurring every other word, held our hands and swore he'd lay down his life for us any time. Dean reflexively yanked his hand away. Realizing this gesture had been important to Zak, whose twenty-year-old pouty face hid his feelings as well as Glad Wrap, Dean replaced it and swore the same. I didn't think twice before adding my promise, forging an allegiance that would see us through the best and worst of times.

We were drunk out of our minds when one of our buddies decided to test his bravado with a civilian who seemed unhappy with our raucous assemblage. This bellicosity was why I shied away from Army drinking buddies. For the most part, my friends were pretty well behaved tonight, except for, a softspoken mechanic from Charlie Company, who, with alcohol serving as a noninhibitor, could pick more fights than a sailor on shore leave. But then, I rationalized, that is typical of guys drinking shots poured out of a bottle of cheap bourbon as big as a harbor buoy.

A tug at my shirt pulled me away from the table, and I followed Dean, Alex, and Zak out of the bar and into the cool, stiff breeze of a Texas morning. Wakeup was two hours away, chemical training in the gas chamber before lunch. I don't know how we made it home.

I do know how I felt the remainder of that day.

By mid-September the division had begun deploying its equipment, moving ten thousand pieces of equipment from battle tanks to humvees, by highway or rail from Fort Hood to the ports of Houston along the Gulf of Mexico. A massive sealift would deliver it weeks later to anxious troops already waiting in the Saudi port of ad Dammam.

Our equipment gone, we soldiers sighed briefly, collectively. The whirlwind was not over as we lined up in unit supply rooms drawing a special issue of desert clothing and equipment. Classes continued on the hazards and customs of a new land. We did not want the reputation of ugly Americans that soldiers in other wars had earned.

Doctors poked and probed, lawyers and legal clerks drew up powers of attorney and wills, and leaders forgetfully repeated their last-minute instructions. The moment was close at hand. Although we were scared, we were ready to go.

Three hours and six operation plan changes later, the 1st Cavalry Division headquarters staff, tense and about to explode after so much foreplay, were ready to storm out of Abrams Gymnasium. It was time to go, commanders began to snarl. Units of soldiers dressed in their still-stiff desert-camouflage uniforms (DCUs) formed in single file to board the buses. Prayers, sobs and children filled the gymnasium. Reality was finally sinking in for those who had until this minute awaited a miracle reprieve, children grasping Daddy's leg, pleading "Don't go . . ." But we have to . . .

It was dramatic for me to watch, but no one was tugging at my clothing to keep me from going. No one was sobbing and giving me a final hug. I watched the personal minidramas with a detached reporter's eye, a way of making up for the feeling in my gut that somehow I was not participating at the same emotional level as those around me. A pattern in my life.

An already scorching sun unabashedly poked its head over the Texas hill country as if not to miss its adieu to the ten-bus convoy winding its way through West Fort Hood to Robert Gray Army Air Field. An MP car, sirens wailing, lights flashing, signaled our tardy arrival.

We were the last of a 17,000-soldier deployment that started on September 16, 1990, when an Air Force C5A Galaxy had taken off from this airfield carrying the division's advance party.

"Don't worry," a specialist said to me.

This was not what I'd expected being sent to war would be like, walking past the 1st Cavalry Division band and television cameras. It didn't seem very John Wayne to fly chartered Northwest Airlines 747s, complete with beverage carts and flight attendants, to a war zone. We were all in uniform, and in all my prior images of going off to war, the planes had at least been courteous enough to get into uniform too.

Maybe now war was civilized. Maybe the Vietnam footage seen on American picture tubes in the 1960s would not be our lot. The good times of "M*A*S*H" episodes seemed possible to a soldier going off to war watching an in-flight movie.

The bullshitting that gradually increased after a fuel stop at Rhein Main Air Base, Germany, ceased ten minutes before landing in Saudi Arabia, replaced by the nervous chatter of young men avoiding con- templation of peril or exploration of the panic and assorted emotions of an adolescent's first shocking view of the real world. The pilot, a former Marine aviator, prepared the cabin for landing.

He ended his usually rote statement with a personal note to us. "Our prayers are with you guys! Semper Fi!"

G.I. JOE

As we taxied past some examples of the might of the Allied air force, gasps of awe filled the fuselage. British Harrier jump-jets, French Mirages, U.S. F-16s . . .

Saddam doesn't stand a chance, I thought. He had to see this too. This unprecedented troop mobilization would be less a war than the greatest-ever show of gunboat diplomacy.

Our plane came to a standstill in the middle of a tarmac. Dhahran International Airport was nothing more than three parallel strips of asphalt surrounded by sand. I assume there was a control tower, but it was lost to my eyes. We emptied our overhead-compartment bins and, leaving the 747, finally left America.

The heat smothered us as we deplaned. This wasn't Texas anymore. We were herded into makeshift hospitality tents, the other half of the 1st Cavalry Division band welcoming us with an eerie rendition of "Garryowen," definitely not the dog-and-pony halftime show they'd given us back home on the parade field for change-of-command ceremonies.

General Tilelli climbed into his humvee after greeting the flight commander, his chief of staff. He didn't wait to see his troops acclimate. Soldiers began drifting into semiconsciousness in the Saudi-made tents holding the bulk of the 1st Cavalry Division Headquarters Company. This appeared a natural way for the human body to react to new surroundings after such a long pilgrimage. We sat in a circle around a box of warm bottled water, blithering, wishing aloud we were anywhere but here. Looking back at the contact sheet of photos from that time, it's hard to imagine the feeling of utter helplessness that overtook us.

That was only the beginning. Being there was different from anything I had anticipated. The numb shock visible in my group seemed a signal that I was not alone.

After what seemed like an eternity later, our hosts herded us outside for a trip to our new home. The Pakistani drivers, who had been haggling for a heftier fee, ignoring the contract they had signed for their work, rolled their mats out on the ground and began to play cards in the shade of the baby-blue buses that were supposed to transport us to the port of ad Dammam, located on the Saudi kingdom's eastern coast.

Major Susan Roma, the division's transportation officer, cursed in disbelief. "Three times in less than a week. Jesus!" Being Americans, we wanted everything now; being Americans in a combat zone, we wanted everything yesterday. *In sha Allah* (When Allah wills) wasn't good enough, she told a Saudi wearing a red-and-white checked headdress.

Half an hour later a crew of Filipino bus drivers arrived with a multicolored fleet of buses. Capitalism would work its wonders and, in either set of buses, we'd be on our way. The heated dialogue between the Filipinos and the Pakistanis was unintelligible to us, as it was likely nearly so to them too. Blackened windows prevented us from seeing anything. All we had was heat and what I think was a Filipino opera sung in Tagalog wafting through the double bass-boosting speakers of a Japanese-made stereo system.

"Don't take the pots off!" our first sergeant screamed.

He never screamed. The Vietnam veteran was as nervous as we were. Kevlar helmets on, we bumped into the unknown.

Pegasus 2, the division's home until word from higher up sent us on, was one of a series of eight empty blank-faced warehouses skirting the water's edge. When 1st Cavalry Division headquarters arrived, half the warehouse had already been occupied. We quickly picked up cots and shoehorned them between the empty spaces left in the sauna we now called home, no more than six inches separating each cot.

Hygiene was mediocre by Army standards, probably substandard if compared to third world living. Latrines were burn-out pits constructed of wood. The smell of human waste carried in the heat from the black asphalt to my nostrils and mouth. Details of privates were assigned to haul out the barrels of waste twice daily, soak them in diesel fuel, and burn the contents. I smelled it, tasted it, and was nauseated.

Showers were also of wood construction. Washed-out oil barrels fixed on top of them held the water supply, with copper pipes and brass fixtures donated by the Saudi government and gravity for water pressure.

Standards gradually slipped as the leadership moved out to field placements and grunts moved in. Pegasus 2 occupants, however, even if they were bathed in sweat, orbited by gargantuan mosquitoes, and tormented by boredom, were certainly better off than the three thousand soldiers living in Tent City five miles away. A collection of Army tents, Tent City looked and smelled like the animal encampment of a poor struggling circus.

As awful as living conditions were, this was the most relaxing period we experienced in-country. Sixteen-millimeter movies were projected continuously on the warehouse wall, interrupted twice daily when the generator needed refueling or when an air-raid siren wailed an overzealous Scud alert. Soldiers were bused to Khobar's shopping malls (wannabe American versions that didn't quite measure up) and to telephones at the Dhahran International Hotel. This wasn't "M*A*S*H" by any stretch of the imagination, but neither was it the jungles of Vietnam.

Leaning against a humvee, the 1990s Schwarzeneggered version of the retired jeep, my body shivered uncontrollably in the ten-below cold of the stretch of Saudi desert we called home. I stared at the desert stars scattered like diamonds across the velvet-black sky. A thin crescent moon perched over the distant horizon, the silhouettes it formed of tanks and tents rising from the desert floor like temples in the night sky.

It takes being ten thousand miles from "civilization" to appreciate fully this beauty, I thought, my observations jarred by the occasional boom of the nightly bombing. I safely assumed they were ours, being dropped on Saddam Hussein's forces courtesy of the Allied air force. Before the next round went off, I remembered reading Ralph Waldo Emerson's elucidation about the stars. If the constellations appeared only once in a thousand years, he wrote, imagine what an exciting event it would be. But because they are up there every night, we barely give them a look. The desert sky was new to me, and I gave it more than a passing glance.

As a young boy I was taught that it was a filial duty to serve my country and give the last, true measure of devotion. Here was the ultimate chance to do so, going to war.

I was not wracked with self-doubt, or praying that my unit would remain stateside, like so many other soldiers unwilling to break with the routine of a peacetime army. I knew this was a serious endeavor, that the personal consequences could be grave, but I also knew that America was right to intervene in a blatant attack against a weak country. Our commander in chief was calling the shots here, and, although fearful of the great unknown that lay ahead, I was proud to play a part.

Sitting in the middle of this arid expanse, I felt like a brown-bagger on a park bench, lost to the world, tapping away on my laptop computer. Who knew how long this Zenith laptop could take the punishment doled out by the inhospitable Saudi desert. If a soldier could have sand lodged in every nook and cranny of his body, and we did, how long could our computer last as sand became encrusted between its keys and in its microchips?

The value I perceived in the role I played in this godforsaken sand dune helped make my life bearable. I knew that the experience we were gaining in putting together a field newspaper was the stuff most journalists would learn about only in the classroom.

Cav Country was the first Army tabloid published in-country. Our base of operations had started as a cot in the port of ad Dammam. We went to press by dragging equipment into the chief of staff's office to print on a dot-matrix printer. Soldiers were so starved for news—words from a home that was so distant—that our newspaper developed a quick following.

Deploying 165 kilometers into the desert, we were soon cramped into possibly the least commodious tent in our encampment. There we set up shop and designed a paper. Once the design had been finished, Captain Phillips and I drove more than five hours to Tehama Press, a commercial printer at the port, manually laid out the newspaper, and made the five-hour return trip while discussing the next week's paper, morale, and often the more personal contemplations of two soldiers. One of us was a captain, the other a private first class, and we saw eye-to-eye on most issues. We considered each other intellectual equals and eventually dropped the pretense of rank, at least in private.

The Stars and Stripes snapped smartly. The desert wind forced sand into every exposed surface with the force a tornado is known to pack when it rams a two-by-four into a tree trunk like a toothpick. In the morning we'd wake and Old Glory would still be there, as in the anthem, though much the worse for wear.

The sand wore away at us—our equipment, our clothing, our skin, our humanity. Because there was no real shelter, no escape, I became something of an automaton in order to survive. Running on autopilot, without feelings, would keep my morale from plunging into the deep—below sea level—depression others had begun to suffer, and that many would suffer long after the war was won.

Private Alex McKinnon was not a Rhodes scholar. He'd earned a GED not more than two months out of basic training, as many soldiers without a high-school diploma do if they ever expect to be promoted.

He had a good heart, though. The more time we spent talking to stave away the boredom, the more we clicked. Until shortly before leaving Fort Hood, ours had been the classic military friendship, carpooling to and from work with friends, sharing a suitcase of Miller Lites in the barracks on a Friday night (if I was not on my way to San Antonio or Dallas). But it was the hours we spent talking in the warehouse and later in the solitude of the desert that cemented our unlikely friendship, as we shared one another's vulnerabilities and fears, knowing they would be kept between us forever. He had a girlfriend waiting back home in Arizona.

I used the line that I was engaged to be married, a cover-up I adopted when asked why I lived off-post. Here we had only each other. This was a friendship, I admit, that helped me through the hell of combat, and although he never said it, I'm sure helped him too.

My conversations with Alex were so removed from my daily living that it was easy to begin thinking in ways that my self-protective ego had never allowed. I asked him about his fiancée to purge myself of curiosity.

After a long silence, during which he didn't take his eyes off of me, he responded slowly, "I'm not sure. My folks are all happy about it. Tammy's elated, but I'm just not as sure as I used to be."

He had still not taken his eyes off of me. He paused and continued meekly, "What about you?"

I evaded his question with another question, and again he paused and laughed. Finally looking away, he continued in a searching voice, like a singer who has begun on the wrong note. "You know?"

When I paused for what seemed to him too long, he chummily touched my shoulder and suggested we play Nintendo.

I didn't understand, much less "know." I did know I enjoyed—needed—Alex's company.

Scattered over barren patches of desert more than 165 kilometers from the safety of ad Dammam, and less than 280 kilometers from the border with Iraq, 1st Cavalry Division units formed self-contained communities linked to higher up by a delicate combination of wire and microwave. Camouflage netting, although far from making us invisible—so the rationalization went—concealed us. More than that, I figured, it offered shade to sun-weary commanders and their troops who, in the searing heat of midday, could not help taking siestas. Mounted guards, some dug into the sand like the aggressively poisonous camel spiders lying in wait under patches of sand for a meal to pass, others stationed on top of buttes and berms, kept twenty-four-hour vigils, their weapons loaded and ready. For them there could be no siestas.

During these times, dust-covered and tired, I sat outside the tent—if a sandstorm did not forbid it—in reflective solitude and read a letter from home or from friends in the States or Germany. The evenings between publications of *Cav Country* brought freedom to while away the time reading, catching up with letter-writing, or falling prey to the boredom of routine and isolation. Better yet, these were the times (if you could not wait until 2100) to nap into the next day—unless you were unfortunate enough to find your name on the duty roster for guard mount that night.

In that case you would wake up at midnight and walk the unit's defensive perimeter in the chill of a cold desert night, wearing full battle gear and carrying a radio, watching falling stars as they made their way to earth, wishing, if your mind could remember to do so, that this were over. The automaton G.I. Joe was functioning perfectly, it seemed. My soul was oddly at peace.

Our job was to chronicle the division going to war. We found ourselves stretched beyond our physical limits. Like all enlisted personnel, along with our official never-ending duties, we were placed on rosters for kitchen patrol, shit-burning details, ammo runs, and perimeter guard. Yet it was also our mission to watch the division through the lens of a Nikon F-4 and with the eyes of a journalist on a daily basis. My job required sending journalists—if I didn't go out myself—to every unit in the division, to observe their training and report on their stories in *Cav Country*. This vicious cycle never ended.

Robyn reported on armor battalions sharpening their gunnery skills on a firing range built specifically for the division. Zak, afraid of his own mortality, captured beautifully on film the bravado of aviators, guarding their helicopters from the harsh elements, who nonetheless, when flying in combat formations, fired everything in their arsenal.

I spent two days living with infantrymen, soldiers more accustomed to the field than most. In countless exercises they pitted their Bradley 25-millimeter chain guns against demo and tear-up targets.

One morning, while airing out my sleeping bag and drying out a pair of socks I had hand-washed after guard duty the night before, the division's sergeant major, a burly Vietnam vet, walked by our tent.

"Good morning, Mr. Editor," he snarled, although he probably didn't mean to. (It comes reflexively with the rank.)

"Morning, Sergeant Major," I returned his salutation, struggling to my feet in a show of respect for his rank and position. The highest-ranking enlisted man in our division had a reputation for being exacting and intemperate.

"Sit down, Zuniga," Sergeant Major Robert Wilson ordered, then sat down himself on a stack of MRE boxes surrounding our makeshift foxhole. "You look like shit!"

Thanks, I normally look eighteen, I thought, but I returned that stony face, not a muscle in my face twitching. This man was reputed to blister paint at fifty feet with his glare. I nodded agreement and explained I had just finished my guard mount and looked forward to a nap before getting back to work on the paper after lunch.

"Wait a minute," he interrupted, a look of confusion on his face. "You mean you don't get the rest of the day off?"

I knew my words would get someone in trouble—mainly our supervisor, who spent at least as much time bullshitting as he did watching out for his soldiers' morale and well-being.

That day Sergeant Major Wilson and I spent many hours together discussing troop morale. We recalled that we had even slept on the desert floor one night when his driver had lost us somewhere between units. Now, we shared barbs—his focused on my writing, mine on the bad example his chain-smoking set. He found my air amusing. I respectfully declined to toss out one-liners I knew would amuse him but could make me cry afterward with the loss of a stripe.

The sergeant major stood up, adjusted his uniform, dusted his boots, and bid me a good night.

"If I see you working this afternoon, PFC Zuniga, your ass is mine! Get some sleep, I'll take care of this," he ordered, then marched off to the next tent.

That night Master Sergeant Fuller ran into our tent and announced that we journalists had been pulled off every detail but security. There is no telling what that did for our morale. I had the utmost respect for a leader who took care of his soldiers. Someday

I would do the same, I thought as I drifted back to sleep, visions of Sergeant Major José Zuniga trooping the line.

Thanksgiving Day was upon us in the blink of an eye. The depressing realization that Christmas and New Year's Eve in the desert would soon follow was temporarily forgotten as the mouth-watering scents of turkey, stuffing, and fresh-baked breads wafted in the air. The president had decreed his soldiers would eat wholesome Thanksgiving dinners, a little taste of home, and we did. The journalists' office sat at our own table, welcoming Alex, our adopted friend, to crowd into any available space and join us in thanking God for our many blessings.

The days went by.

Unlike Thanksgiving Day, Christmas begged for privacy to allow soldiers to mope and lament how far away we were from our families. No words needed to be said. An informal Christmas party lasting ten minutes was held in the main tent, with an exchange of gifts following a traditional Christmas carol. We eventually returned to our cots sulking. Each of us did what we had to to get through the day: Zak slept. Dean and Alex played on the Nintendo Gameboy Dean's fiancée had sent him for Christmas. I pulled a hefty box from under my cot, which had arrived three days before from home, the words *Merry Christmas* scrawled on the butcher-block paper wrapping by well-wishing mail handlers.

Tearing it open, I saw a cornucopia of canned foods, toilet paper, the usual assortment of magazines. There was also a gift-wrapped box protected by a dozen pairs of olive-drab socks wrapped around it to absorb the shock of transport to the ends of the earth. *To G.I. Joe from Mom, Dad, and Sis,* the tag read. The wrapping paper took seconds to shred. A Sony Walkman. Thanks. But there was also a cassette tape in the box. I fumbled nervously to get the tape into my new Walkman. The sounds of home, my mother's sweet voice, brought tears to my eyes and magnified the desolation I felt sitting in the middle of this vast ashtray on what would normally be one of the happiest days of the year.

Feliz Navidad, Pepé . . . I realize that by the time you hear this message Christmas may have come and gone. Whenever this gets

to you, know that your family is with you in spirit. . . . Don't let
yourself get down at this very special time of the year. I know it
may seem difficult not to focus on the loneliness, but you must.
I am praying for your safe and quick return home. I know God
will grant me the miracle of seeing you soon. Until then, keep
the faith.

I can't go on, my heart screamed. There was a sense of relief to
hear her voice this day, and for several days after as I replayed her
message. But there was also an utter sense of loss festering inside my
heart. With every quake in her voice, every cough, I feared never
seeing her alive again. I didn't want to lose her, but it was inevitable.
I buried my face in my hands.

God grant us a miracle, I prayed.

Alex walked over to my cot and sat down. Nothing of any great
significance was said, yet for quite some time I felt graced with such a
feeling of love. When he spoke, the words were about the bond we
had created, but it was clear that the words were not doing justice to
the underlying emotions.

Eyes without speaking confess the secrets of the heart, St. Jerome
said.

"Merry Christmas, Joe," he whispered before leaving the tent.

Merry Christmas, Alex.

A TIME OF WAR

I WAS WALKING THE REAR DETACHMENT'S DEFENSIVE PERIMETER ON January 17, the morning the air war started, with my Walkman's headset hidden under my helmet. Frantic broadcasters informed the world that Saddam's transgression was being punished by an Allied air offensive. Their exact words escape me now, but at 0200 the thuds of what we later knew were U.S. cruise missiles fired off the Saudi east coast made exact words pointless. My guard buddy and I ran to the first sergeant's tent to tell him the news, not thinking he may have heard the pounding too.

"I know," he said from the comfort of his sleeping bag. "The United States and her coalition partners have launched a massive air campaign to dislodge Iraqi troops from Kuwait," he added, as if reading the evening news from a teleprompter. It seemed everyone in the encampment knew. For the last two weeks we had all slept with one ear planted on a makeshift pillow, the other listening to military broadcasters on the radios set up in each tent.

We knew our time for battle was that much closer when the division rear was ordered to "jump" (a tactical move forward) to a position not more than twenty-five miles from the Saudi-Iraqi border.

As Robyn and I packed our computer equipment for the jump, she facetiously reminded me how unhappy I had been in being so far from the front. True, I had experienced my best moments in-country when out with a line unit covering a story in the farthest reaches of the desert. Far from the relative safety of our tent, I thrived on the oneness of a unit of soldiers relying on one another for the solace needed to sustain everyday life. "Maybe now you'll be happy," she said, a nervous tone blurring the line between reproach and jocularity.

In a two-hour convoy to our new patch of sand, the silence was raped at least three times by the anxious scream of a chemical-attack alert, forcing us all to don our protective masks and gear. But then, better safe than dead. Iraq was launching Scud missile attacks in response to losing control of its airspace. Who knew what payload they carried? While negotiations continued worldwide, with a sense of hope that the massive air campaign might bring Saddam to his knees, we continued our training.

Within a week of arriving at our new location, the division was fine-tuning its maneuvering capabilities. Our secret reassignment to VII (U.S.) Corps units freshly deployed from Europe confirmed the rumors spreading like wildfire of an imminent start to the ground war. No more clues were needed when General Tilelli ordered all female medics assigned to battalion-level aid stations back to rear-detachment aid stations and hospitals, creating empty medical slots that could only be partially filled by male medics.

A nervous feeling that I would be one of those sent forward because of my medical training was confirmed late one evening when Captain Phillips paid a rare visit to our tent, asking everyone but me to step outside for a minute.

"I could fight to keep you here," Captain Phillips said, a hint of self-doubt betraying his knowledge that such a plan was probably futile. "In the end, it's not my decision, or even yours, unless you make one now."

My options were to rejoin the rear-detachment medical battalion to which I had been first assigned at Fort Hood or join a forward armored medical platoon in desperate need of medics. As easy as it would have been to remain near headquarters, a second's worth of soul-searching made clear what otherwise would have been an agonizing decision. What had John Wayne and Salvador Zuniga taught me?

Two days later I relinquished the *Cav Country* editorship, packed my bags, and awaited orders to report as a combat medic to the 2nd Battalion, 8th Cavalry Regiment (more precisely, to a platoon of ten medics, two physicians' assistants, and a doctor in his third year of residency at Darnall Army Hospital). Britt volunteered to drive me forward—it would be a great opportunity to get some shots of forward units training, he said. I knew that, deep inside, it was his way of delaying our goodbye.

Alex had secured permission from his section chief to join us, a routine communications or commo-line inspection, he said. At the last minute, though, he was called off to fix a commo-link foulup and sadly said goodbye before leaving, promising he'd catch me on the radio wherever I was.

"Wait!" I heard Captain Phillips scream. I saw him running—as much as you can run in sand that is like talcum powder—toward us. "You can't go yet."

He called into the tent for everyone to come out; he hadn't noticed that everyone was already outside wishing me good luck. Britt and I got out of the humvee and joined the crowd, as confused as everyone else when Captain Phillips called us hastily to attention and ordered me to post myself front and center. Clutching a sheet of paper firmly in his hand, Captain Phillips started to read:

> This is to certify that the Secretary of the Army has awarded the Army Commendation Medal to Private First Class José M. Zuniga, for exceptionally meritorious achievement from 9 August 1990 to 16 December 1990 while serving as designer and editor of the 1st Cavalry Division's Desert Shield command information newspaper, *Cav Country*. PFC Zuniga, under austere and hostile conditions, produced a highly informative professional newspaper for the command. His efforts have resulted in heightened morale and improved information flow within the First Team. PFC Zuniga's duties reflect great credit upon himself, the 1st Cavalry Division, and the U.S. Army. Given under my hand, Leon J. LaPorte, Colonel, Chief of Staff, and Michael P. W. Stone, Secretary of the Army.

My arrival at Task Force 2-8 Cav's headquarters was met with considerable disdain. The commander, first sergeant, and most soldiers had known me as editor of *Cav Country*. There was much speculation about who and what I was. Many had envisioned and grown to envy my life of leisure in a Dhahran hotel, putting together a newspaper they fed on for news of the war and word from home. Britt having chauffeured me to my new assignment didn't help to change that impression.

"Boy, are you in for a surprise here," the first sergeant said menacingly, before radioing the medical platoon sergeant to pick me up.

Surprise could not even begin to describe the shock of seeing the reality of how front-line units lived. Because of security restrictions, journalists had not been allowed to group and report stories about these units once they'd jumped so far forward. The beauty of this place, less than ten miles from the reality of war, however, struck me as my eyes absorbed a stretch of desert so saturated with reds and yellows that it looked as though Frederic Remington had spilled his paintbox.

A stocky staff sergeant came barreling toward the first sergeant's tent. He was my new supervisor, and he didn't look all too happy about it.

It must have been the intense look in my eyes that won me his favor.

"Relax, Zuniga," he said in what sounded like a Puerto Rican accent, then grabbed one of my duffels and led the way. "I'm Sergeant Hector Morales."

February 10, 1991

Dear Son,

Your friend Alex called us a few days ago with the news you have been transferred to a unit closer to the front lines. He gave us your new unit's name so mail would get to you quicker. I pray that this letter is reaching you.

All is well here, you need not worry about us. Know that I am praying for you. Remember that even when we march in battle into the pits of Hell, God's shield will always protect us from all harm. Have faith, Pepé.

Your father is very proud of you, we all are. We all miss you and anxiously await the end of this war. I'll close for now, knowing that whatever the future may bring, God will insure your safe return home.

Your mother,
Raquel

Notwithstanding the initially hostile drop-off, acclimating to my new surroundings was made easier when Sergeant Morales called a platoon meeting to introduce the newest addition to the medical team. He then offered me five minutes in which to dispel the speculation that I was, in military lingo, a REMF (rear-echelon mother fucker), the worst possible reputation a soldier can garner. My mile-a-minute monologue, not a word of which I now remember, must have been convincing, because they opened their arms to me.

Still, life in the front took getting used to. From whores' baths, during which we poured frigid water over one another to bathe, to a lack of hot meals, to the irregular delivery of mail, nothing contributed to making it any easier.

Alex finally reached me one night on the radio through some feat of technological wizardry to share, if only long distance, in my misery. It pained me to hear his voice. I missed the closeness we had developed but was relieved my transfer had meant that closeness would go no farther, even if it had been possible.

For the first time in my enlistment I was feeling emotionally attached to a human being in a way that scared me. I had shut the door to my heart when I signed my name on a dotted line, swearing my allegiance to the Army. I had made a conscious decision, a promise to myself, to repress any and all sexual and emotional feelings.

I had been largely successful. Although most of my Army friends were either gay men or lesbians, and my attraction to men was never squelched, I was an asexual soldier.

With the security of many miles between Alex and me, burying any thought of this matter under mountains of denial, I would keep my promise.

By early February, Allied commander General H. Norman Schwarzkopf laid out, in secret, his battle plan. Critical to accomplishing this plan was fooling Iraqi tacticians into believing an imminent large-scale attack or breach would be attempted through the Wadi al Batin, a valley near the joint borders of Iraq, Kuwait, and Saudi Arabia. Until late January, this area had been secured by the British Army's 1st Armoured Division. General Schwarzkopf's plan called for the First Team to serve as a decoy front. A series of massive artillery raids and reconnaissance-in-force missions northward into Iraqi defenses was meant to draw the Iraqis' attention. If the deception worked, the 1st Infantry Division, otherwise known as the Big Red One, would breach the enemy defenses in southeastern Iraq, more than a hundred kilometers west of where Saddam was anticipating a full frontal attack. Remaining VII (U.S.) Corps armored units would roll in, envelop, and annihilate the formidable Iraqi presence in western Kuwait.

The key to the plan's success was making the deception credible. The 1st Cavalry Division drew closer to the border. Allied air and artillery barrages flying directly over our heads reminded us how close we were to our enemy. The sky at times was illuminated like a lightbulb's filament—surreal lighting over the northern horizon. The boom of impact blasts provided realism. If we winced at the mere thought of the destruction, how was it for Iraqi troops to live through it?

As effective as the air campaign had been—hundreds of Iraqi soldiers, defeated by the deafening nighttime barrages, were walking south through the deadly minefields their army had planted to surrender to Allied soldiers—it was becoming obvious that a ground offensive was inevitable. By mid-February, our platoon was providing medical support in a series of cross-border raids near the wadi, the majority of our aid going to enemy prisoners of war. In keeping with the Hippocratic Oath, medics made no distinction between friendly and enemy casualties.

Military intelligence reports indicated that Iraqi infantry and armor divisions were now entrenched a stone's throw from the Wadi al Batin area. The deception was working. Slowly, using the First Team as a decoy, the remaining Allied players began positioning themselves for the battle that lay ahead.

I wrote in my diary an account of Task Force 2-8 Cav's activities the night of February 20, 1991. The following excerpt was published in the division's official written history, *America's First Team in the Gulf*:

> "Let's go, let's go," growled Command Sergeant Major Marvin Loris as he approached us around midnight. "We've got a mission."
>
> We were to support a recon into Iraq, retrieving the injured or dead. I drove an armored personnel carrier. As we inched along

the berm, my commander reminded me that one jolt on the gears could send us over a mine.

The lead tanks rolled across the berm. Artillery fire lit the sky. We medics knew we'd be busy tonight, but the mission ended without friendly casualties. The task force did take several prisoners and we treated them.

The Iraqis were so glad to see us. They were cut off from their supply lines. An Iraqi lieutenant tearfully told us in broken English how grateful he was that he didn't have to be in the rain anymore. We brought them to the battalion aid station, worried about having the enemy in vehicles with us. But they were so tired and miserable that the last thing on their minds was escape.

One Iraqi had been hit by shrapnel, but most of them had trench foot and other problems from exposure. Wet socks stuck to their rotted feet and we had to peel them off. I don't know how they managed to walk.

We completed treatment and sent them to the prison camp. Wondering about their fates ... Anyway, our mission is over. Time to sleep. Bad dreams, though. Can't get the picture of that Iraqi jeep out of my mind. It was still smoldering, the metal white like aluminum paper. Inside there were three bodies, all of them charred black ... Gotta sleep ...

Sergeant Morales and I slept, exhausted from the night's mission and the constant megaton pounding noise impinging on all hopes of tranquil rest. The battalion chaplain, a man I had met only once, woke me by gently nudging my shoulder and asked me to join him for a walk. The sky was still dark from an overnight rain storm. Our platoon leader accompanied him, the grim look on his face telling me more than any words could.

As the chaplain blithered something about faith and peace, my mind wandered elsewhere. At this moment I felt a helpless frustration that brought me near tears, frustration that none of his consoling words could assuage.

I was an ocean away, and I knew Mother was dying. Her illness was not new, but she had been in a slow fade for so long and the arrival of an official bad news delivery party meant either the end had already come or it was imminent. Worst of all, they couldn't give me an answer about her status. They were honest enough to admit that even with satellite and microwave, the details of the drama playing itself out in a San Antonio hospital were beyond their knowledge.

Within less than an hour, orders authorizing my emergency leave were signed by General Tilelli himself. Regardless of the speed with which words could be transmitted over miles, there was no way to transmit my body by the technology science-fiction writers had invented. I couldn't just ask Scotty to beam me home.

The company commander personally offered to drive me to my first destination at battalion headquarters. From there, I was to fly by helicopter to Dhahran International Airport.

Despite the beginning of the ground offensive, great efforts were made to get me on a C-130 back to the United States faster than I'd ever seen the Army's bureaucracy work before.

This plane was no commercial jumbo jet commandeered to whisk a fresh army off to war. This was a plane that opened its bowels to swallow tanks. Passenger seating was netting attached to the cavernous fuselage. Stepping into the cargo bay and taking the first available seat, I looked around me at the other passengers on the flight. Many of them had enjoyed the luxury of a shower and the benefit of a change of clothes before boarding. I, however, was coming from the front line where such niceties of civilization no longer existed. I carried with me only the sweat- and oil-stained uniform on my body; I had not changed either last night after the recon or while waiting for my orders from higher up. I felt as if I had been in the sandbox so long I didn't need a bath, I needed a run through a car wash.

Such trivial thoughts were of short duration as I fell into a deep sleep that lasted the nine-hour flight to Torrejon Air Force Base in Spain.

"Is that you?" my father asked exasperatedly when I called him from Spain. "Where are you?"

It didn't take long for us to brief each other, having learned the simple art of omitting unnecessary words and sticking to the point.

"She swore she saw you tonight," he said, choking with an emotion I had never seen or heard in him. "Hurry home, son."

I knew she was still alive, but that did not make my frustration and pain go away. I could not sleep. No matter how hard I tried, thinking eclipsed sleep on this ten-hour military flight to Charleston, North

Carolina. I thought of my mother, who just days before had written to tell me to have faith in my new assignment, never once mentioning how ill she really was. I reread one of her letters I had just days before stuffed into my pocket. Her poetic letters, written almost daily while I was away at war, had woven by means of alliteration, juxtaposition, imagery, and symbolism the story of a life unlike what I had known or assumed hers to be. It was a covenant shared between two repressed artists. Through the umbilical cord of pen and paper, I came to know the woman who was my mother. I suppose then it was the possibility of mutual loss—mine to a bullet, hers to a pathogen—that allowed us to tear down the barriers of sham intimacy that family relationships often require.

My thoughts shifted to my buddies at Task Force 2-8: Alex, Dean, Zak, Robyn, Captain Phillips . . . The ground war was well on its way now, and although I had seen a fair share of action, it would come and go so quickly that I would have to see its end on CNN like any other American.

A Delta Airlines flight delivered me to San Antonio a day later and I took the first cab to the Baptist Memorial Hospital. The strange glances people shot my way as I made my way through the hospital and up the elevator to the intensive-care unit added self-consciousness to the witches' brew of emotions percolating inside me.

Although it was well past visiting hours, the nurse on duty, seeing my uniform, wretched as it was, escorted me quickly to my mother's bedside. There on a hospital bed, ensnared by glistening lines and swathed in plastic tubes, lay a remnant of the woman on whose forehead I had planted a goodbye kiss six months before. She was asleep. I heard Bernard Shaw on a television set in the corner, commenting about the war as if it were a football game.

"Your mother demanded to have a television hooked up and on all day for the latest news about you," the nurse explained. Father had told me in our telephone conversation yesterday that whenever she was conscious, she either watched CNN or listened to National Public Radio. She made sure, even in the intensive-care unit, that she was caring for her child.

I leaned over and gently kissed her free hand, not wanting to wake her from what seemed a pleasant albeit sedative-induced slumber. Her eyes quivered open, at first slits, finally wide open. She strained to say something, but no words developed.

112

That's okay, I whispered, wiping the tears of joy from her eyes. "You were right," I said as she clung to my hand like a baby. "God did get me home safely."

A nod of her head indicated she understood. Her eyelids began to droop. Don't fight the sleep, the nurse said. But she tried anyway. Her nails dug at my hand three times until she could fight the sleep no more and drifted into slumber.

WELCOME HOME

WELL BEFORE THE START OF THE FEBRUARY 24 GROUND OFFENSIVE, most Iraqi line infantry divisions had experienced severe attrition, even though their officers had laid minefields and fire trenches to prevent a retreat. Instead of retreating, Iraqi soldiers were left with the option of walking forward to surrender. To their forces' credit, the mechanized and armored formations proved cohesive and willing to do battle; yet in little more than ninety hours, overcoming tough logistical challenges in a 150-mile sweep around Iraqi lines, Allied forces crushed their foe. During the fight and afterward, the Allies captured or destroyed more than 5,200 pieces of enemy equipment and took (received, in many cases) more than 22,000 prisoners of war. But what is more important, the Allies achieved the goal they had set in the summer of 1990.

Kuwait had been liberated.

Watching the hundred-hour war on CNN was surreal. I had the special knowledge of reality from having been in the field. I knew Iraqi troops were likely being bulldozed alive, their trenches becoming instant graves. I was seeing the war through the rosy haze of victory through which the American public saw it. But I knew it to be only a shadow of the true, grim horror. I knew the first reported atrocity, the miles long "Highway of Death" littered with destroyed Iraqi armored vehicles, was just the tip of an iceberg. Guilt shadowed my joy that the war was over, though I knew my rightful place had been by my mother's side as she lay in what the doctor predicted would be her deathbed.

Within a week, her son home and no war for him to go back to, my mother miraculously recovered from her near-death state. She would still require chemotherapy to kill off the cancer left behind in this round of surgery, the doctor predicted. But the doctor also told us she required love and care in what he termed her "remaining cane-assisted days."

She was not dead yet. An early frost had not wilted her desire to live.

My emergency leave over, I managed to persuade Fort Hood officials to authorize a temporary assignment as a medic at Fort Sam Houston's Brooke Army Medical Center, which was only a ten-minute drive from my parents' home. A two-week authorization allowed me time to request and have processed compassionate reassignment orders.

On the eve of the authorization's expiration there was still no response from Army officials. With each phone call, the common response was that word was still out. Until today, I had been buoyed by each answer that wasn't a no. I needed a definite answer now or I would be forced to return to Fort Hood. The doctor's advice that I remain in San Antonio here had a special resonance for me. I could see how frail Mother had become.

Stepping around the partition surrounding the orders clerk's desk, I was elated to find him there. This was the first time I actually saw this man, although we had communicated by phone at least twice daily over the last two weeks.

"They were denied, man," he said, not looking me in the face.

What? I remained silent a minute too long. His words had hit me like a Mac truck.

"I'm sorry, Zuniga. You know if it was my decision to make . . ." His words faded into nothing. No, I didn't know he'd make the right and human decision. For all I knew he was as heartless as the computer terminal in front of him.

My mother's complexion paled as I communicated the bad news. I swore to continue trying through the personnel office at Fort Hood. My words turned into stammering.

"At least you're not a world away," she said.

I was back in Killeen that night.

*　　*　　*

115

The division sergeant major rallied the troops outside the American University dorms for a pep talk before our big event. This was the 1st Cav's golden opportunity to make our country and fellow cavalry buddies proud. We would march before George Bush, the president of the United States, and show him from what mettle we were made; the commander in chief's victorious legions returned from the throes of war in the Persian Gulf.

General Tilelli, recently promoted to major general, arrived a good ten minutes late; of course he would say *we* had arrived ten minutes too early. Tardiness is par for the course for generals, who are notorious for their elastic concept of time, except when relating to golf, appointments with higher-ups, or war.

Dean and I had been assigned to cover this parade and the ticker-tape version in New York City's Canyon of Heroes. We jumped at the opportunity after the boring task of chronicling in *Cav Country* the division's redeployment and postwar hibernation. As we ran up and down the parade route, following the band and vanguard, we shot roll after roll of film and video of the general and his staff waving at the throngs of grateful Americans who lined the route. There had been controversy about the war, but the support shown here for the returning men and women forgave such differences.

It wasn't until that night, as I struggled to catch a glimpse of Barbara Mandrell singing the "Star-Spangled Banner" and the fireworks illuminating the night sky in a symphony of light, that the magnitude of this weekend really hit home. Many were the service members in the audience that night who shed tears of joy at the respect and adulation with which our nation was showering its newest heroes.

Our Vietnam era comrades-at-arms were also partaking in the celebration. We extended our arms and hearts to them, to include them in the celebration they never received. Many of us were aware that their welcome home—along with that of many of our fathers, uncles, and brothers—had been neglected in the din of political protest. They too had sacrificed their all for a country that exacted a price in tears and blood, many having watched buddies die in their arms in the name of liberty. Tonight our welcome home was theirs too, and as we listened to Whitney Houston's "God Bless America" flow out of the skyscraper-high speakers towering over the stage, our hearts were one.

It was during the lull that seemed to blanket a weary division of troops that I came to fully understand that my love for Alex went beyond the usual closeness and camaraderie produced in combat. We had talked about homosexuality a number of times, about as many times as we talked about almost everything else in the multitude of late desert afternoons when boredom drove you to bullshit or sleep.

"I don't know," Alex would say, jokingly slipping into a lisp and effeminate body language that lasted only seconds.

A native Californian, he confessed to having seen and heard it all. I could never quite get the definition of *all*—I really didn't care then. Now, I knew he was married, but not the happiest married man around. It was interesting to hear him talk about some of his best friends and the fact they were gay. I ribbed him constantly, hoping he would defend these people—or perhaps defend some of the feelings I was trying so hard to repress. Since I could turn him in no matter how close he thought we were, I rationalized, even if he felt the same as I did, he would never admit it.

He mentioned having gone dancing a few times at predominantly gay clubs. They were cooler, he added. I didn't fess up to my own dance experiences, much less to my last roommate and his friends.

The facade I maintained had been constructed years before when my father and my Church explained to me the perversion of being gay. The facade was reinforced after a simple farm boy was used to hammer home the military's requirement for being an effective warrior. Did Alex sense my inner conflict? Or was he baiting me? And if he was baiting me, was it because he wanted to share his confusion too—or was he a pawn in this witch-hunt? Could I be an object of his affection?

I'm pretty sure Alex was not gay. I'm sure, too, that if I had shared my secret with him then, he would have been tolerant and helped me find inner peace.

Coming out isn't a come-on, Mr. Falwell. My bond with Alex did not depend on sexual gratification.

I distanced myself from Alex, afraid my secret would be discovered, even though he seemed so unprejudiced. I could not afford to explore these feelings as I tried and failed to years ago—I couldn't even own up to them now. I knew I was gay, but my heritage, my Church, and society had all taught me that being gay was wrong. I was in denial, ashamed of my preservice sexual experiences, and, although I'd been tempted to try again, I resisted and kept my gayness in shackles.

Alex was reassigned a few months later. As Army buddies usually do when parting ways, we both abstained from the teary goodbye. Instead we both looked froward to the day when we could sit down somewhere and think back on the good times over an ice-cold beer. I wonder if we ever will.

How deep was our friendship when I never let him near the real me? Did he know the real Joe Zuniga, or did he know the cardboard cut-out, the model soldier? His departure signaled the end to any thought I had of exploring my developing emotions, philosophically or otherwise, with him, I concluded. I managed to convince myself that Alex was the only man in the world who could bring to life, as if by command, feelings that would otherwise remain dormant. It was now time to dedicate myself to settling down into the monotony of military life.

I was making rank and friends in high places quickly. The military lifestyle fit me like a glove, with one exception: I was a twenty-one-year-old single career soldier.

There is no written rule, but it is common knowledge that a spouse is needed in this family values–laden society to avert questions. *Marriage*. That was what society, more specifically the military, expected.

The fact that I had not set down roots was also a source of disappointment for my dying mother. Marriage would be a backdrop, a curtain behind which I could hide from the zealots who would never see past the glossy photo of a lovely wife that would sit on my desk. And as self-deceptive as it would make me feel, marriage, or "settling down," would be a dose of tranquility I thought my mother deserved.

THE PERFECT
MARRIAGE

Department of Defense Form 1966/2, Question 27a: Are you a homosexual or a bisexual? ("Homosexual" is defined as: sexual desire or behavior directed at (a) person(s) of one's own sex. "Bisexual" is defined as: a person sexually responsive to both sexes.) *Question 27b:* Do you intend to engage in homosexual acts (sexual relations with another person of the same sex)?

MY RECRUITER NEVER ASKED THE TWO QUESTIONS LISTED UNDER the "Character and Social Adjustment" heading, just as he never inquired about illegal drug use. These were but two of the nonwaivable moral and administrative disqualifications listed on Line C of an A-to-Z table of disqualifying factors under Army Regulation 601–210. Seven detrimental traits were listed on this line, with homosexuality ranked fifth behind "questionable moral character, alcoholism, drug dependence, and sexual perversion" but above "history of antisocial behavior and history of frequent or chronic venereal disease."

Stone-faced determination had gotten me through the screening process. As long as I passed the physical and didn't have flat feet—not good for marching—I knew I was in. The recruiter had before him a twenty-one-year-old, physically fit, college-educated man volunteering to sign his name to a piece of paper guaranteeing the military eight years of his life. He had something the Army wanted, and he was not going to let me slip away back into a $30,000-a-year job on technicalities. If I had been asked questions 27 a and b that day, I am not sure what my response would have been.

By the age of seventeen, I had begun to dabble in the value system that dictated that only the appropriate manifestation of love and sexuality—being with the opposite sex—was acceptable. I went out with girls in high school and college, but the relationships remained platonic and were limited to movies, dinner, and proms. I did not think of myself as gay, through some combination of denial and rationalization.

Now, if I wanted a military career, and there was never a question I did, I would need to be married. Besides, with the number of soldiers being discharged for homosexuality, I needed all the protection I could get. As I waffled between marrying or not, all I had to do was listen to stories of other gay and lesbian service members caught up in the Gestapo-like nets.

A friend of a friend, Anne was in a similar predicament—she was gay but husband-hunting to meet social norms. A twenty-seven-year-old schoolteacher in rural North Dakota, Anne feared the repercussions from her family, friends, and employer if they found out her secret. We met in my apartment in Killeen and hit it off. We felt we could be useful to each other.

I proposed, using her girfriend's ring, and we were married that same day at the Belton County Court House. Nervousness and apprehension permeated the courtroom air as the judge delivered the marriage rites.

"You're letting her keep her last name?" The judge seemed to be joking. "That's where it *starts.*"

We laughed despite ourselves. If he only knew, I thought.

"You gonna kiss the bride, son?" he asked with a smirk.

I had not anticipated this moment. How to kiss her? Full on the lips? We had just met, I reminded myself.

A quick peck on the mouth and we were married. My mother would question Anne's decision to keep her last name; it was not the old way. Why not hyphenate? There would be no answer. We had the pictures we needed for our desks, the rings on our fingers. A week's leave of absence to celebrate our marriage and we were each back on our own, living our individual lives. My life was in Texas, where, beyond the occasional question about Anne's welfare and activities, being married exacted no costs in the context of my career and reaped only benefits. The story was that Anne and I had separated amicably shortly after our wedding and were working things out.

Anne's life was in Ohio with a career that we mutually agreed was too important for her to give up by moving to Texas. The perfect marriage.

A marriage that had been an advantage to me during my rise in the military weighed heavily as an albatross around my neck in 1993 when I was agonizing over whether or not to come out. What consequence would my actions have on her well-being, including possible exposure to public scrutiny of the private life she treasured?

"I'm married," I confessed to my attorney during our initial interview.

He sat slack-jawed. "Are you . . . bi?"

"Not exactly. It's more a matter of mutual convenience. You know how it is."

In a matter of seconds the former Army prosecutor was digging in his satchel, a look of consternation crossing a face that moments before had seemed serene. Of course he knew about sham marriages.

"Article 1xx . . . 1xx . . . 1xx . . . 72 . . . Serious cause for concern here . . . Where is she on this? Does she know? Why don't we start at the beginning . . ." he said a mile a minute.

Despite the possibility that her rights to privacy might be trampled on, Anne supported my crusade to change the world, exacting only the promise of absolute discretion about our marriage. I was successful in that regard throughout my discharge and in my national speaking tour. To the charge I may have broken the promise, I can only respond that I have done so to further illustrate the tragedy of the closet.

Soldiers, like members of any other profession, have long married for reasons other than love. After all, long before there was a United Nations, long before there was mediated arbitration or conflict-resolution conferences, there were prearranged marriages among friendly or warring tribes to settle farmland disputes. Randy Shilts in his book *Conduct Unbecoming* referred to the practice in the military between hetero- and homosexual service members. Most major works dealing with gays in the military have debated the practice. But there was no real reason to listen; none of the highly publicized cases garnering media attention had focused on sex per se. Anne and I, with our story, become living examples of the murky depths to which society pushes us to hide ourselves.

I have thrown aside my mask. Someday I hope that Anne can too, by her own choice, since we are brother and sister in the same fight.

FREE TO FLY

=========

THE USUAL THREE-HOUR DRIVE FROM KILLEEN TO SAN ANTONIO seemed eternal, with the twenty-one years of my life flashing across the windshield of my mind as I raced down Interstate-35 at close to seventy-five miles per hour. With each frame on the reel my guilt increased. Tears welled up wherever it is they originate, but I could not cry. I cursed myself for having lost touch with the humanity Mother had valiantly tried to instill in me. Only a week before, I had canceled plans to visit her because my father had insisted she was doing fine. A routine hospital visit on Wednesday, he said, for an MRI. There was no company chaplain warning me otherwise.

Was I going to make it home on time? Frame after frame passed before my stinging eyes.

Three-year-old Pepé in a miniature sailor suit, Mother lifting him onto a kitchen chair to blow out the three candles on a homemade birthday cake . . .

Mother combing Pepé's hair back for an elementary-school year-book photo . . .

A proud mother, her delicate body ignobly dwindling to something less substantial, a remnant of the woman I once knew in a hospital bed, smiling from ear to ear as she poses with her son in cap and gown before his high-school graduation . . .

An Aggie cadet and his mother posing in front of a newly refurbished house in San Antonio, struggling against gravity to a standing position for this special occasion . . .

A grown-up G.I. Joe, no longer little Pepé, sitting on a cot in

Saudi Arabia listening to Mother's Christmas wishes playing out of a Walkman headset . . .

Mother, wait for me! My aching heart screamed as I was seventy-five, fifty, twenty-five miles from home and closing fast.

Pulling into the hospital parking lot I felt the urge to jump out of the car and bound up five flights of stairs to the oncology ward. I found what seemed to be the last parking space in the entire structure, turned out the headlights, and shut off an overheated engine. The elevator ride was predictably long, the shrieking noise of a baby not helping to speed up the process.

I headed to the nurses' station. I knew the place well, having spent many days visiting Mother in her trips to this floor. I did not need to ask anyone for her room number, as I saw my father standing stoop-shouldered by a closed doorway.

Our eyes met and I knew I was too late. There was no embrace, not for the Zuniga men. Zunigas huddled together crying cathartically was unimaginable. But I took my father's hand, squeezed it, and felt myself weep somewhere deep inside. He looked at me quizzically, choked back his own tears, and proceeded, with me following silently, back to the private room in which my mother lay dead.

Her body was still warm; she had gone in her sleep not thirty minutes before. I imagine she simply closed the door and murmured a prayer. A smile graced her deceptively youthful, now serene face.

Peace often comes only with sleep, a poet once wrote. My mother was at peace, I knew. Glancing over to the medicine counter beside her bed, I saw a family portrait we had posed for a few years before. I glared at the color-enhanced photo for what seemed an eternity, wishing that, when my focus shifted back to the bed, my mother's eyes would be open, and blood again coursed through her veins. But my mother was dead.

"I should have been here earlier," I said softly, more to Mother than to my father or anyone else in the room. I felt as if I were accursed, and I begged to be damned further.

The mortuary attendant waltzed into the room and gently spat out a list of the regulations that had been broken by keeping my mother's corpse in the room so long. I walked out and tried to fix blame on myself for not having been with Mother as she took her final breaths. The fact she was in a coma did not play into my calculations. She died on a Wednesday. I'd been planning to drive down to San Antonio that weekend. I already carried a private burden of guilt about the lack of attention I had lavished on my dying mother, of which I was reminded numerous times by an alcohol-emboldened father. My absence at her deathbed cemented that guilt.

It was a rainy August morning but the sun was stationed in its midday post, its rays piercing through the two or three rain clouds scattered in an otherwise cobalt-blue sky. A frosty breeze, uncommon in any Texas Indian summer, blew steadily. Fifty of Raquel Vaca Zuniga's family members, closest friends, and those who felt it a social obligation to attend such events, regardless of their connection to the deceased, gathered under a pin-striped blue awning that at once shaded us from the sun and protected us from the rain, to return my mother to the earth from whence her religion said she came.

Until the moment her rose-hued casket was lowered into the ground, the past week's events had seemed unreal. Now they seemed surreal, with Franz Kafka or Rod Serling as the unseen master of ceremony. My heart paused as the casket disappeared into the cement vault that would house it beside the river she'd fallen in love with in the days when she could let its water trickle through her toes as she played games with her two young children.

I was so busy making last-minute funeral arrangements and playing family spokesman, dealing with people who came to pay their last respects, that I had forsaken my own mourning time. I did not cry; there was no physical manifestation. I probably could not cry. Duty called, and as my father and the military had so proficiently taught me, the mission comes first. Laying my mother to rest was my mission, and I was the only one assigned to the task, as my father had shut down, at least as far as helping with arrangements.

I had thought at first that he might break down. Now he stood straight-backed and resolute, shedding no tears. An inner strength seemed to seize control of him the day she died, and he made it through the most traumatic of times. It was a method of dealing I would have found impossible to copy had I not been in the most extreme denial. I was impressed by his austerity. To each his own defense.

Just a month before Mother and I had spent hours talking in her bedroom. I remembered helping her back into her bed after a short walk to the bathroom for a glass of water and her medications. Her hands clutched my shoulder blades as she settled into position, thanking me for my gentleness. I couldn't imagine having been otherwise; at that moment I couldn't bear the thought of losing her, although I knew I already had. The sense of being together on borrowed time was palpable. She had lost her bloom to the disease, and like the stray strands of hair she hid now and then beneath her wig, she looked to be dying but was attached to the root, some remote vitality she used to possess still lingering.

Her eyes as soft and dark as a night's deep sleep watched me, absorbing every aspect of my being. I had always been her favorite, I knew, although I had not always been the perfect son.

It wasn't until after I enlisted that she endorsed my career, knowing that I had finally settled down, even though she didn't really approve of the military for me. She knew almost everything about me, for it was always with her that I shared my problems and my victories. What I did not share she could probably see. To her, my walls had crumbled long ago. Such is life when your father is emotionally inaccessible.

But there was one part of my life she was not aware of, or at least I thought she was not. Since I had expertly masked my sexuality during my strict Catholic upbringing and into my school years, her being in the dark would not have been a surprise. Yet we had such a close bond that on some level I'm sure she knew since my teens that I wasn't simply a bit on the sensitive side, I was gay. She had never asked the wrong questions, but she also safely avoided the right ones.

Today, for an unknown reason, she chose to confirm her suspicion by asking if I was ever planning to have my recent civil marriage to Anne blessed in the sanctity of a Catholic church. She had to know this union did not merit such pomp. She had to understand that my instant rejection of a church wedding weeks before was a refusal to commit sacrilege before God by elevating this union into something it really wasn't.

"No, Mama, and I think you know why. Trying to advance in the Army's futile if you're not married."

I felt I had said a lot, yet so much remained unsaid. Could she place the right weight and emphasis on my carefully chosen words? Could she, in her frailty, still read between the lines with the incendiary intelligence she once possessed? Had I said too much to a dying woman, a dying mother? The calm tears of this dying woman with whom I shared much more than lifeblood radiated undiscriminating love, forgiveness for my lie of omission, and, I hoped, a new respect for her son's truthfulness. I felt absolved as I sat by her bedside the rest of the morning, quietly basking in her emotional warmth.

That evening I sat on the twin bed I had slept on through my childhood, composing in my head a one-page obituary I would later type on my father's 1930s Remington. My mission was to tell the world about the great loss it had experienced. Maybe in this way, I too would come to accept the reality of her loss. It is remarkable the change the death of one woman can bring for an entire life. My father withdrew into a shell from which he still struggles to emerge.

As for me, one thing became abundantly clear: The minute my root to Texas died, I was free to go.

PART 3

PART 3

WITCH-HUNTS

SPECIALIST ANDREA THOMPKINS WAS A TOPNOTCH SUPPLY TECHNI-
cian, recognized over and over for her proficiency and dedication.
Her job as supply clerk for a 350-soldier company kept her on the
go constantly. Amazingly, she possessed what most supply clerks in
the Army don't: an intense desire to help fellow soldiers through
any bind. Where most supply clerks would make soldiers jump
through hoops when they needed supplies, Andrea would go out of
her way to solve a problem. Fortunately, because of her great capacity to care for any soldier, her lesbianism was overlooked by most:
Everyone in the company knew about it; no one discussed it.

A year into my assignment at Fort Hood, a gung-ho armor jock
joined our unit as a training noncommissioned officer. This staff
sergeant had been trained by the best the Army had to offer and
felt it was now his turn to pass on his knowledge. He was a welcome
addition to our unit because he brought with him an enthusiasm
about what he taught. He also brought, however, a voracious sexual
appetite and he seemed ready to prove it.

What seemed at first like a platonic friendship between Andrea
and the sergeant became one of the most talked-about scandals on
post. It was viciously rumored she had agreed to have sex with him
to prove she could. When she refused to continue the sexual dalli-
ances, what could have blown over became a vindictive campaign
to destroy her career. We exacerbated his wrath by mocking his
involvement with a known lesbian. Evidently, he had not known. At
the same time we allowed him to lead us by the nose in his personal
campaign of vindictive harassment: degrading remarks, hostility, and

crude jokes. This kind of misogyny had been taught us in basic training. Within three weeks Andrea was booted out of the military with a dishonorable discharge.

The havoc this created in her life stirred my inner conflict. This was a good human being, a model soldier, whose life had been destroyed because she loved someone of the "wrong" sex. What of me and my inner turmoil? What of my complicity in this wrong?

They sat him at the far end of a conference-room table in a dimly lit room, Marc recalled vividly as he told us about the nightmare interrogation he had endured. Just two days ago his lover, a medical service corps officer, had been hauled in for questioning by the military police. In exchange for an honorable discharge, he'd made a bargain with the devil and given military authorities intimate details about his relationship with Marc. Tears welled up in Marc's eyes as he recounted details of the interrogation that had taken place not more than a few feet from the dining facility at which four closeted gay soldiers now sat. He had been offered an honorable discharge if he cooperated and provided a list of all his gay and lesbian friends. Marc held firm.

Crying and frightened, he faced an investigating officer who said he would call Marc's father, a sergeant major, first thing in the morning to tell him that his son was a *fag*.

"This is not a threat," he remembered the softer of the two agents explaining after reading him his *Miranda* rights, "but if you don't cooperate we'll have to expand the investigation. . . . You done anything else wrong?"

The CID's modus operandi, most soldiers I'd heard explain, was virtually to dictate statements and force suspects to write what the agents wanted. The soldiers felt the very real fear that further measures would be taken if they continued to deny being gay. Although Marc was able to resist their intimidating scare tactics, "what hurt most was becoming a pariah among my colleagues and friends," he said. Until then Marc had traveled in our motley circle. Those who weren't gay knew everyone else's secrets and were cool. Marc had anticipated this reaction from some in the group, but, as was evident by the fact that only Mitch, Eleanor, and I sat here tonight, he'd been unprepared for the full-scale retreat of his social network.

Marc was afraid to go out, knowing someone was spying on him. With obvious pain he urged us not to risk our careers by associating with him; although he needed the support of friends to help see him through. Marc knew he was a drowning man. We, his best friends, rationalized that we had let him down because we knew we couldn't save him.

Marc became a pariah not because people deplored his sexuality but because no one wanted to fall into the fine net of his investigation—where to be suspected was to be found guilty. Because of his resistance to cooperate in the witch-hunt, the CID redoubled its efforts to catch other people in the net. His discharge was delayed two months while an extensive investigation was conducted.

We were relieved we slipped through the holes. But we couldn't help feel the pain as we witnessed the slow death of a career and couldn't even send a sympathy card. Marc, like thousands of gays and lesbians before him, was branded with an indelible mark on his Department of Defense Form 214, Character of Service: "Narrative Reason for Separation: Admission of Homosexuality/Bisexuality." Today I thought of my marriage as a life-preserver. It could not rescue Andrea or Marc, but I was safe so long as I maintained the facade.

When my orders to report to the Presidio of San Francisco arrived at company headquarters—an unplanned but fortuitous transfer—I was relieved. I would be escaping the traps laid for us at Fort Hood. Yet I was also apprehensive, rather paranoid. San Francisco was the gay mecca. Should I not worry even more about getting caught? Would a five-by-seven glossy of my wife be enough to deflect suspicion?

TONY

My new home was hidden behind an ornate iron gate and spread out across a vast rolling hill perched in the shadow of the Golden Gate Bridge on the edge of the Pacific Ocean, the San Francisco Bay. The Presidio of San Francisco was a far cry from Fort Hood, where curled paint peeled in long strips like hangnails from the facade of nearly every house and building because of the sun. This seemed a million miles removed from the strange synthesis of urban detritus and military prowess of my last assignment.

Despite the Presidio's postcard quaintness—1,480 acres of land in the corner of one of the most densely developed cities in the nation, (more than two square miles of picturesque forests and fields surrounding a golf course, a hospital, and almost five hundred historic buildings)—I missed Fort Hood. With a fierce smugness I had once considered myself better than the country bumpkins who were my neighbors, friends, and colleagues in Texas. I didn't feel that now as Shangri-la surrounded me.

I was treated like a prima donna from the first day of my assignment to the Sixth U.S. Army's public affairs office. My combat record as a journalist and the numerous awards I had received while with the 1st Cavalry Division spoke for themselves. The combat medical badge worn on my uniform over my heart—awarded to front-line combat medics for service in Operation Desert Storm— made me something of an instant war hero, since most of the soldiers assigned here were either green recruits fresh out of basic training or seasoned officers awaiting their retirement papers.

The public-affairs officer, Lieutenant Colonel Steven C. Fredericks, was a man with an intellect both powerful and passionate; he took on the world with an insatiable appetite. He was so unlike the majority of those assigned to this post, people for whom pedigree was surpassed only by the rank one sported on a uniform. Like me, he learned the Army way in the field. I ate dust as a cavalryman; he pounded dust as an infantryman. With this common ground, he and I established a relationship that would aid my quick rise in rank and position, although it could not protect me from the initial jealousy and resentment of some in the office.

The Sixth U.S. Army's command information newspaper, the *Star Presidian*, was Lieutenant Colonel Frederick's greatest headache. He had been hauled onto the Old Man's carpet on more than one occasion, he confided, because of the newspaper's second-rate production and mediocre writing. Since both General Mallory and I had come from Fort Hood, proprietor of a metropolitan-sized newspaper heaped yearly with lauds from Army public affairs, we both knew the difference between quality and hodgepodge journalism. A tour of the office provided the first reason behind the newspaper's miserable state: It was not computerized, so it was misery just putting it together. At least I wouldn't have to work out of a tent to put this paper out.

Taking me back to his office, where he spoke slowly and carefully and rarely in longer than two or three sentences, Lieutenant Colonel Fredericks laid out my mission: to revamp the *Star Presidian* into the top-notch newspaper it could be. Don't miss the staff meeting today because, he said with a wink, there is going to be a change.

I buried myself in work from day one, convinced that by doing so, as I had done to remedy problems in the past, I could solve my moral dilemma and carry on pleasantly with my life of denial. But my attraction to men was continuous, and it affected me in so many disparate and confusing ways that I felt myself faltering. My life was in emotional upheaval. God, don't let me be wrong. At work I maintained the facade of a happily married heterosexual, wearing the snug straitjacket I'd worn in public since my high-school days. I hid the search for self-knowledge masterfully behind the camouflage of serenity and security. A wedding photo graced my desk, although Anne and I were "separated and in marriage counseling."

I created and maintained the life of duplicity needed to dispel any rumor that might arise.

In private, I began spending time in the Castro, San Francisco's predominantly gay district, people-watching in cafés and bars. My self-questioning became unavoidable.

The move to change editors did not become a back-stabbing power play. A civilian employee was currently the editor of the *Star Presidian*, his journalism experience limited to radio and television programs he had produced while a Navy broadcast journalist. Lieutenant Colonel Fredericks and key decision-makers within the office had privately arranged the change out of respect and empathy for a loyal employee. They didn't want to criticize him publicly; the general's vicious attacks on the paper to date had sufficed. Despite resentment from some soldiers, two of whom outranked me, there was a general feeling of relief when I was named acting editor.

With twelve years of Army experience under his belt to my three, Sergeant John McGarrah said the journalists wanted to be saved from mechanical, thoughtless reproduction of ubiquitous stories about the post's impending closure or spouses' club meetings. Having recently been assigned here from Korea, where Army publications win kudos left and right, John would become my right hand. I made no promise to liberate the journalists from their mundane assignments, not knowing how far the command would let us veer from the path the *Star Presidian* had traditionally taken. But we would all try to make our assignment here at least intermittently interesting. One thing I did promise Lieutenant Colonel Fredericks and myself: The *Star Presidian* would never again be ridiculed by the three-star down the hall. I vowed that the *Star Presidian* would never again be the laughingstock of the Army public-affairs community.

Within a month the newspaper had been redesigned—a complete facelift, not just a nip and tuck. General Mallory expressed his pleasure in the form of a three-star commendation memo addressed to Lieutenant Colonel Fredericks and his staff. Forces Command (the command above the Sixth U.S. Army) public-affairs officials welcomed the resurrection of what had once been the best military newspaper on the West Coast. The once fractious journalists now worked as a team.

Changes, however, did not come without making enemies among those who opposed what they considered change for the sake of change. These were the traditionalists who had stifled progress and thwarted the efforts of numerous journalists before me, including John, to jump-start the newspaper. This time they lost the fight. Over time, with the newspaper's added recognition, a desire to share in the limelight turned even these enemies into friends, some of whom would be foot soldiers in the next phase of reconstruction: covering socially responsible issues.

In the early 1970s, Representative Phil Burton, a Democrat from California, recognized the potential for the Presidio to serve as a model for peacetime conversion of surplus military real estate. He wrote and shepherded through Congress a federal law requiring that the Army turn the base over to the National Park Service if the military decided the land was no longer necessary for national defense. After World War II, the post had suffered like a bulky dinosaur foundering in the primeval ooze. So when the Pentagon put the old Spanish *presidio* ("garrison"), with its rows of red brick Romanesque barracks, pine and eucalyptus trees, and views of the Golden Gate, Pacific Ocean, Marin Headland and San Francisco Bay, on the list of surplus facilities in 1989, visionaries, planners, and dreamers began planning the future of a civilian Presidio.

But what of the military? Until now military and civilian employees of the Presidio were privy to little if no information. That changed as our *Star Presidian* dedicated space to transition and downsizing information—all of these stories with quotes directly from the horses' mouths instead of the press-release stories of old.

As important as it was to monitor the progress of the 1989 Base Realignment and Closure Act and its impact on the Presidio's military and civilian community (speculation and more speculation), the *Star Presidian* was missing something—depth and humanity. It wasn't just enough to provide information, I argued with Lieutenant Colonel Fredericks. We owed our readers some social contribution, and that could only come in the form of personality features tackling

137

issues of importance to soldiers and civilian employees in the 1990s. I began pushing my superiors for, first, permission, and then backing, to write a particular feature story I knew would push the boundaries of the *Star Presidian*'s past and ruffle some feathers in the command. After much haranguing, permission was granted, but no indication was given about the likelihood of the story running in this or any Army publication. Nonetheless, I pursued the story, confident the command would understand my message was one of hope: to educate an ignorant generation of people my age who might feel less susceptible to AIDS by virtue of their youth and a stash of condoms.

Tony was happy when he was on the drugs that killed the pain that would otherwise ravage his frail body. Sobering up, he was the most remorseful man I knew, gay or otherwise. He learned he was HIV-positive at eighteen. Long before he began to lose his hair, before weakness had chained him to a bed, he attempted, in vain, to craft what remained of his life. His health began to fail in 1990 when his T-cell count slipped below 200. He was forced to accept medical retirement after a two-month bout with viral bronchitis.

An Air Force captain with a flourishing military career not more than a year before, he was now medically retired and listed as a terminal patient at a local San Francisco nonmilitary hospital.

My method of journalism is to immerse myself completely in the subject. See what he sees. Hear what he hears. Attempt to feel what he feels. Writing a feature about a human being afflicted with a terminal disease was one of the most enervating experiences of my writing career. It drained me to see a man of about my own age, a man with whom I shared many of the same visions and aspirations, wither away to nothing before my eyes with every passing day. As much as I wanted to chronicle his struggle for the benefit of others, it was also my plan to force the Army to allow stories of social importance into our newspapers, even if they dealt with difficult issues. My story would acknowledge the captain's sexual orientation, not let the reader assume in an alarmist way that it had been contracted from a tainted blood transfusion. I wanted to teach.

This was news, and the valid subject of a feature story, should the command decide to pull its head out of the sand and face the 1990s.

Although he was semi-conscious on this particular cold December night, his pale blue eyes stayed open in an unblinking stare, and he moaned in a constant, low rumble, like an engine's idling. I pressed the neon-red button marked with a hieroglyphic that looked more like a cocktail waitress than a nurse. After ten minutes of investigating, the nurse realized his IV line had clogged; he wasn't getting his doctor-ordered dose of Demerol and the ravages of his diseased body were making themselves apparent with increasing manifestations of pain.

"Don't be stupid, Joe," he rasped, when I reluctantly confessed that I was unhappy about my sexuality. "I screwed girls too before I got screwed. . . . And you know what?" He attempted to grab his crotch and failed, but the message was clear: "All that matters is that you're happy."

A few seconds' break to sip water, swish, and swallow. He went on with his advice, sound and unlike the words of a man in his twenties, more like the chant of a dying older man sharing lifelong memories with a man his own age. He seemed to hope I could learn from the mistake he'd made—denying his sexuality until he became HIV-positive.

"My brothers laughed at me, my dad kicked my ass out of his house, and the Army kicked my ass out of the service almost as fast as I was diagnosed. But that doesn't matter. You know why?" he asked, hitting the mattress with all his remaining strength. "Because I am at peace with who I am."

I, who was so much better off, had not yet achieved this inner peace. I would be an eager student, hopefully able to learn some valuable lessons without taking the same missteps.

Looking into his bloodshot eyes, blurring past the splotch of purple science calls Kaposi's sarcoma that had blighted the right side of his otherwise beautiful porcelain face, I saw a solitary tear.

"Do I look like the devil to you? Not that I believe in that. Don't let those son-of-a-bitch biblethumpers tell you different! Be proud!" His voice faded, the words trailing into an indecipherable fragment, as I walked down the creaking stairs leading to the outside world of unregulated oxygen. I suppose he knew I had left for the day; if not, someone would remind him I would be back tomorrow, as I had every day in the past week.

The feature ran on Page 5 of the post paper with a teaser tagline and graphic on the front page. I had to strike a bargain with Lieutenant Colonel Fredericks for it to run. The feature would be accompanied by an informational sidebar of statistics showing how the AIDS pandemic affected the Army. As expected, higher-ups made their disapproval known, although they must have realized the significant contribution the piece made to our military community.

Tony died three weeks later. The command, as expected, declined to run an obituary, but I swore that one day I would memorialize a fallen serviceman's death, a brother's loss. In a small way, he helped me see what a life of misery and denial could lead to. I had learned much in our short time together.

"Your life will be all smiles, kiddo," he had toyed with me once, as we wheelchair-raced down the fifth-floor hallway, catching the ire of several nurses, " 'cause those who do for the betterment of others are rewarded. You just never know when that God in the heavens is going to say: Let's go."

I had learned. Hopefully some of my readers had also. The feature won several awards, about which my commanders, with Lieutenant Colonel Fredericks as the only constant supporter, were at best ambivalent.

I drank before this period of time usually in the spirit of jubilation. I drank now because I wanted to deny responsibility for my emotions; the Army and drinking were now as much a tradition as the other Army vice—smoke 'em if you got 'em. Thankfully, a side effect of my red-wine binges was introspection, and the writing that flowed from that was a reflection of my guilt-ridden soul. But I forced myself to move on to the next assignment, a little numb, a tiny piece of me gone, but still functioning as an integral part of the military propaganda machine. Tony's story was just the beginning. In the following months the *Star Presidian* would tackle sexual harrassment, drug abuse, abortion, and alcoholism.

* * *

I bicycled to the top of the hill without stopping. That was important: Stopping along the way meant lack of commitment, and I was not about to let my resolve waver so quickly. Through the many hills the ride required, I maintained my strength by meditating on the descents on the other side of those arduous ascents and lingered for a rest on each peak. It was cold and gray this Saturday morning, and the wind seemed to sweep in my general direction, forcing me to lower my head. But my unwilling legs had pedaled valiantly and were now taking a well-deserved break as I caught my breath, soaking in San Francisco from one of the Presidio's unique vantage points.

The hill rolled away beneath me, the bay beyond, and San Francisco and Marin joined by the neatly arching Golden Gate in the distance. I had not hopped on my bike, though, and exerted this much energy to see the eucalyptus sway in the breeze or the occasional sunlight dance on the waters of the bay. This was not a "this is great" leisurely ride. This was my time for self-reflection. One never knows what lies on top of the tectonic fault of emotions until one explores. I had lost two friends with whom I shared a spirit of playful adventure back at Fort Hood to the ruthlessness of a policy against gays. Yesterday I had lost my friend Tony. The Army had in the end shafted a victim of the plague by denying him military medical aid and forcing him to depend on an already overburdened civilian medical sector. As I stood on this hill overlooking a glorious city, I was beginning to assimilate the loss, to develop a corrosive contempt for that which was directly responsible for the loss—bigotry, hatred, and ignorance.

DoD Directive
1332.14

Homosexuality is incompatible with military service. The presence in the military environment of persons who engage in homosexual conduct or who, by their statements, demonstrate a propensity to engage in homosexual conduct, seriously impairs the accomplishment of the military mission. The presence of such members adversely affects the ability of the Armed Forces to maintain discipline, good order, and morale; to foster mutual trust and confidence among service members; to ensure the integrity of the system of rank and command; to facilitate assignment and worldwide deployment of service members who frequently must live and work under close conditions affording minimal privacy; to recruit and retain members of the armed forces; to maintain the public acceptability of military service; and to prevent breaches of security. Homosexual acts are crimes under the Uniform Code of Military Justice.

*Department of Defense
Directive 1332.14 Section (1) (H)*

I LOOKED UP THE DEFENSE DEPARTMENT'S DIRECTIVE BARRING HO-mosexuals from military service on a lark, or at least I was trying to convince myself I was. Hiding the document behind a stack of newspapers, I read its meticulously crafted words repeatedly.

Tony's death had sparked in me a desire to see justice met. Friends were talking about candidate Bill Clinton's pledge to reverse the policy. I had not put much stock into his promise until now. For years, the nation had resisted the notion. The courts' precedent-setting rulings favoring the military placed the issue on the political backburner, especially for any serious presidential candidate. Then again, it seemed the country was figuring out how to deal with this issue more honestly than before, rather than hiding behind slogans.

There was no question it hit a raw nerve in the public consciousness. The religious right, unchecked, applied hot pincers to the raw nerve and was beginning its campaign to encourage hatred and divisiveness. What with the fall of the Berlin Wall and democracy desperately attempting to take root in Europe, homosexuality and racial issues were edging out communism as America's obsession.

Pat Buchanan won rousing applause by attacking "multiculturalism," scoffing at those who argued that the world's many cultures were of equal value. "Our culture is superior," Buchanan told a group of two thousand Christian conservatives at a September 1993 meeting of 1996 GOP presidential prospects. "Our culture is superior because our religion is Christianity and that is the truth that makes men free. . . . We cannot raise a white flag in the cultural war because that war is who we are."

A subtext of Buchanan's harangue was that gays and lesbians have no political rights because of fundamentalist doctrine. We are witnessing the consequences of this belief in fundamentalist political maneuverings. They are not limited to codification of the military's gay ban. An all-out war is being waged to erase bans on anti-gay discrimination around the country using local anti-gay ballot initiatives and Colorado-style referendums.

The campaign of cultural cleansing sparked a growing recognition in the civil rights community that gay rights equals civil rights. Among many other national civil rights organizations, the NAACP, the Southern Christian Leadership Conference, the Japanese American Citizens League, and the Chinese American Citizens Alliance joined more traditional supporters in condemning anti-gay discrimination and endorsing civil rights protection for gays and lesbians. The American Jewish Congress said in its statement supporting the boycott of Colorado: "As Jews, we are especially concerned with any attempt to deny civil rights or access to the courts to any particular segment of the population. Our experience has taught us the consequences of such policies. We know all too well that when a society is willing to limit the rights of some, no one is truly safe."

Army Colonel Margarethe Cammemeyer, Navy Petty Officer

Keith Meinhold, former Naval Academy Midshipman Joseph Steffan, Navy Lieutenant Junior Grade Tracy Thorne, and Army Sergeant Perry Watkins* were among the valiant gay and lesbian service members already engaged in the battle for equal rights.

I wasn't needed, I told myself. Besides, I enjoyed the adulation and caresses, the feeling of being a successful, pampered, cheerful sybarite on a career ladder going up. But it saddened me to know that eventually, all this could end, to know that with a Freudian slip or a stroke of bad luck I too could face the inquisitive eyes of the witch-burners who resented our presence in the world over which they lorded.

---

*Biographies of these key military players are in Appendix A.

THE DETOUR

THE INSIDE OF THE BAR WAS DARK WITH ALMOST EVERY AVAILABLE surface, inside and out, painted a matte black. Spotlights pierced the thick, smoke-filled air. They pointed at nothing in particular, but people avoided them. A black felt-topped pool table and a chain-link fence running the length of the bar were the only decor, unless you considered the patrons permanent fixtures, rooted to the beer-soaked bench lining the wall. The Detour, a gay bar with grunge music, has the reputation of entertaining San Francisco's "dirty white boys," or those who try to escape the drab reality of their lives and fit that mold.

The evening of February 8, 1993, will forever remain enchanted in my heart because of the events that would follow my chance meeting with the man I believe destiny hand-selected to be my soulmate.

I had made the trip to the Castro out of necessity tonight. Sunday, after spending an hour in the rain snapping photos of the Chinese New Year's parade downtown, I took a cab to the Castro to have a medicinal drink at Café San Marcos. I feared catching a cold but had promised my sister pictures of the parade and would have felt like a wimp telling her I couldn't deliver because of some drizzle.

After a few schnapps, I thought of my ten-year-old iron, which had been acting up for quite a while (forcing me to spend already committed money to dry-cleaning expenses); this morning, with an electrical burning smell, it had finally given up its ghost.

Although there was a Walgreen's just outside the Presidio's front gate, (they are about as abundant as McDonald's), Monday night I craved the aura of the world's gay mecca. Despite a predicted 60 percent chance of rain, I threw on a suede jacket, left my umbrella in the closet, and embarked on the one-hour bus ride to the Castro. I've thought back to that night a lot in the last few months and know I wasn't seeking solace in the neighborhood. I had enough money in my pocket for a beer or two, bus fare, and had some time to kill. Another night in the drab, Romanesque barracks I lived in held no appeal. But I also didn't have very much money to blow on cover or drinks. The Detour. I vaguely knew its reputation, good music was pumping out its open door, and besides, I'd seen a fifty-cent draft beer ad in the local gay rag. What the hell!

The decor did nothing for me, and my musical tastes tend more toward screaming divas than grunge. But I bought a fifty-cent draft beer anyway and found a place to stand among the wannabes huddled in the middle of the bar. People-watching has always been a pastime. I'd inherited from my mother an almost anthropological interest in the way people act. I thought I was giving off an aura of unapproachability, yet a fairly drunk and unkempt gentleman in his late forties, early fifties, approached me and extended his hand, obviously unable to read my body language. The tweed jacket and green cap looked familiar. I had passed this man on the street a hundred times. But now he tried striking up a conversation. Talk of his summer home in Tahoe, his Mercedes-Benz, and the ketch bobbing fetchingly in the Marina was supposed to pique my interest, I suppose. I tried to ignore completely the overture. He was unrelenting. I started giving terse, one-word answers, hoping he would sense my lack of interest in him and his accumulated wealth. Although I abhor rudeness, I began casting glances about the bar. Like an immigrant longing for the sight of a familiar stranger, I suppose I was beseeching any nearby soul to save me from this predicament. I avoided eye contact with my tormentor.

Standing behind me was a group of three younger guys who, although they appeared a bit too clean behind the ears for the Detour, could see my distress. Would they come to my aid? I was able to make eye contact with one of the three, and he edged over to join our "conversation."

"Hi, I'm Dave," he said in a prairie-flat drawl.

In the Detour, professionals hide their credentials rather than display them. This is not the Midnight Sun, where boys who work retail try to hook professionals and others worthy of bringing home to Mom. The Detour is boots, not loafers. Anyone stumbling in wearing something requiring dry-cleaning wouldn't bother ordering that first drink but instead would do an about-face and head to a more hospitable environment.

The Detour has its share of professionals as patrons, but these are Generation X professionals, many of them postliterate nonconformists who have had their synapses rewired to fire faster and who consider the coat and tie a form of drag. Here the doctors, lawyers, and accountants wear costumes reflecting their desire to shirk their responsibilities—as if by throwing on a pair of strategically ripped jeans and sporting a fuck-you smirk and projecting a fuck-the-world attitude (or at least wearing a fuck-the-world T-shirt), they could clear their minds and calendars of lingering anxieties, short-fuse deadlines, and impending projects.

My ally, who, under the dim glow of a spotlight barely lighting his face, looked more like an eighteen-year-old kid than the thirty-one-year-old professional he was, admitted he was a third-year psychiatric resident. He wore his disguise well. We made a bit of smalltalk, enough so that the man who had intruded on my peace of mind retreated to a corner of the bar, shooting drunken glances my way every few minutes.

Noticing my brush cut, Dr. Dave Kilgore asked, "Which branch of the service are you in?"

Most of the boys in here had shorn hair. I could have mistaken many of them for soldiers except for giveaway anti-establishment, appearance-altering clues such as the occasional pierced lip, nose, or eyebrow. Would he ask that question of anyone with short hair? I answered tentatively, sure he had not heard me over the din of the blaring speakers hanging overhead. Not bothering to repeat myself and hesitant to continue, the conversation quickly tapered off. Dr. Dave rejoined his group and I recaptured my solitude.

It was clear that Dr. Dave was being debriefed about his encounter with me, and that this debriefing was being pursued most intently by the member of the group whom I found most attractive—perhaps because, like me, he didn't really fit in but was attempting to. Sporting a Mickey Mouse baseball cap, Doc Martin boots, jeans, and a hooded flannel overshirt, he almost blended in in a crowd where it's chic to look as if you have not. He had an intensity that gave him away as a wannabe club kid, not the real thing. Simultaneously exuding a look of seriousness and playful jocularity, his was a magnetism I could not then (and to this date cannot) explain.

I made the required eye contact and we shared a half smile, but I couldn't seem to draw him closer. I was plastered in place, not wanting to be seen as making the first move. Rejection has always been one of my key anxieties. As if by fate, my tormentor started back toward me. With this as my catalyst, I approached the boy in the Mickey Mouse cap, and half-jokingly asked him to save me. He did.

Mark Keeney, the most reserved of the three, was an accountant at a multimedia software company. He was out tonight only because it had been a rough weekend and, although he professed not to drink, added that the Detour was a good way to get over the hangover. Dr. Dave had already disclosed his profession. Dave Falik introduced himself as a "lawyer slash club kid," pointing out that he was more the latter these days, having taken leave from a large "law firm slash sweatshop" after being diagnosed with work-related depression.

"Take a V," Mark said sarcastically (meaning Valium).

Dave did not answer. Instead, he sipped on his drink and looked at me. It was a glint in his eyes that captured my attention. We studied each other for what seemed an eternity. Dave seemed in no great hurry to make his interest or intentions known. Advice Dean offered on a drunken night spent at a Killeen strip joint months before suddenly came to mind: "Men who don't chase women are really only asking to be met halfway. Why waste your time pursuing a woman who acts as if she's doing you a favor by simply letting you stand in her presence?"

Dr. Dave soon cut through the silence by reminding Dave that, apart from him, everyone had jobs. Mark followed up, ribbing Dave about his Bohemian lifestyle. They were ready to go. Did this mean time alone with Dave? Dave asked them if they needed a ride home.

1. My father, Salvador Salazar Zuniga, celebrating Christmas in 1964

2. My mother, Raquel V. Zuniga, posing with horses in Kentucky in 1968

3. At four months of age, moving away with my mother in 1969

4. Celebrating my first birthday in 1970

5. With my sister, Sandra, in 1975

6. Cadet Colonel Zuniga (front row, second from right) and his headquarters staff, Wheatley High School Junior ROTC, 1986

7. With my father in 1987; I'm wearing my Texas A&M ROTC uniform.

8. Shining combat boots during basic training at Fort Bliss, 1989

9. My official Army photo at Fort Bliss, 1989

10. In the Persian Gulf (front row, left) before Operation Desert Storm—the 1st Cavalry Division Public Affairs Office, November 1990

11. Designing the *Cav Country* newspaper in Saudi Arabia, December 1990

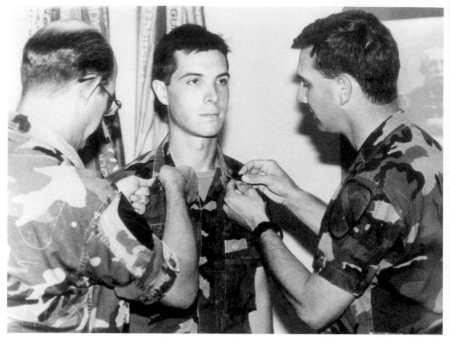

12. Private First Class Zuniga promoted to specialist in a ceremony at Fort Hood, July 1991

13. The Presidio of San Francisco, overlooking San Francisco Bay, January 1993

14. General Mallory gesticulating during the Soldier of the Year ceremony, March 1993

15. Me and Dave in our apartment

16. James Kennedy backing me up as I prepare to mount the podium during my coming-out ceremony, April 1993

17. Coming out

18. With singer Melissa Etheridge

19. With Laurie and Robert Bray at Old Postal Square

20. Jesse Jackson comforting me after the March on Washington

21. With Keith Meinhold (to my left) and James Kennedy and Tracy Thorne (to my right) during the March on Washington

22. With Tom Stoddard on the "Good Morning America" set at the Washington Monument

23. In half-uniform, posing for the *New York Times Magazine* piece

24. With MTV reporter
Tabitha Soren

25. With a hunky
parade participant
after the Oklahoma
City Gay Pride
parade, 1993

26. With the drag
Miss U.S.A. in
Oklahoma City

27. Addressing a post-
parade crowd, San
Diego Gay Pride Day,
July 1993

28. With (from left) Paul Tsongas, Peter McHugh (the mayor of Milpitas, CA), and Laurie, October 1993

29. With Dave, Laurie, and Teardrop at the Russian River in California, 1993

30. Recharging my batteries in Puerto Vallarta after four months of nonstop activism

31. With Laurie and Dave in our San Francisco home, January 1994

Dr. Dave accepted, while Mark said he would walk the two blocks to his apartment.

"How're you getting home?" Dave asked me. "Can I offer you a ride?"

Without thinking, I reflexively said no. "Damn it, Joe, are you crazy?" I thought. I had been dying for him to ask—not because I necessarily wanted to make more of this than meeting a couple of new friends, but because it was late, it was drizzling, and I didn't relish the idea of taking the No. 22 Fillmore bus home, or walking a mile from the bus stop to my barracks.

"Look, it's drizzling. I'm going to be up for a while, but I'm tired of standing here." He was almost pleading. "Really. I'm just offering a ride home."

The ride to Dr. Dave's flat was fun. Listening to the two exchange barbs like catty pros was welcome comedic relief. It reminded me I had not laughed as much in months. I guess there had been few reasons to laugh in a life of nonstop work and no play. The laughs stopped after we dropped Dr. Dave off and headed toward the Presidio.

It was with some trepidation that I engaged Dave in a conversation. His speeches at the bar had tended toward arrogance. I really did not want to endure that alone tonight. But I felt conversation was the least I could do for a Good Samaritan who was going out of his way for a complete stranger.

At the Detour, he had shown me a picture of Teardrop, his eighty-six-pound Dalmatian, pasted haphazardly on his gym identification card. Coincidentally, the two of us were members of the same gym, only I pasted no picture on my card. Having broken the ice with this whimsical factoid, the subject of his wife had been broached in such a nonchalant manner that I dismissed it as a joke.

Now I shrank into the soft leather passenger seat as the Acura sped down Franklin Street, the light drizzle bouncing off the sunroof, making harmony with the purr of the defroster. My reaction had little to do with the driving and plenty to do with the driver, who in less than ten minutes of unsolicited monologue had managed to shed his role as savior and take on that of tormentor. Just a half hour earlier we had been standing face-to-face in the Detour, engaged in nominal chitchat, asking and answering the basic array of questions that are part of the accepted getting-to-know-you ritual: name, profession, weather forecast, favorite Beatle.

I suppose I was guilty of starting the monologue by asking him to explain his comment at the bar about having a wife. In a few moments, information turned to lecture as he painstakingly explained that he was a member of an elusive breed: the Bisexual. He professed an attraction to women but added that he rarely found a female with physical attributes he deemed hot who was also intellectually interesting. He'd married Laurie because she generated lust but was also his intellectual match. She too was an attorney.

With men—or boys, as he preferred to say—it was another story. Smarts really didn't matter, and "limited-purpose people" had a friend in Dave. Boys are simply sex toys, I translated. He was cute but crazy. Well, not crazy, but our values did not come from the same marketplace.

The car came to a screeching halt as he realized he wasn't going to make a changing light. My seat flung forward on its track, jerking me forward.

"Manufacturer defect," he said apologetically, placing his hand on my knee for a fraction of a second.

What torture! To like someone while actively disliking who they are or who they are making themselves out to be. The ride became insufferable. Longer than any bus ride. Longer than walking across town from post to the Castro. Could he see me squirming in the seat? Was he enjoying his delivery and the nonverbal reaction it was getting? Dave's social etiquette seemed to be from a world foreign to mine.

As we passed through the Lombard Gate I let out an audible sigh. He had finished answering my questions. It was my turn to talk about myself. I answered the few questions he asked with terse answers. I could not open up to him as he had to me. My most profound answer came after he asked about my past relationships. Thinking of Russell and the pain I had suffered, I answered there had been none. I confessed to having secretly loved someone once, thinking of Alex, and said I could never love again with that same intensity.

He looked at me sadly for a moment. "I hope for your sake that's not true."

"Do you want to come in?" I asked as we sat in the parking lot alongside my barracks.

He declined, claiming he had a doctor's appointment early the next morning. He scribbled a telephone number on a strip of paper he had torn off a club flyer. "Give me a call if you want to get together sometime," he urged. "I've got time on my hands."

I could not tell whether he was feigning the nonchalant attitude or if he was really indifferent. Feeling that common courtesy demanded it, I jotted down my number for him—though I reversed the last two numbers.

"Good night," he said out the window as I left his car and ran inside to the comfort of my world.

Good night. I threw off my clothes and slid into bed, replaying his words as if rehearsing lines from a play. My head was throbbing from so much thinking and rethinking. I slipped in a video to relax. Early morning tomorrow. A seven-mile run at 0500.

LOOK BEFORE
CROSSING

═══════════

"YOU READY TO WIN, SERGEANT ZUNIGA?" SERGEANT FIRST CLASS
Donald Banks, the public-affairs supervisor, asked me while I was
in the middle of a telephone conversation with my branch manager.

The telephone conversation ended with my manager's promise to
expedite orders assigning me to the 2nd Infantry Division at Camp
Casey, Korea. I had grown weary of the low morale at this dying,
downsizing installation, and had asked for a transfer. I would not be
locked into an assignment with a unit whose only mission was to
pack all its belongings into boxes and move to some unknown location. Better the bitter cold hell of a Korean winter than the boredom
of a beautiful San Francisco day spent in a poorly ventilated building
doing what I'd done every year of my childhood.

After closing a file on my computer, I walked to Sergeant First Class
Banks' desk. His question had been about the Sixth U.S. Army Soldier
of the Year competition on February 25 in Reno. A show of confidence
from our former supervisor, who had retired a month after my victory
at a Headquarters Company Soldier of the Month competition (which
I had won in October 1992), had evolved into this. The Headquarters
Command Battalion Soldier of the Month and 1992 Presidio Soldier
of the Year honors fell somewhere in between. Even more than my
work as a journalist or my combat experience, this exposure cemented
my standing with the command, primarily General Mallory.

*   *   *

Despite having promised myself not to call Dave, and ensuring he could not call me, two days later I broke down and called him. Something about him had intrigued me. A little smalltalk and then we made a date to have dinner or catch a movie. Six tonight? Great!

"Tried calling you at the number you gave me. I think you jotted it down incorrectly," he squeezed in before I could hang up. Was that reproach I heard in his voice or was I just feeling culpable?

"Really?" I said, feigning innocence. I gave him my office number and felt my act of contrition complete. "See you at six."

A late assignment to cover a lecture series forced me to postpone at the last minute, I convinced myself. I was lucky to catch him at home before he ran out to run some errands and meet up with me.

"That's okay," he said quietly. "Maybe tomorrow."

As Dave pulled his Acura into the parking lot outside my barracks two days later, a tinge of guilt suffused my memories of our first verbal repartee. All my life I had feared rejection more than anything else. And REJECTION in flashing neon letters was exactly what I felt the night we met as he had rationalized and argued his point about bisexuality, striving to make it as bulletproof as possible. In the luxury of leisurely retrospect, he seemed more intent on justifying his existence than on selling me on the idea that his view was right for all. A part of me dreaded climbing in and going to dinner by way of the torturous route we had traveled a week before. I was afraid to learn of any other character flaw that, like his bisexuality, would cause a flashing red light to go off in my brain.

Such disclosures had terrified me in the past, but now some great unknown reduced the red light to a look-before-crossing warning. Dave's had not been one of those false and pretentious displays of instant love and affection for which some gay men are infamous. I would get to know him, explore what was behind the facade. It had to be a facade!

A final thought crossed my mind as I ran out of the barracks to go out on my first date with Dave, my first date with a man since I had enlisted in 1989. Apart from the sting of his refusal to come in that night, I remembered my amazement at how effortlessly his life became exposed to me, layers upon layers of himself unfolding as easily as a well-written dissertation. Every story related to deep personal values and views of the world. Much talk and contemplation, none of it trivial.

Dave wanted me to meet his wife, Laurie. But our weekday schedules conflicted and her nights were overcommitted with her volunteer work in the San Francisco Bay Area chapter of the Gay & Lesbian Alliance Against Defamation (GLAAD). I woke Dave with a phone call Saturday afternoon.

"Let's meet at Café Flore, say about three?" he suggested.

"Fine," I said nervously. "Is your wife going to be there?"

He laughed. "See you at three."

Dave and I sat at a table near Flore's counter a good hour, sipping on Diet Cokes and chatting about nothing in particular, when Laurie and Mark joined us.

"Nice to meet you," she said tersely, then asked if I knew Mark.

I nodded my head. Dead silence. A few platitudinous questions about the Army. Again dead silence. I was never quick to reveal my feelings, much less to a woman. She was not impressed, I could tell. She quickly gave up; she was not the kind to put much effort into someone in a different social or intellectual stratum, and she started talking to Dave and Mark about *Backlash: The Undeclared War against American Women*, the Susan Faludi book she was reading.

Right then I knew more about her than she of me: not only that she was brash and demanding, but that she was fully immersed in the culture of activism. Her choice of reading material frightened the conservative in me. I had mixed feelings about Faludi's book. I felt she had superbly chronicled the women's movement, but I also felt she'd editorialized to the point some could use her textbook as a crutch to blame everyone but women, from late-Victorian religious figures to political leaders, "for a spiral of four revolutions that constituted a counterassault on women's progress over the last decade."

I guess I didn't know what to think. At least Faludi was able to capture my attention and that of millions more.

Laurie's inquisitive green eyes intrigued me. Inside that bitchy exterior shell, I thought I saw a little girl smiling broadly at the world, fondling the ends of her shortly cropped blond hair, asking questions, waiting for and caring to hear answers. For some un-known reason, destiny was pitting us against each other.

Dave decided to walk back to the apartment for a nap, and I gladly joined him. He'd drop me off at the Presidio after dinner.

"Nice meeting you, Laurie."

"Same here, Joe."

I could tell that her social pleasantries were just that and no more. She seemed, like me, to pigeonhole people upon first meeting them—to see a fragment, in this case my silence and thinly veiled ambivalence, and interpret it as fault.

Although we would spend much more time together in the next month, the brick walls erected on that first day at Café Flore would be hard to bring down. Only time, patience, and a mutual commitment to get to know each other would start the bricks crumbling.

DAVE

THIS WASN'T THE FIRST TIME I'D SLEPT WITH A MAN. THIS WASN'T even the first time I'd lain in bed with Dave. We'd lain in bed in his apartment watching television many times before. But for some reason, I was afraid to look at him tonight because I feared I wouldn't know what to say or do. As a child, I would have crawled into my mother's lap rather than face such uncertainty. Until this afternoon, while walking back to his apartment from Café Flore, we had not even held hands. Smiling sheepishly, he plopped his figure on the sofa and extended his legs. Now our knees touched in such silence that their contact was as clamorous as church bells to the godless.

When I finally did dare raise my eyes to his, I realized I could no longer keep my promise, a promise that had at times squeezed blood out of my heart as I struggled to suppress my wants and desires. Tonight I would permit myself to put down the luggage of my life and live. I used my fingertips to caress his single stud earring, the angularity of his face, the warmth of his navy sweater, his jeans . . . sharing an intensity of feelings beyond what, as a neophyte, I could express in words. He understood.

Caught in excruciating tenderness, my mind battled the confusing state of rapture my body was enjoying. Spiritual ferment, thoughts of my father, the religious condemnation of my sin . . . hell and damnation—all these years these fears had plagued me. Was sex a sin, or was the sin in two men having sex?

The out-of-focus blur of romantic memory brought me back to the present. I had always imagined sex to be romantic, dramatic, and accompanied by an orchestral crescendo. This was much more. Our faces contorted in ecstasy, our bodies were one; this was love shared between two souls, not just two bodies. When we were finally exhausted, he held me in his arms until I fell into a blissful, childlike sleep. My mind slumbered while the imagination of my dreams ran riot.

The alarm buzzed at 0400 and a half-asleep Dave drove me back to the Presidio. I asked him to come in for a second. We wound up cuddling on the sofa bed in my private barracks room. "I love you, Dave," I whispered into his ear at around 0530. It was time for calisthenics and a five-mile run.

I came back to my spartan room at 0900 to wake him with a kiss. After showering, shaving, and getting dressed, we said goodbye until dinner. Before he left, I gave him a copy of the novella I had finally finished. Dave had asked to see it after I mentioned it on our first date.

JOHANNES AND SOLOMON

DAVE READ MY NOVELLA OVERNIGHT, HE ANNOUNCED THE NEXT day in an unexpected phone call to my office that would become a midafternoon ritual. Excited and nervous about the first critique of my first serious literary undertaking, I wanted to run through it now point by point, scene by scene. My mind, most likely my ego too, hungered to discover his educated conclusion about a love story I gave birth to over four years, several dozen bottles of red wine, and on ninety-six single-spaced sheets of paper. The characters, schizophrenic clones of me, had fallen in love at age seventeen. In the safety of type, Johannes, the scared and repressed teenager, submitted to Solomon, the lust-filled, curious nemesis kept locked in an abyss. The novella, dark and terrifying in its conclusion, had been a catharsis for me; writing it had helped me decide I did not want to end up like either Johannes or Solomon. Plotting the demise of Johannes at Solomon's hands forced me to continue repressing the deviance and depravity I associated with my feelings.

"It was amazing! I feel I've known you all my life," he said, my required ego-stroke quota for the month met by the first three words. "It's like being handed an instruction manual, a look inside."

I heard approval. This could not possibly be rejection; if felt too good. But, a doubt burst in, was his critique just an effort to be polite? Rationality countered quickly with a resounding *no*. Dave went far beyond what he would have had to say if courtesy were his goal. Indeed, some of what he said had disturbing undertones. Did I want anyone to have my "instruction manual" and thus have the control that comes with knowing what buttons to push?

"Remember, it's fiction. Please, don't jump to any conclusions about me," I said, taking an extended pause before requiring another pat on the back. "But, you liked it?"

"It was beautiful. A little terrifying, at parts, but . . ."

"I hope you don't think I'm a psychopath or anything like that," I cut him off at midsentence. "And besides, I still think it needs much work."

A few seconds of quiet seemed to be ending our conversation like the hush of a city silenced by a fresh blanket of snow.

"Wanna hang out tonight? We can catch a movie," he suggested.

Okay, that was confirmation. There was no underlying rejection, the snooty little voice in my head said in an I-told-you-so tone.

"Something light. A comedy. I've had a hard day and I think laughter would have medicinal value," I said, still processing the fact he had just validated not just my work of four years but, in essence, a large part of my soul.

We made plans to see Bill Murray's *Groundhog Day* and perhaps have a drink or two afterward.

Concentration on my work—a feature series about sexual harassment in the Army—was periodically, spasmodically, interrupted by thoughts of Dave. Didn't I dream about him or had I forgotten? Images of last night replayed themselves in my head. Because the piece wasn't due for three weeks, I could afford the time for the contemplation I had dedicated to few important turns of events in my life. I deserved a break. At twenty-three I was eating Maalox tablets as if I were fifty.

Until today, I had worried that this lawyer slash club kid with an Ivy League education thought I might be his intellectual inferior. The misconception that service members are all half-a-brain-cell, muscle-and-brawn grunts was one I had heard, but I felt he did not share.

Although Dave and Laurie constantly joked about who was smarter, deep down they knew a rough parity existed. They were philosophical soulmates who shared everything without becoming co-dependent or parasitic in the process. In the same breath, Dave had added that he had not held the few boys in his life, so far, to the same standard. He had explained that people need not be your everything to be incredibly meaningful and important in your life. The look-before-you-walk caution lights were blinking when they should have caused me to bolt for cover instead. Why was I interested in someone who seemed to feed my self-doubt?

SOLDIER OF THE YEAR

SERGEANT ARMANDO YEO AND I ARRIVED AT THE HEADQUARTERS, Sixth U.S. Army, building well before 0700 and our driver was already waiting in his vehicle, engine idling. Armando and I were the Presidio's candidates for the Sixth U.S. Army's soldier and noncommissioned officer of the year competition in Reno tomorrow. A 0900 flight would deliver us to the gambling city and kick off a day and night of nervous, last-minute cramming, checking alignment of awards and decorations on our uniforms, and cramming some more to win the coveted titles.

The United flight attendant refused to hang our garment bags in the garment closet on the plane. "First class, sorry, guys." We angrily folded our crisp, dry-cleaned Class A uniforms in half and stored them in the overhead storage bin. Another thing to do once we get to Reno, Armando complained, wondering if there would be a dry-cleaning service at the Peppermill Hotel and Casino.

I woke up at 0430 the next morning, assuming I slept at all that night, and hit the slot machines down the hall from our room. If I wasn't ready by now, I thought, I'd never be ready.

At 1300, after watching fifteen other competitors walk in and crawl out of the conference room where a board of sergeants major from throughout the Sixth U.S. Army seemed to be eating candidates alive, I knocked on the door and waited for the word, "Enter!"

"Sergeant Major, Specialist Zuniga reports to the president of the

161

board!" I reported to Command Sergeant Major Otto Copeland Jr., the Sixth U.S. Army's command sergeant major and General Mallory's adviser on enlisted matters.

Seven sergeants major sat at a table, like the vultures of my dream last night, teetering, veiling, and rocking in expected malediction. After a thorough inspection of my uniform they began firing off questions with machine-gun rapidity.

What is the Mission Essential Task List?

What is the maximum effective range of an M16A1 rifle?

Name five of the nine principles of training.

What is involved in Step No. 3 of an After Action Review?

Describe eight of the twelve symptoms of shock.

What are the three types of supply?

Name the three approaches to counseling.

What five field manuals cover Army leadership doctrines?

With each answer they paused, twisted their mouths in thought, took down notes, and continued. After forty-five minutes of question-and-answer, records review, and getting-to-know-you banter, the competition was over. As usual, I had been the last candidate—with a last name like Zuniga there is rarely anyone following me in alphabetical order.

"Born of War, sergeants major!" A crisp salute and an about-face followed the Sixth U.S. Army's battle cry, and I was out the door.

I had won. I knew it in my bones. And still I was nervous.

Twenty minutes passed before Sergeant Major Copeland stepped out of the conference room to announce the winner.

"You all did a magnificent job. Unfortunately, there can only be one Sixth U.S. Army Soldier of the Year, and for 1992 that soldier is Specialist José Zuniga, Headquarters Command Battalion, Presidio of San Francisco."

I was promoted to sergeant a week later.

I didn't know it then, but this honor would be the precursor for one of the greatest changes in my life. I called Dave that afternoon, not to tell him the news—because I imagined he didn't much care about these matters—but to check if, as promised, he might make the trip up to Reno and meet me. The felicity of the afternoon was slightly disturbed by an answer contrary to what I had expected. He couldn't make it. I would nonetheless celebrate my victory here tonight and return home on Saturday night.

"By the way, I gave Laurie the copy of your novella like you asked me to," Dave said, his voice still sounding apologetic. My prayer was that Laurie, with whom I'd had rocky relations until now, would see my struggle in the novella. I had always bared my soul in my writing, and this novella was no exception. Laurie might understand my pain and personal struggle. Her sad, soulful eyes spoke of a deep struggle within her as well.

Laurie, I whispered into my pillow that evening, I do not want to hurt you ... I need help in finding myself. I am scared of losing my will and becoming Johannes or of losing control and becoming Solomon. Either way I fear death. . . . I love Dave. . . . I fear losing Dave. . . . And I fear loving you. . . . Loving you? Is it possible? And if I love you, I must fear losing you, too. . . . But first, is it even possible?

TO LOVE A
WOMAN

═══════════

FINALLY, IT HAS HAPPENED TO ME, RIGHT IN MY FACE, AND I JUST CAN-
not hide it....

Dance diva CeCe Peniston's throaty voice and a backup singer's
swoon cut through the dance space, like lovers tongue-tied by delirium. Rhythms dissolved into synthesized tracery. This was the atonal
call-and-response music of the San Francisco dance scene. And at
Product this Saturday night, the crowd filed to the dance floor like
Los Angelenos flocking to the beach.

Dave, Laurie, and I were out clubbing. We belonged to a generation in constant, hard-charging pursuit of active recreation twenty-
four hours a day. We worshiped the diffuse Eurodisco cues, the
throbbing electrorhythms of house music. We prayed to escape the
hard realities of our lives. Here we could shove all worries aside and
revel alongside fellow worshipers, even the modern-day avatars of
chic with their shockingly dyed hair in hyperreal blues, greens, reds,
and yellows. I was also here to escape the voices within my mind,
voices whose tones sounded like General Mallory three days prior
at the Soldier of the Year luncheon. The electricity of the sounds
penetrating my eardrums would, I prayed, exorcise his voice from
my consciousness.

Watching Dave and Laurie dance, I couldn't help envying their
lives. There were no demons in their lives—except for maybe me,
Laurie might say. They were happy. I felt sorry for myself. Dave

and I were gradually building our relationship, but with Laurie as a third party I felt left out. Sure, Laurie and I had developed an intellectual bond. Having read my novella, Laurie felt closer to me and we had started over instead of continuing down the bumpy road we had initially chosen. I was desperately trying to understand the calculus of a three-way relationship that seemed unpredictable and awkward to maintain, much like trying to balance a triangle on its point. It scared me. But I was trying. I was opening myself up to her as much as my heart would allow. Our conversations were rambling soliloquies that flew off on tangents and circled back to where they began; our individual points were made a dozen different times. I was growing to feel for Laurie what I had never felt toward another woman. Yet the emotional bond was still missing.

I left the dance floor, voices echoing in my mind. Time to indulge in alcohol—wasn't that the attendant excess of both military and urban gay life? Three shots of peach schnapps and a Tanqueray Collins. That seemed to quiet the bastard!

A tap on my shoulder. Laurie. What she must think of me, of my self-hatred, my drinking problem, my utter lack of emotion toward her.

"Get away from me!" I screamed drunkenly. I falsely accused her of sunny superficiality.

She accused me of being too drunk to tell the difference.

Laurie! I am just a life that wills to live, in the midst of other life that also wills to live! I was beseeching compassion, confronting the fact that I loved two people, one of them a woman, and demanding inclusion in her life. I wished I could rip my trembling heart from my chest and pin it on my sleeve. The words I wanted and needed to say were locked away, and for the life of me I could not find the key. Maybe Laurie was right, maybe I was too drunk to tell the difference.

"I love you," Laurie whispered into my ear.

Hah! She said that as if those words could quell my turmoil. But they did. Her whisper, louder than the blaring 140 beats per minute that should have made it impossible for me to hear a shout, much less a whisper, was the key.

I love you too, I thought.

Looking into those green eyes that had intrigued me so long ago, I began to sob. "I love you too."

Still facing me, Laurie took my hand and drew me behind her, down the stairs and to where Dave danced solo to Sunscreem. We were leaving, she told him. He nodded acknowledgment, then gave me a knowing smile, eyebrows raised. I returned an unknowing smile as I walked out with her. I have never been where you suppose I'm going, I wanted to shout back to Dave. She led me unflinchingly from the depths of the dance floor crowd. Maybe I don't love her, my mind suggested. We were still holding hands as we climbed into the cab, her small hand in mine.

Teardrop greeted us as we stumbled into the apartment.

"Hi, Tear-Meister," I slurred.

He jumped up on me, begging for food. Teardrop had eaten earlier, even if his winsome brown eyes tried to communicate the opposite.

Laurie had thrown off her clothes and was taking a shower while I played with an attention-starved Dalmatian. Sensing that I might be uncomfortable with her T-shirt and shorts (I was), she leapt into bed.

"There's no pressure," she whispered and turned away from me, allowing me to remove my clothes without inhibition. I took a shower.

"Dave's boxers and T-shirts are in the hall closet," Laurie announced. Of course, I already knew that, but she was providing me an option.

Throwing on a pair of boxers and nothing else, I crawled into bed. She moved closer to me, holding me, placing her head on my chest. I had the sense of peering over a parapet. Her purity rendered me mawkish and miscast. I closed my eyes, meditating on the ways in which our bodies touched and didn't touch. So close, they touch and do not.

Sleep.

She woke me just before sunrise by dangling her hair across my face and making, at 0530 on a Sunday morning after our debauchery, a surprising but appealing request. "Let's jog!"

Driving to the Marina Green, I stared at her in groggy vulnerability. "You know, I wasn't too drunk not to know what I said last night," I said, squinting against the morning sun, our future shimmering with bright uncertainty over the calm waters of the bay.

"What *did* you say?" she asked, grinning knowingly.

THE HAIGHT

We were smack in the middle of San Francisco's Haight-Ashbury, a neighborhood still caught in its 1960s flower power heyday. The counter-culture, one could easily assume if shown only this area, had outlived the Summer of Love and, twenty-five years later, was alive and well. Hell, some of the original hippies and their wannabe younger brethren might yet take over.

With my conservative, sheltered background, each foray into the Haight was not only an adventure but a lesson in 1990s society. Dave's warnings could not possibly prepare me for my first trip into what fellow Army colleagues had warned me was one of San Francisco's scourges, the Castro District being the second and more reviled. As we walked down Haight Street from Masonic toward a McDonald's across the street from a makeshift homeless encampment in Golden Gate Park, I heard the constant murmuring from every soul who passed us by or stood along our route. A stiff breeze, the droning of passing traffic dodging double-parked cars and momentarily stranded Muni buses. The noise pollution alone was enough to make most mumbling incoherent.

My Army-issue hearing impairment from the Persian Gulf rendered these noises all but inaudible. I assumed these were the city's down-and-out seeking food and shelter, or simply the professional panhandlers finagling money for food (beer money) from gullible passersby.

Something seemed odd, and my paranoia took over. They didn't seem to be begging in the way I had witnessed in other parts of the city, particularly downtown. These shadows of what once must have

168

been some mother's pride were whispering words I couldn't make out but assumed were probably not good. If they had been, I asked myself, why the whispers?

Afraid to admit a flaw that until now had remained a secret from Dave, I did not immediately mention my auditory inability to hear anything near a whisper, a handicap I attributed to an artillery piece firing not more than ten feet away from me during the war. When I expressed my anxiety at not understanding why these strangers seemed to be verbally attacking us, Dave chuckled.

"They're selling drugs, honey," he explained. "I wouldn't expect you to have heard about three quarters of the things they're selling," he added in a clear attempt not to make me feel foolish.

I blushed, then began quizzing him about the street names of the drugs being pushed by muttering men and women hanging out in dark doorways, unafraid to make transactions on street corners or at busy intersections. The dealing was small time, Dave shared from his experience with the law, but the panoply of illicit pharmaceuticals available on this street rivaled that of over-the-counter and prescription medications in most corner drugstores. Having grown up in the city, and being quite a bit more streetwise about such things, he was usually able to provide a translation for the cryptic utterances I was beginning to understand.

In the daytime, to my own surprise, I enjoyed walking this street, people-watching, window-shopping, and exploring its alternative boutiques. Once I got past the initial irritation with the blatant proliferation of drugs, the neighborhood's historically liberal bent made me realize this was one of the safest neighborhoods in the city for people like me, and I ventured there more often, even when not connected to an appointment at Bladerunners. I wondered what this area must be like at night. I was in no hurry to find out. I have yet to.

Bladerunners was an eclectic but funky mix of post-modernism and 1950s retro. Screaming neon lighting and two rows of black barber chairs suggested the cult movie whose name the shop had adopted. The retro turquoise couches were reminiscent of "I Love

Lucy" set furniture. Deena fit in perfectly with both the tone and the setting.

Dave took me in for my first haircut with Deena while I was still on active duty at the Presidio, well before the thought of coming out had even crossed my mind. This haircut absolutely had to comply with Army regulations and meet the personal appearance standards expected of the Sixth U.S. Army Soldier of the Year. Deena ably adjusted her style to cater to military regulations.

I learned in a few visits that, should a patron engage Deena in conversation, a half-hour shampoo, haircut, and style could easily stretch into an enjoyable hour. Much of what she said seemed so foreign to me in our first appointments. Gradually, with at least a few of the reading assignments completed in my personal course on Gay Studies 101, her words made much more sense. I never failed to learn a lesson or two in diversity from her random comments. Deena and I would teach each other much more in the coming months.

Deena always wore elaborate cocktail-party-type dresses culled from her frequent excursions to thrift stores. Her dresses, more costumes than simply clothing, frequently matched the garish pastels of similar costumes in colorized black-and-white movies on late-night television.

Deena was something of a character. Taped to her workstation mirror, alongside her California cosmetology license, one could always find a flyer promoting offbeat dramatic productions in which she was always involved, despite a full work schedule. The shows tended to beg for campy staging in converted warehouse spaces rather than in any of San Francisco's many small theaters. Her need to act was occasionally expressed in a corner of Product, our favorite Saturday night gay dance club, where she danced on a dancer's box wearing a spacesuit, or was engaged in some other form of performance art. At once she seemed bizarre, yet so safe and friendly that the word *bizarre* carried an insulting connotation I would never wish to make. She was the radical 1990s persona packaged in a "Father Knows Best" box.

"What's wrong with this world is that there are too many rules and laws to tell us what we can and can't do," Deena summed up, making explicit a point she had been trying to make by example for the last ten minutes. I agreed with her analysis wholeheartedly. Thus far I always agreed with Deena, who articulated in her own foreign tongue much about some of the newer gay political issues to cross my mind.

"I'm bisexual," she blurted out during one of our sessions. It should not have come as any surprise to me, but it did. For a minute I felt like those who have listened in stupor or awe as my relationship to Dave and Laurie is explained. My jaw dropped embarrassingly, as I focused in on her perfectly made-up face instead of my own image framed in the mirror of her June Cleaver–style mirror.

"I thought you knew," she said, surprised that I didn't.

"Bisexual" is not a label I affix to my name or my existence, although others in similar circumstances might choose to. I suspect that if it were not for enormous monosexist pressures from both the gay and straight communities, many more people would identify as bisexual. If I had my way, no labels would be used to define a man or a woman. At times it seems we are advocating a grocery list instead of recognizing the human capacity to love. In my heart I feel that human identity, even in love, is a process rather than a fixed state. But I know we shall never achieve consensus about this subject. I label myself a human capable of loving a man or a woman because they too are human.

I had allowed myself to imagine that people who are targets of prejudice have an almost instinctive sensitivity to the mistreatment of other minorities and avoid engaging in it themselves. Unfortunately, I found out that this is untrue. Oppression makes some people more sensitive, but it is just as likely to make them hard, bitter, and suspicious. When Dave, Laurie, and I revealed our relationship to close friends within our own community, the best many could do was express that the concept of bisexuality seemed abstract (read: a little weird) to them. But it is wrong to imagine that bisexuality is uncommon in our community, my psychiatrist said, although even he appeared taken aback at first.

The politics of homophobia have warped this issue. There are straights who disavow their homosexual feelings and oppress those who do not. Many lesbian and gay people, naturally enough, respond in mirror fashion by creating their own communities and choosing to separate themselves completely from the straight world. Humans seem to have a need, born of suspicion and fear, for sharp differences and boundaries. Many of *us* have much of *them* within us; the conundrum is that when we hate *them*, we also hate ourselves.

The greater message of love and humanity must prevail over prejudice and derision. The hackneyed myth that "everything goes" for bisexual people is nonsensical and demeaning. Laurie would learn firsthand the pain that perception can cause when she disclosed our relationship to her parents six weeks after my coming out. Seized with fear, they let their imaginations rule for many months, and as in so many families, grueling arguments gave way to long silence. She is lucky, for bridges are slowly being rebuilt.

Love transcends sex. Love is an emotional, intellectual, political, and spiritual matter that comes from the heart and mind. My bond with Laurie was not sex-driven. What happened between us was driven solely by love—a love that didn't ask why it was happening against the natural tendency of my sexuality.

In the eyes of a world intent on labeling everyone with a permanent marker, my public identity was moving from "straight" to "gay"; while at the very same time I was loving a man, I was getting more and more involved with the only woman I'd ever loved.

A Life Decision

In January 1993 I won the Army's Journalist of the Year
Award. An invigorated Congress was in session. The electorate had
exiled President Bush more than two thousand miles from the Beltway, at last making true on his promise to return home to Texas.
Gay men and lesbians across the country had coalesced and mobilized like never before to help make the dream of ending the seemingly eternal Republican reign in the Oval Office a reality.

How a little-known governor from Arkansas with a spotty record
on gay issues attained the position of the gay community's political
messiah come to save us from the claws of right-wing aggression—
and who just as quickly fell from grace—tells much about our naïveté
in the brutal world of politics. While campaigning before the Iowa
caucuses, in response to a reporter's query about lifting the ban on
gays in the military, technocrat Paul Tsongas responded, "Everybody's in, nobody's out." A lemminglike frenzy ensued among Democratic presidential prospects. Candidates who didn't themselves
broach the issue had their positions, or lack of them, outed by gay
activists.

Clinton became the front-runner and began actively to court the
gay community. Was it moral conviction or political exigency that
practically forced Clinton to echo Tsongas's stance? Political expediency would, ironically, later force him to capitulate on the issue of
gays in the military. Gay politico David Mixner, a long-time "Friend
of Bill," rallied community support for a Clinton presidency months
before the New Hampshire primaries. With Mixner's strategic advice and fundraising prowess in its corner, the Clinton campaign

173

would, in the coming months, lead gay men, lesbians, and bisexuals to believe change over issues of importance to the community was on the way. Our votes and dollars could, and in fact did, become a key factor in positioning Clinton for victory.

Clinton's campaign rhetoric at a high-profile gay and lesbian fundraiser before the California primary helped cinch the gay vote. In retrospect, with the benefit of a tagline and 20-20 hindsight, the politician's pontification takes on more of the appearance of a Lettermanesque punchline. Clinton told his audience that the country "[could ill] afford to waste the capacities, the contributions, the hearts, the souls, the minds of gay and lesbian Americans." He seemed choked with emotion as he acknowledged the community's leadership role in the AIDS struggle.

Clinton walked out of the Palace Theater in Los Angeles with the gay vote in his pocket. If gays were not flipping the lever for him in the remaining primaries, they were almost assured to do so in November. Just in case, he secured high-octane financial backing for his campaign. Hope overpowered the footnotes hidden in the rhetoric. It was so blinding that the "Slick Willie" charges were discounted and the rhetoric was wholeheartedly believed. Oh, the naïveté, the crushed dreams.

Bush, architect of the Persian Gulf victory, had never been known to complete a sentence, much less express a vision of America, if he in fact secretly harbored one. In contrast, Clinton expressed a vision of gays and lesbians seated at the table of American opportunity, playing an active role in his America. Although even then I doubted the sincerity of his words, the Arkansas governor's words inspired the gay community as the Reverend Martin Luther King Jr.'s Dream had inspired African Americans fighting for civil rights. Gay leaders interpreted Clinton's message as being akin to a presidential edict to integrate the community's equal rights agenda into the nation's civil rights movement. The smell of impending victory justly titillated even seasoned activists. By God, Bill even promised to lift the ban on gays in the military by executive order!

Although gay Republicans, including me, were skeptical of the Democratic candidate's discourse, the GOP convention in Houston managed to alienate all but the most dyed in the wool. I sat in my barracks room watching the live convention coverage, my stomach acids worked up as gays were offered to the lions. Gay Republicans chose not to support the party nominee with their money or their ballots. Holding our noses, most would vote for Clinton on a hope and a prayer. My question, and one I predict was asked by many of my fellow gay Republicans, was how to help Clinton make his vision a reality.

I fumed as the "reverends" Pat Robertson and Lou Sheldon, bestriding the conceptual world of spirituality like colossi, inveighed against the deterioration of "family values" and painted a party of exclusion. Their words betrayed just how venomous the party's far right could be. I thought of writing President Bush a letter begging him to shun the politics of hatred that fellow party members were espousing. But what good would that do?

Suddenly I realized my blood was boiling over something that would not affect me if I maintained the duplicitous life I had lived for more than three years. Why did I care? There was no immediate answer, but the more I thought about my life and that of my few military and civilian gay friends, the more I reeled at what I was hearing. As Stalinist Russia and Hitler's Germany had their villains, queers in America were the new pariah threatening to unravel the fiber of American society. The anti-gay rhetoric was reminiscent of an earlier age when the combination of an absurd race theory and pseudoscientific myths about homosexuals was the basis for Nazi actions against gays. Any chance of Bush's reelection dwindled with the utterance of each cruel syllable.

Eleanor called me from Fort Hood on the night that Republican spin doctors tried to use a bandage to stop a hemorrhage. Mary Fisher, the daughter of a prominent GOP contributor, was called upon as an "innocent victim" of the AIDS pandemic to address the convention from the still seething-hot pulpit from which some had hinted AIDS was God's punishment for fin de siècle lifestyles. My eyes watered as Fisher made an impassioned plea for AIDS sufferers, her voice quavering with the only hint of humanity shown that night. Fisher, a heterosexual who'd contracted HIV from a blood transfusion, brought the convention to tears. She begged for increased funding for research and education. "Don't do it for me—do it for my children, do it for your children," the shaken woman implored.

I thought of Tony. I thought of two other military buddies who had been diagnosed as HIV-positive since I left Fort Hood. Images of "Common Threads," a Lifetime special presentation about the NAMES Project AIDS quilt, began haunting me. Twelve years of Republican rule had mostly ignored the AIDS pandemic, the greatest medical scourge to threaten this country in years. If the Republicans were unwilling to tackle the subject (the disease's existence itself was all but denied during the Reagan years), they would never tackle the issue of equal rights for gays, lesbians, and bisexuals. Hell, they even dared inveigh against my TV journalism idol Murphy Brown.

Was Clinton offering political hope or just political bullshit?

The repercussions of the religious right's vicious attacks were not limited to the negative reaction of the gay community, as party insiders deluded themselves. In the closing months of the campaign, national polls indicated that a large segment of society had decided that Bush's party of exclusion was out of touch with the changing attitudes of the 1990s, focusing exclusively on values America considered secondary to such issues as the economy and racial, cultural, and societal change.

As the electoral college waited to cast its preordained lots, the gay community turned its organizing energy to the passage of a federal gay civil rights bill. With Clinton in the White House and what seemed a perceptible shift in the country's outlook on homosexuality, there was a sense of buoyancy and confidence that passage was assured. If not right away, it would happen at least in due course.

Showing a good measure of political innocence, gay leaders expended little political and monetary capital to follow up on candidate Clinton's campaign pledge to rescind the military ban. Skeptics and mainstream political analysts argued Clinton's pledge had simply been a lure for gay voters. The majority in the community, however, believed that an executive order awaited presidential approval. Minimal, almost token opposition from Congress was expected. Conservatives would beat their chests, lamenting the loss of morality in Western civilization. But the deed would be done. Clinton appeared to be the first progressive president to occupy 1600 Pennsylvania

Avenue in more than twelve years. More important, he was the first chief executive for whom the word *gay* was neither a synonym for happy nor a pejorative term.

The community's logical syllogism was easy to follow: Everyone knew Clinton's position on this issue was based on a moral belief in the value of gay men and lesbians and their inherent equality. He had promised to stand by his conviction. This was a new breed of politician, not the traditional demagogue. Clinton seemed to despise anything that smacked of half-truth or falsehood. Besides, a democratically controlled Congress wouldn't countermand its first triumphant presidential candidate. Indeed, most political analysts concluded Clinton could lead the Congress anywhere—even out of gridlock—at least for a reasonably lengthy honeymoon period. With those logical and factual assumptions as a general premise, the gay community's political machine shook off its postinauguration hangover and fought to extinguish the right wing's brushfire attacks on local and state civil rights protections.

Unchaperoned, the gays in the military issue was lost in the gradual shuffle of a new administration into the Beltway. No transition staffer was chosen to manage this potentially volatile issue. A few prominent members of the gay community were asked their advice. But like so many of the administration's first steps, the issue floated aimlessly. News-starved reporters speculated on the issue even before the administration could devise or implement a plan of attack.

Sam Nunn, a Democratic senator from Georgia who serves as chairman of the powerful Senate Armed Services Committee, announced with a snort of moral indignation that an executive order lifting the ban would not go unchallenged. Was Nunn being vindictive because Clinton had not offered him the position of secretary of state he was known to covet? Was it maybe a little muscle-flexing and political posturing? Or was it bigotry and homophobia? Nunn threatened to push for codification of the current policy.

The issue took on a life of its own with the media as its incubator. Speculation, not facts, rapidly filled what was otherwise a news void. With every homophobe-quoting news clip, every front-page article invoking the morale and discipline argument, every talking head

177

babbling about the president's expected retreat, my thoughts about coming out evolved into a decision.

Nine days after his inauguration, Clinton allayed fears that his campaign rhetoric had been "a sea of empty promises" by reiterating his intention to lift the ban. The ongoing media feeding frenzy seemed to force the president's hand in the first days of his presidency. In what some considered a political retreat, the president imposed a six-month deadline for the Pentagon to submit a nondiscriminatory policy for his signature. Dreamers—I include myself among them—predicted that July 15, 1993, would stand in history as a sweeping indictment of the far right, the day the last vestiges of sanctioned bigotry would die at the hand of our elected savior.

A formidable political force, the right wing had moved swiftly to oppose Clinton's position, launching a nationwide television, radio, and print campaign of misinformation well before he was even elected. Just as *The New York Times* had warned in a November 1992 front-page story, the religious right and family values organizations mobilized overnight, activating phone trees and flooding White House switchboards with more than 400,000 messages on one of the early days. Incoming mail from "concerned citizens" urged to write their elected leaders and voice "their" opinions inundated the White House mailroom at a rate unmatched since the 1963 assassination of President John F. Kennedy.

The military leadership, headed by Joint Chiefs Chairman General Colin Powell, seemed to forget the oath to diligently follow the orders of the commander in chief. By jumping on the anti-gay bandwagon, they staged something of an unprecedented military coup. Their contributions to the national dialogue were apocryphal predictions of the havoc lifting the ban would wreak on unit morale, cohesion, espirit de corps, discipline, and the blood supply. The media tried illustrating the correlation between the gays in the military issue and the integration of blacks in the late 1940s by using the fact General Powell was the first African American chairman of the joint chiefs in part because of an historic executive order opening the military's ranks to blacks. Powell's vehement, absolute rejection of the notion he was denying gays what others had once denied blacks made front-page news.

The issue gained further press momentum as the press, smelling blood, began to pit the military institution itself against its new commander in chief. Story after story ubiquitously drudged up Clinton's lack of a military career. How could a draft dodger be in touch with his subordinates' needs and concerns? The frightening fact was that the military command was engaging in behavior that encouraged the grunt on field maneuvers, the artilleryman at his ammo point, officers on break huddled around the office water cooler, to mock the commander in chief to whom they had sworn allegiance.

I wonder what would have happened if Clinton had signed an executive order in January 1993. The American electorate had made it clear his lack of a military career was not a liability by placing him in office.

Why was he so desperate to please everyone on a subject on which he could not? Clinton seemed to be whistling Barney's song, "I love you, you love me . . ." Where were his political advisers to point out he was proving himself unable to command by coddling such blatant insubordination? Why didn't anyone tell Bill Clinton to grab his balls and say "I'm in charge here! How dare you question my orders? You're fired!" President Harry S Truman had done so without hesitation when General MacArthur, a greater American hero than any soldier alive today, stepped out of line.

I'll try to help you, Mr. President. I'll give up my career to provide you ammunition. I can't provide courage, though. It's not a commodity item. "Courage," I had read in *The Anatomy of Courage*, my father's choice tome, "is a moral quality . . . a cold choice between two alternatives, the fixed resolve not to quit."

If the leader of the free world can't affect change, then those Americans who hear my story will.

Dancing Along the Precipice

PRESIDENT CLINTON SHOCKED MANY DURING A PRESS CONFERENCE in March, when he floated a trial balloon proposing the segregation of gay troops from military combat units. A surprise declaration or just a slip? It did not take long before his first balloon crashed and burned. Within hours of the first Clinton press conference, activists expressed angry frustration at what seemed a presidential retreat. We went from being treated like second-class citizens to being treated like lepers. And this repugnant rhetoric was being introduced into the public dialogue by the very man who, intentionally or not, had thrust the issue into the media spotlight by proclaiming his belief that all Americans should enjoy equal protection under the law.

On March 23, Clinton delivered another blow. "If you can discriminate against people based not on what they are but who they are," he told the press, "then I would think you could make appropriate distinctions." Activists, already upset that Clinton had not included a ban-lifting order among the stack of political bombshell executive orders (including lifting the ban on fetal tissue research) signed postinaugurally to deflect media firestorms over each individual issue, were witnessing political retreat.

Segregate gay troops from the throes of combat? What about Colonel Margarethe Cammermeyer, a highly decorated Army nurse with a stellar twenty-eight-year military career, including a tour of

180

duty in Vietnam during the Tet Offensive of 1968, for which she was awarded a Bronze Star? What about Air Force Technical Sergeant Leonard Matlovich, whose unblemished military career included three tours of duty in Vietnam, for which he had been awarded a Bronze Star and the Purple Heart? And what of my service in the Persian Gulf? The president's backpedaling was unbelievably frustrating.

I danced along a precipice during my long walks along the high rocks and bluffs surrounding the Presidio, trying to escape the dreariness of my existence by communing with nature. General Mallory's diatribe, Clinton's empty promises, and Nunn's threats all blurred into a cacophony of bigotry and ignorance distracting me from the regal beauty surrounding me.

Although it seemed predetermined by a pro-ban bloc in Congress backing the Pentagon, the outcome of this battle might swing in our favor, it seemed to me, if more gay and lesbian service members stepped forward and destroyed the myths and lies with the powerful weapons of their careers. After the president announced his intention to reverse the policy, a *Time*/CNN poll asked whether "gays and lesbians should be banned from the military." A formidable 57 percent of the sample responded that gays should not be banned. A month later, a *Newsweek* national poll found that 72 percent of 663 adult respondents believed that "gays [could] serve effectively in the military if they keep their sexual orientation private." At least the debate seemed to be effective in discounting the long-held denial that homosexuals could even serve in the military.

I weighed my options carefully and made the decision to step forward and stop taking Clinton at his word. He had proved to be an ineffective leader. My experience in the military had taught me that when a commander orders something, it tends to get done. "It ain't no democracy," my father told a twelve-year-old boy questioning one of his directives. Apparently, Bill Clinton wasn't let in on that secret. The fairy tale of candidate Clinton's promise, delivered on a cold October day at Harvard University, was not going to win our battle.

Once upon a time there was a young candidate who promised to end institutionalized discrimination in the armed services and deliver the gay community from evil by exposing America's institutionalized discrimination against gays. He was elected president and became a great hero to many as he continuously promised to right a wrong that destroys thousands of careers (and lives) yearly. But then one day, faced with opposition from ogres who recoiled at the prospect of change, he threatened to promote a form of segregation eradicated in the 1940s by another hero, long since dead. From that day hence, the hero began to lose the people's faith. . . .

The close and intimate conditions of life aboard ship, the necessity for the highest possible degree of unity and esprit de corps; the requirement of morale, all these demand that nothing be done which may adversely affect the situation. Past experience has shown irrefutably that the enlistment of Negroes (other than for mess attendants) leads to disruptive and undermining conditions. It should be pointed out in this connection that one of the principal objectives of subversive agents in this country is attempting to break down existing efficient organizations by demanding participation for "minorities" in all aspects of defense, especially when such participation tends to disrupt present smooth working organizations.

It is considered also that the loyalty and patriotism of the minority should be such that there be no desire on their part to weaken or disrupt the present organizations.

—Department of the Navy Memorandum on Negroes
December 24, 1941

"Prejudice," journalist and author Walter Lippman said, "precedes the use of reason." It also prevents the emergence of reason. So it should be no surprise that many of the arguments used during the late 1940s to debate integration by race were based on the idea that African Americans engaged in different behaviors from those of white Americans and that those behaviors would be disruptive to the effectiveness and morale of the military—stereotypes invoked verbatim in the gays in the military issue almost fifty years later.

When President Truman ordered an end to racial segregation in the armed forces in 1948, he received virtually unanimous advice from his senior military officers that it would be disruptive. In 1948 the generals were wrong. The cataclysmic upheaval predicted by the military brass never happened. Truman's strong leadership (or, as some cynics now note, his campaign strategy) turned the country in the right direction. Executive Order 9981 ordered that the desegregation policy "shall be put into effect as rapidly as possible, having due regard to the time required to effectuate any necessary changes without impairing efficiency or morale."

President Truman was denigrated in the annals of history until his memory was resurrected by Clinton, and by those who saw the similarities in their fights. Today his bust sits behind Clinton's desk in the Oval Office. The irony of it all.

Was Truman's defeat in 1952 the fate Clinton feared? Was he so preoccupied with the prospect of his own re-election in 1996 that he would barter away the rights of a segment of society whose rights weren't even acknowledged, much less protected? If in the glaring lights of the 1990s the original arguments against integrating blacks into the service are repulsive, how repugnant the anti-gay policy now seems, supported by the identical failed rhetoric of another, less enlightened generation?

Yet retired Lieutenant General Calvin A. H. Waller, deputy commander of the U.S. Central Command under General Schwarzkopf, testified before the Senate Armed Services Committee that allowing open homosexuality in the U.S. armed forces would eventually lead to the creation of a second-rate military.

In his opening remarks, General Waller, who is black, said, "I suppose the one thing that upsets me more than anything is the comparison that so many individuals . . . make between the integration into the armed forces of homosexuals and the integration of African Americans into our armed forces. To compare my service in America's armed forces with the integration of avowed homosexuals is personally offensive to me."

General Waller, your offense is misplaced and gives free reign to society's most destructive impulses. True, the black soldier was considered inferior to whites. Given the opportunity to prove he was not inferior, he went a long way toward dispelling that theory. Homosexuality is perceived as being a moral issue. The problems and solutions with respect to gays in the military will be somewhat different from those that surrounded the integration of blacks into the military. When the perceived "inferior" element was allowed to prove his worth, the inferiority tag faded into insignificance. The "immoral" element is not even permitted to prove his worth. The immoral tag cannot and will not fade into insignificance while homosexuals are considered less than two-thirds of a human being.

Have you reviewed recent teen suicide statistics, direct responses to the stress of having to play into the strict sex-role behaviors children must exhibit to avoid bracing ice-bath ridicule? Or to parents who would rather a gay son or lesbian daughter perish than impugn the family name? A 1989 Department of Health and Human Services report (Gay Male and Lesbian Youth Suicide, Report of the Secretary's Task Force on Youth Suicide) presented evidence that lesbian and gay youth are two to six times more likely to attempt suicide than other youth, and they accounted for thirty percent of all completed suicides among teens. In 1988 alone, the National Center for Health Statistics reported that nearly 5,000 Americans ages fifteen to twenty-four died of suicide. The destruction of our children is the net result of your bigotry.

For more than forty years, the truth about the irrationality of the policy had been in the hands of Pentagon officials and numerous administrations, and no action was ever taken. *Vincit omnia veritas*, "truth conquers all," did not apply here. If anything, the government turned a blind eye as millions of homosexual service members were drummed out in the name of national security.

The March 1957 Crittenden Report stated, "The concept that homosexuals pose a security risk is unsupported by any factual data. . . . The number of cases of blackmail as a result of past investigations of homosexuals is negligible. No factual data exist to support the contention that homosexuals are a greater risk than heterosexuals."

Officials also ignored the findings of the Nonconforming Sexual Orientations and Military Suitability study of December 1988: "The values that any society places on social acts are subject to change. . . . The lessons of history tell us that the legitimacy of our behaviors, customs, and laws is not permanently resistant to change. Customs and laws change with the times, sometimes with amazing rapidity. The military cannot indefinitely isolate itself from the changes occurring in the wider society, of which it is an integral part."

Another study, titled Preservice Adjustment of Homosexual and Heterosexual Military Accessions: Implications for Security Clearance Suitability (January 1989), noted that "the preponderance of the evidence presented in this study indicates that homosexuals show preservice suitability-related adjustment that is as good or better than the average heterosexual."

The culmination of years of million-dollar studies eaten by the family dog or lost in the mail was the DoD's Policy on Homosexuality study of June 1992 that asserted, "Major psychiatric and psychological organizations in the United States disagree with the DoD's policy and believe it to be factually unsupported, unfair and counterproductive. . . . Further, the Secretary of Defense and the Chairman of the Joint Chiefs of Staff have recently acknowledged that homosexual orientation is no longer a major security concern."

No studies incensed American taxpayers more than two specific U.S. Government Accounting Office (GAO) reports that looked at the issue from another perspective: money. A 1984 study requested by Representative Sala Burton, (D-Ca.), indicated that $3.3 million was spent on outprocessing homosexual service members alone. The study concluded that after adding the $176 million cost to train and maintain these soldiers, and the $3.7 million spent in investigations and prosecutorial activity, taxpayers shelled out more than $183 million to discharge 14,311 gay, lesbian, and bisexual service members in a ten-year period.

A 1992 study requested by representatives John Conyers Jr. (D-Mich.), Ted Weiss (D-N.Y.), and Gerry E. Studds (D-Mass.), determined that more than $493 million was spent in one-to-one replacement of 16,750 enlisted men and women and 169 officers discharged for homosexuality from 1980 to 1990.

Someone with the power to right this wrong had to have read these reports. The numbers in these reports were based on fact, not fear. Yet too few Americans searched very hard past their personal beliefs and bigotry. They were blinded by the visual and linguistic swamp created by extremists. The government was playing a game of Chinese boxes that ended in the same conclusion: Ban the queers! Money and lives wasted. The values of a nation cheapened.

*　　*　　*

185

The look of surprise on the faces of Dave and Laurie when I nonchalantly announced my decision to come out wasn't surprising. Although we had often jokingly discussed the possibility, I was still readying myself for deployment to my new duty assignment in Korea. Laurie immediately played devil's advocate, although she knew my gut-level decision was the right one. I understood their concern not to want to feel responsible if my action went awry. After all, the negatives, including a possible prison sentence and alienation from my father, seemed to outweigh the advantages.

My mind was made up.

April 1, 1993

Joe,

We just dropped you off in the neighborhood after spending a few hours together. It was a very awkward evening for me, in that I knew only the vague outlines of what was really troubling you, and that there was probably very little I could do or say to help you even if I did know.

My only glimpse of the real nature of what was on your mind came as we were getting drinks together. . . . You said you felt as if you had "thrown something away today." I know I have no right to presume I understand the true weight of that. What I do know is that whenever I have had to make one of those turning-point decisions in life, the immediate aftermath always consists of intense brooding over the negatives and the risks that were part of the calculus. I'm sure I don't have to tell you that you did not make a wrong choice; I have never regretted a major decision in my life, for very good reasons, and I know you haven't either for the same reasons. This will not be the first, because what you are doing is moral, courageous, and right, and you will achieve stellar success as a civilian just as you have as a soldier.

But none of this diminishes the tragedy inherent in the choice that a discriminatory government is forcing you to make. I know how much you love the military, and at least one aspect of your state of mind right now is the pain of acknowledging how serious the flaw in that love relationship really is.

You will play an important part in righting this great wrong, but I know that reality does nothing to mollify your anger and frustration. If there were anything at all I could do to help dissipate those feelings, I would. But I know the only things that will have that effect are time and a pen.

Laurie

Operation
Coming Out

The following afternoon I phoned Keith Meinhold's attorney, John McGuire, in Los Angeles. I did not hear what I'd wanted to. He strongly recommended I reconsider my decision to come out, citing the many other cases clogging the judicial system. His advice seemed myopic, at best. Similar advice was forthcoming from Keith himself when I spoke with him. I suspected the reasons behind their advice, but chose not to lend credence to them. They had both accomplished so much. Did they believe that admitting others were needed in the fight lessened these accomplishments? We were all on the same side, weren't we?

Two weeks after the Soldier of the Year ceremony, I saw David Drake's one-man play, "The Night Larry Kramer Kissed Me," with Dave and Laurie at the Life on the Water Theater in the Fort Mason Center. One of Laurie's gay co-workers had offered her an extra ticket at the last minute. With less than fifteen minutes to get ready and drive to the theater, I changed from the sweatsuit in which I'd lounged that Sunday into a pair of Dave's dress pants and starched shirt.

Drake's closing story was "... *and The Way We Were*," a utopian look at a future America where everyone is afforded the opportunity to live happy, productive lives and homophobia is a reviled relic of the barbaric times when publicity-grabbing evangelical extremists roamed the airwaves unchecked. His performance was moving; not one audience member stirred as the lights dimmed into darkness.

Besides the added perspective the twenty-nine-year-old playwright and actor had inspired in me, tonight had also sparked a chance meeting with a woman who would help change my life. In the audience that night was Elizabeth Birch, the chief of litigation for Apple Computers and co-chair of the National Gay & Lesbian Task Force. After the play, Laurie introduced us. The sparkle in Elizabeth's eyes as I told her I was ready to come out and take a stand gave me hope. More than that, though, I saw in Elizabeth's beautiful, wise face a caring spirit. A shrewd executive, she was also human. We need help, Laurie added. Elizabeth pledged not only Task Force support but her own too.

The next day Laurie and I conference-called Robert Bray, the NGLTF's media coordinator. He had just had a week from hell coordinating a historic Oval Office meeting April 19 between President Clinton and selected leaders of the lesbian, gay, and bisexual community. Through April 24, he was frantically preparing for the 1993 March on Washington. Flustered, Robert did not immediately grasp the potential political impact of the Army's Soldier of the Year announcing he was gay. His initial response was ambivalent to jaundiced.

"I'm sorry, you'll have to talk to Tanya. She's our Military Freedom Initiative director," he said apologetically, excusing himself because he was late for a meeting. Two days later Robert called back, raving about how he'd thought it through and saw how hot this coming out could be. He asked for the biographical information we had tried to provide him the first day.

Tanya Domi, a fifteen-year Army veteran, had climbed the ranks from private to captain, serving as a drill sergeant and company commander along the way. Now the nationally recognized spokeswoman on gays in the military was on a cross-country bus tour, which was called Tour of Duty, speaking at town halls, press conferences, and meetings, and appearing on local radio and television programs to discuss the issue directly with Americans in the heartland. She could not be reached. In frustration, Laurie and I called on Elizabeth again.

"Why not present him as a surprise speaker at the Honoring Our Allies reception?" Elizabeth rhetorically asked Torie Osborn, the Task Force's new executive director.

An inspired idea! Thousands of gays and lesbians were expected to attend. Senator Edward Kennedy (D-Mass.), an outspoken advocate of gay equal rights, and Representative Patricia Schroeder (D-Colo.), who in 1992 introduced legislation to overturn the ban, were among the honored congressional guests. The entire contingent of military veterans legally challenging the ban would be on hand. Most important, there would be maximum press saturation.

"Do you have legal representation yet?" Torie asked. She realized my coming out would be a public-relations coup to fight the military prohibitions, but the Task Force would not commit activist extremism; they were unwilling to sacrifice an innocent for the cause. Torie wanted to be sure I'd be working with a safety net to save me from potential military repercussions.

"We're working on that," Laurie assured Torie and Elizabeth.

That night I finally reached Tanya in an Atlanta hotel. Dave dialed the number and handed me a telephone that looked as if it could order up an entire nuclear war. Within minutes, a groggy Tanya was on the line.

"Are you sure you want to do this?" she asked after I answered a battery of questions.

At one o'clock in the morning, her time, Tanya explained she feared the Tour of Duty might face the same fate as that of the first Freedom Riders in 1961. Traveling through Alabama, the Freedom Riders were met by mobs of angry protesters. The result was one bus fire-bombed, the other assaulted by the violent mobs. It was hard to picture someone with such a take-no-prisoners mentality feeling scared, but it made no difference in making my decision.

I was willing to take whatever was hurled my way. Anointed with the Task Force's approval and using the media spotlight focusing on the Honoring Our Allies event, I would become a new military poster boy. The multitude of other cases were now in the midst of legal wrangling that seldom made front-page news. Time to get us back on the front page, if only for a day.

*　　*　　*

"I don't want to say that," I said with about as much patience and tact as I could muster—basically, none. I was tense and frustrated. I also detested being edited. My nerves were on edge as they had never been before as Dave, Laurie, and I sat at a corner table of Café Flore, the Castro's coffee central, putting the finishing touches on a speech that would derail my military career but would make persuasive headlines for the great Undecided. I shook my head to clear my mind of all else. A couple seated nearby turned toward us, asking in the characteristically brazen (but friendly) curiosity of San Franciscans what we were working on with such diligence.

I hesitated, since my announcement was a well-guarded secret.

"A coming-out speech," Laurie answered matter-of-factly, returning her gaze to the computer printout in a fraction of a second.

"That's great," the two chirped in tandem, a lack of comprehension or a measure of disbelief showing on their faces, like they were customers in an automobile showroom.

This café was a San Francisco institution complete with tile tables, hanging plants, and an outdoor patio—*sans* heatlamps; that's too L.A. Flore is a place where the likes of David Geffen and some stunning young boy sip on coffee, eat half a pastry, and discuss God knows what in self-prescribed anonymity. They serve the best double mochas in the city, and, using them with the skill of a schoolyard pusher, Dave had taken me from a coffee avoider to a coffee addict. Today I was on regular coffee, with cream and sugar.

This was meeting No. 5, or maybe No. 6, in preparation for D.C. It seemed that all we did lately was think, plan, strategize, drill, and rehearse. Robert had warned us the media could be a double-edged sword. If we played our cards right, it was a vehicle with which to raise public awareness and knowledge. But we needed to be prepared for the remote possibility the press might ignore the story, he added.

Sipping coffee or Diet Cokes we debated the different ways to spin answers to reporters' questions, while Alison Moyet's soulful wails flooded the air. "Spin," Robert explained, "is like taking a lump of bad news, throwing it on a pottery wheel, and hand-shaping it to the best form possible, given the available material." I also learned the diversity of views in the queer community on each issue. Calling on my experience as a journalist, I asked probing questions and listened to the answers. The political correctness issue gave me the most trouble: *sexual orientation, not sexual preference*, I was drilled repeatedly. The tendency to use the other forbidden word *lifestyle* was exorcised from my speech with Laurie's every stern gaze and occasional verbal cattle prod. I was truly fortunate. Louis XIII had Cardinal Richelieu. The Medicis had Machiavelli. I had Dave and Laurie to advise me and help prepare me for a required metamorphosis.

Laurie's zeal reminded me of that of militant suffragettes. Dave was the calming force gapping the rifts between propriety and confrontation. Pausing with a soup spoon halfway to his mouth, he would speak in well-turned paragraphs but be reduced to silence when he realized he'd gone off on another tangent. Eventually I caught myself picking up my interlocutor's ragged questions, performing reconstructive verbal surgery, and delivering incisive, politically correct answers.

"The issue here is . . ." Laurie began, and I tried finishing.

"The issue here is that our community will reject any compromise that would result in service members continuing to live in the closet. The comfort level of farm boys in the ranks should not be the issue."

A pit-bull snarl from the two suggested I might want to tone down my statement. "Farm boys?" Dave asked quizzically.

"People enter situations with personal likes, dislikes, prejudices, and biases. All of these feelings are deemed detrimental to unit cohesion and are subjugated by the military." I paused for dramatic effect. "So should the prejudice against homosexuals be subjugated by government-mandated military policy."

The goal of our brainstorming was to establish positions on issues that until now seemed foreign to me. I staked out positions I was comfortable with, even if they did not gel with the positions of others in our community. I did not wish to be the movement's mouthpiece and trumpet. I was fairly conservative, still a registered Republican, and I wanted to remain my own person rather than adopt others' views wholesale. I believed my politics must be compatible with those seen from some well-worn porch swing in Kansas or Montana. But most of all, I didn't want to be a lumpen protoplasm molded into something I didn't want to be. There would be no idol maker!

Of course, there was much more to our lives than planning our contribution to the gays in the military fight. Our lives were complicated enough without the extra homework. Dave and Laurie had just closed on a house. With that, a year-long process had finally come to its fruition. By the time we started the move from an apartment two blocks from Castro Street to a house on upper Market Street, we had already stopped brainstorming at Café Flore because the tables were too close together and the potential for a leak was too high. Our all-nighters found a new home.

Laurie bounded up the stairs of the new house, dodging boxes and Teardrop on the way to the kitchen, where Dave and I were on a well-deserved break. We had managed to clean out the apartment on Diamond Street and supervise the movers in hauling our belongings into the new house. Ahead of us was the daunting task of unpacking and planning the house layout. There was so much stress in our lives that we vowed to reduce it by unpacking immediately instead of living out of boxes.

At first glance, James Kennedy was not at all what I expected when Laurie called from a gays-in-the-military seminar she had attended this Saturday morning. Although they were confident they could provide sound legal advice, Dave and Laurie knew that the Uniform Code of Military Justice was a foreign system and that, even with their help, I would need someone schooled in its particular intricacies. Laurie called late that morning, proud to say that she had invited one of the speakers, a former Army prosecutor, to join her home and discuss my case. Redheaded, with a beard and a slight paunch, as the *Wall Street Journal* would later describe him, he did not fit the stereotype of the former Army prosecutor. Yet in his eyes was a glimmer of the warrior ethic. As I relayed my intention to come out at the March on Washington, his face grew grave.

"Do you realize the potential consequences of your actions?" he asked, not giving me time to respond before he opened his leather satchel, pulled out stacks of Army regulations, and began his consultation, peppering his dialogue with legal citations and Uniform Code of Military Justice references. I expected we would talk fifteen to twenty minutes. We ended our conversation with a firm handshake three hours later.

The former Army prosecutor was not going to blow sunshine to persuade me to help the cause. He had resigned his commission quietly when his orientation became clear. He said he could not bear to live a lie and prosecute soldiers because they were gay like him. So for three hours, he laid out the worst possible scenarios, each pitfall, and each possible punishment. He gave me the information that allowed me to rethink my position. After listening to his three-hour discussion of the possible outcomes of a public announcement, especially as public as we planned to make it, I found myself dashed by doubt and worries. I knew I would probably be thrown out of the Army, but the very real possibility of being thrown in jail was not something that had entered my earlier calculations.

His words reverberated in my head as we ate the sandwiches Laurie had run out to get us from the corner deli. My decision was easy. I would come out because it was the right thing to do. Whatever retribution the Army chose to dole out would reflect only on their willingness to quash anything that challenged them. My punishment, if out of proportion to that usually doled out, would further expose the illegitimacy of the policy and spotlight the witch-hunt mentality. James Kennedy and I would fight this one together, I knew, because vicariously he was fighting the same monolithic institution that through its malevolence had forced him to foreclose a promising career. He'd resigned instead of fighting then. He'd fight his own fight now by helping me wage my battle. We would not be just another blip on the timeline.

I received this letter of recommendation for my impending transfer the morning before my last strategy session with James:

21 April 1993

Major Russell Peterman:

Sergeant José Zuniga will be joining your team shortly and I wanted to tell you something about this exceptional young journalist and noncommissioned officer.

Sergeant Zuniga came to Sixth Army from the 1st Cavalry Division. The Cav thought highly of him and recommended him to me. When Joe arrived at the Presidio, I put him on the *Star Presidian* staff. Shortly thereafter, I had him completely redesign and change the focus of the paper. That was four Fourth Estate Awards ago. Under Joe's direction, the *Star Presidian* has evolved into an outstanding newspaper. I would also be remiss in not mentioning that he was selected as the Forces Command Journalist of the Year for 1992.

I consider Sergeant Zuniga not only a superb journalist, but also an exemplary soldier. From the beginning, he has proven to be a willing and capable leader, able to quickly take the leadership of a team and move it firmly and harmoniously ahead. I mentioned the word "exemplary"—Joe is a Primary Leadership Development Course honor graduate and the 1992 Sixth U.S. Army Soldier of the Year.

I think you can understand my enthusiasm for this young man. It's a pleasure to send you someone of his caliber. While Sixth Army hates to lose him, our loss is now your gain.

Steven C. Fredericks
Lieutenant Colonel, Infantry

James answered the door wearing tropical Army fatigues, the kind he wore when assigned to Panama. Time for some final contingency planning before his flight to the nation's capital on April 21. Short on cash, and with only a promise from me to pay his fee when possible at some point in the future, James had to leave early to make use of generously donated frequent-flyer tickets.

I started by showing him the letter of recommendation Lieutenant Colonel Fredericks had written to my next commander in Korea. To James, this letter served as another piece of ammunition to use against the Army.

"Picture it: a conservative Catholic boy, born into a family with a proud tradition of military service, discarded by the Army not for misconduct, not for any action nor because of any behavior, but for telling the truth." James was almost giddy.

I had almost cried after reading my boss's letter, feeling even more like a traitor.

Time to change the subject. Until now we had never discussed what would happen if our plan unraveled. After all, almost every news organization in the country had been clued in to the upcoming event. The Army could call me back off leave and demand I fly back to the Presidio on a moment's notice, he said.

"Could they detain me?" I asked nervously.

Yes. But just until an attorney ordered me released. They had no reason to incarcerate me, James assured me. I was neither a criminal nor a flight risk.

That said, James wished me luck in my remaining days at the Presidio and said he'd pray for my safe delivery to Washington.

From your lips to God's ears, I thought.

YOUR LOVING SON

THE ARRANGEMENTS FOR MY COMING OUT SEEMED TO BE GOING without a hitch. No one in my office suspected anything, or at least I thought not. Confirmation came in the form of an office flyer advertising a farewell party in my honor after my return from leave on May 5. It broke my heart to hear my friends and colleagues plan a party for me, a party that would never happen because after the night of April 24 I would no longer be Sergeant Zuniga the co-worker and friend, but Citizen Zuniga the queer, the pariah. Even if my co-workers didn't feel that way, I would probably have all my time consumed by the process of being thrown out. Either way, the farewell party seemed unlikely to occur.

This matter, although troublesome, was minor compared to that of finding a way to warn my father about the life-altering step I was about to take. Should I call him? I feared hearing him answer, or worse, the click of the receiver on its cradle. Should I fly down to Texas and face him with a truth that would surely devastate him? Again, I feared his answer. Nothing in the twenty-three years I had known my father hinted that he would do anything other than physically remove me from his home and disown me. But he had to be warned, I knew. I could not bear the thought of his reading that his son was gay from the local newspaper; it would hit like a bullet shot at point-blank range.

Sitting in my barracks room, a family portrait positioned atop the computer monitor, I began to write him the first letter I had ever written him in our twenty-three years together. How to start? I flipped through a photo album, turning to the few photos of us

197

together. There had been a definite warming in our relationship in the years since my mother's death. He and Sandra had even come to visit me in San Francisco, shortly after my transfer to the Presidio.

During their visit, I had told Sandra I was gay and was considering coming out of the closet publicly. She was accepting, but expressed concern over the effect this would have on Father. I finally felt that Sandra was my sister.

I don't want to lose you, Father! You're all I have left! Will you understand? Can you understand? I'm doing this as a matter of honor. Can you understand? Will you be proud of me ever again?

This is the letter I sent:

April 20, 1993

Dear Father,

I expect that April 24, 1993, will be a day I will never forget because of the magnitude of consequences that a ten-minute speech I will deliver in Washington, D.C., might bring. I am not disturbed that for the most part my going through with one of the most difficult decisions of my life will be greeted by a negative response; I fully expect that. What does concern me is the possible effect my actions may have on you and Sandra.

Before I expand on my decision, I must confirm something you may have already suspected. I am gay. It has taken me this long to admit I have come to terms with who I am. I wish I could be with you now in person, but although I am not there to gauge your reaction to this confirmation, I think I know what your reaction will be. For this reason, I ask that you understand that what I am does not make me any less of a person. From the day you proudly watched Henry B. Gonzalez pin the rank of cadet colonel on my shoulder boards in high school to the day two years ago when you saw the video of me marching down Constitution Avenue in Washington, D.C., after Desert Storm, you were witness to my desire to emulate those qualities in you that I most admire: perseverance, honor, and selflessness.

Father, I have followed your lead as well as I could. I may not always have been the perfect son, but then how many perfect sons are there? I know you were disappointed when I didn't accept the nomination to West Point. You were further disappointed when I abandoned the Aggie Corps of Cadets to pursue journalism instead of a commission. But it is my greatest hope that you have been proud of me for being one of the best noncommissioned officers in the U.S. Army.

It is when I think of your sense of honor and integrity that my conscience cannot rest. It is with that thought as a preface that I tell you I will "come out" of the closet. I do this because many of the people who know and respect me favor the ban on gays in the military. I hope my example will help them realize the ban's irrationality. Above all, though, I can no longer live the farce that my life has become.

A month before Mother died she told me how very proud of me she was. Because I rarely heard those words in my upbringing, I knew there was more to her statement. She then asked me if I was happy with my life. My answer to her question was a weak yes. She knew that I truly was not. It was with a tenderness that only a mother possesses that she told me she still loved me. She didn't quite understand the *why* behind who I am—I am not sure any of us does—but she made clear that my being gay would not preclude her from loving her only son. I felt a huge weight lifted from my chest as her words flooded my mind, washing away the doubt.

If you should offer me a fraction of that understanding I will be among the luckiest men alive, knowing that you will at least not have disowned me as many of my friends' parents have. Please do not follow in the footsteps of other parents who begin to question where they might have gone wrong. I am sure I was born the way I am. It took me so long to own up to who I am only because society forced me to repress so much of myself. It was you, however, who taught me to fight for what I believed was right. The battle I wage now is not only right, it is just. I ask you to remember that what I admit to being today does not change who I have been in the twenty-three years of my life. Your loving and loyal son,

José

AN AVERAGE JOE

I WORE THE BASEBALL CAP, BAGGY JEANS, AND UNFLATTERINGLY large jacket Robert had suggested I wear as a disguise. I assume I was as conspicuous as a rookie CIA agent tailing a seasoned terrorist, but I was playing it safe. Robert had requested this guise as an insurance policy against the military's Gestapo. James, although doubtful the military police or CID would show, saw no harm in indulging Robert's paranoid request. After all, it was James who, fearing that the Task Force phone lines might be tapped, advised code names from the day he took on the case. I became "Luke," he became "Obi-Wan Kenobi," and General Mallory became "Darth Vader." Dave and Laurie became "Han Solo" and "Princess Leia," respectively. Washington, D.C., became "Out East." My coming out became "The Event." Our codes were successful. The public-relations assault was set in full motion when two of twenty embargoed interviews (one with *Time* magazine, the other with the *San Jose Mercury News*) took place at home the night before my flight to Washington, D.C.

Glancing over my shoulder a few times, I swore I saw someone looking somewhat suspicious following me through the crowded San Francisco International Airport. Just as I spotted him, though, he would disappear into an adjoining concourse or board a plane at a gate behind me.

Paranoid? I had every reason to be. No one suspects anything, I thought, trying to calm my dilated synaptic firings.

A memo in my in box the afternoon before my leave started with news of a goodbye lunch on May 5. *It's official: Sergeant Zuniga is leaving.* I felt awful but nonetheless said goodbye to no one. As far as the Army was concerned, Sergeant Zuniga would be on leave until one minute past midnight on May 4.

American Airlines Flight No. 1674 into Dallas was late in arriving. I made a full-speed sprint to a connecting gate on what seemed the opposite side of Dallas-Fort Worth Airport. The morning wasn't going well. The leisure travel office on post had issued the tickets. I didn't bother to notice the less than fifteen-minute leeway between flights, and I cursed myself for not having checked, but at least I was in shape. Thinking back, I probably could have made it to Gate 12 by walking briskly, but scenes out of *Hudson Hawk* kept popping in my head. What if the MPs flew here to detain me? Was that why I ran? Was I afraid to face the music? Of course, there was no such scene. From the hundreds of travelers buzzing from terminal to terminal to the haughty gay man sitting in the aisle seat beside me, I was just another faceless passenger, and that's just what I wanted to be.

I let out an audible sigh as the plane bounced onto the Dulles runway. I knew the plan could yet be foiled, but I felt relief.

"Are you here for business or leisure?" my bright-eyed companion asked.

"Both. You?" I shouldn't have asked. A rambling answer swallowed the time between taxiing and deplaning, followed me off the plane, and ended abruptly only when I shook his hand in the gate lobby and said, "Pleased to meet you."

My sense of relief increased as I walked down the passenger ramp into the airport. Our plan had worked. Bags in hand, the notes I had scribbled for my coming-out speech while on the plane stuffed in my back pocket, I was ready for my last night as a private citizen in public service. In twenty-four hours I would become a public figure thrown out of public service.

Plans called for a *Time* magazine assistant photographer to pick me up at the baggage-claim area and drive me to a photo shoot in a Georgetown studio. His instructions were to look for a tall, lanky, twenty-three-year-old, sporting a Mickey Mouse baseball cap and sunglasses. This individual would respond to the name "Luke."

To my surprised dismay, a balding man holding a sign with the words TIME: JOSÉ ZUNIGA etched in fire-engine-red two-inch block letters greeted me at the gate. So much for security. I threw off my sunglasses in disgust.

"So, how was your flight?" he asked.

"I'm exhausted."

ZERO TOLERANCE

Pentagon Report Tells of Aviators' Debauchery

WASHINGTON, April 23—In a devastatingly detailed account of drinking, debauchery and sexual abuse within the military, a Pentagon report released today said that as many as 175 officers may face disciplinary action as a result of their involvement in a drunken revel two years ago in a Las Vegas hotel.

The report, by the Pentagon's inspector general, makes it clear that the scope and nature of the abuses at the Tailhook Association convention of top Navy fliers in 1991 were even worse than they appeared in previous news and official accounts.

According to the report, 83 women and 7 men were assaulted during three days of boozy parties.

"The assaults varied from victims being grabbed on the buttocks to victims being groped, pinched and fondled on their breasts, buttocks and genitals," the report added. "Some victims were bitten by their assailants, others were knocked to the ground and some had their clothing ripped or removed."

Naval aviators and their guests also engaged in consensual oral sex and sexual intercourse in full view of other participants, contributing to a "general atmosphere of debauchery," the report said.

The report rejects the claim by some top military officers that the Tailhook scandal was an isolated incident. The abuses at the convention, the report concluded, were not significantly different from those at earlier meetings and were widely condoned by the Navy's civilian and military leaders.

The Pentagon report released today is the second part of the inspector general's inquiry into the Tailhook convention. The first part, released in September, assailed the Navy's official in-

203

quiry into the episode charging that senior Navy officials deliberately undermined their own investigation to avoid unflattering publicity.

—*The New York Times*
April 24, 1993

The Pentagon's second report on the 1991 Tailhook Association convention in Las Vegas was released to every major media outlet and reported without censure on the very day of my arrival. What good fortune to have this testament to the existence of unbridled, military-sanctioned heterosexual machismo and misogyny available for the public to inspect as the handwringing debate about gays in the military focused on the subjects of foxholes and showers. On the eve of the March on Washington, Laurie and I read about the report in *The New York Times* front-page story in utter disbelief at the magnitude of the debauchery the article or, more accurately, the Pentagon described.*

"Maybe we should ban heterosexuals from military service," Jay Leno joked on the "Tonight Show."

The Navy would re-evaluate its sexual harassment policies and educate sailors about the "zero-tolerance" of such behavior, Admiral Frank Kelso, chief of naval operations, announced at a joint news conference with Marine Corps Commandant General Carl E. Mundy. Ironically, Kelso was among the more than four thousand Tailhook Association members attending the 1991 conference.

"Tailhook brought to light the fact that we had an institutional problem in how we treated women," Kelso said, adding he would not resign as the Navy Secretary did after the first Pentagon investigation.

Clinton said he was disturbed by the report but added, "It should not be taken as a general indictment of the U.S. Navy."

Grown men, good sailors one and all, attacking women for no

---

*Excerpts from the Pentagon Inspector General's second report on Tailhook 1991 are reprinted in Appendix B.

reason other than their gender? Should heterosexual males be banned from the military based on rape statistics? Since every espionage case in recent history including Ames, Pollard and Miller has involved heterosexuals, are straight men a security risk? Has it gotten to the point where we can no longer trust heterosexuals in the military?

Imagine if the words "gay" or "lesbian" were suddenly substituted in the Senate Armed Services Committee's debate with words reflecting ethnicity. Take the words of horror applied to the prospect of a "gay sailor" in the submarine shower room and substitute "African-American sailor"; a "lesbian Marine" in a two-man tent and substitute "Asian-American Marine"; a "bisexual soldier" in a Persian Gulf foxhole and substitute "Mexican-American soldier." The Tailhook issue, like the issue of allowing gays in the military, was one of defining and putting in place enforceable regulations governing sexual misconduct, not sexual orientation. Even the most outrageous fantasies about military gays concocted by Senate Armed Services Committee members could not exceed the reality of Tailhook 1991.

Until now, Tailhook news accounts had failed to report in detail any conclusions reached in the first Pentagon report. Although somewhat familiar with the story, Americans were mostly unaware of the scale of sexual misconduct. I have often wondered if the conspiracy of silence was initiated by the highest echelons of military leadership because disclosure could substantially weaken the Defense Department's stand against gays in the military. Oh well ...

Screaming headlines proclaimed the Navy's shame now. A black-and-white photo of an aviator wearing a "Women Are Property" T-shirt accompanied the syndicated articles running on the front page of metropolitan dailies across the nation.

PROUD TO BE GAY

Robert Bray and I were scheduled to meet this after-noon in the lobby of the Hyatt-Dupont Circle. This would be our first and last meeting before the event tonight, a time to iron out any wrinkles that might somehow have survived the full-steam press of our diligent advance preparations.

He walked in at precisely 2 P.M., as promised, in stark contrast to my expectation of one who belonged to a society that viewed timeliness as something for drones or for people with no class—my definition of "queer time." I'd formed the image of a centenarian activist. The youthful and vigorous man standing before me was shockingly unexpected. "What's wrong?" he asked. "You look like you've just seen a ghost."

"It's just that I pictured you to be much older, much more—well, 'older' is the right word."

"Well thanks, I'll take that as a compliment."

Even before our meeting today, he had imagined me as the quintes-sential image of the all-American boy, he confessed. "You have to be clean-cut, unobjectionable, and sympathetic to the mainstream as an average Joe, only just a bit more above average, refusing to fall victim to politics based on ignorance and fueled by a handful of righteous, holier-than-thou extremists, feeding the fears of the many and focusing a cultivated bigotry against you and your brothers and sisters. . . ."

He stopped himself, blinked his big doe eyes, and started again. "You've gotta watch that, becoming a quote 'whore' turns people off, especially the media. It's more facts and image today. Have you noticed?" He was appealing to my senses as a journalist. "Images have actually helped decide the outcome of a war. It's not enough to win, you have to look good winning too."

He was right, of course. The information superhighway replaced the Yellow Brick Road ages ago, destroying much in our society with information overkill.

Pulling a notepad out of his backpack, Robert began to drill me on minor technicalities he had dreamed about the night before. He had not yet seen my speech and with every question seemed to hint at his strong desire to read it before its delivery tonight.

"I hope your focus isn't just on the constitution and the oath to defend one's country and how pathetic it is we're fighting for the rights of Americans other than ourselves," he said, baiting me to hand over my text.

"No," I answered tersely.

"Good, because that is so overdone sometimes, so cliché."

Robert, it's when you combine that clichéd message with a hint of human suffering that the people will listen. He noted a soothing confidence in my gaze and pressed no further.

"Your life is going to change. Don't let yourself get caught up in the whirlwind," he warned with a brotherly warmth.

"But I already sometimes feel as if my life has been distilled into one thought—one important message that must be repeated again and again."

He paused a minute to search for words. "The message will change too. You don't have to watch the 'Joan Rivers Show' to grasp the societal importance of its impending change."

"And what if I can't change with it? What if I can't keep pace with the struggle?" I played devil's advocate.

"Joe, you're not being asked to outline a military policy. You're just one soldier taking a stand. After that, you take it one step at a time." With a chuckle, he said, "You could become a sultry letter-turner. They pay quite well."

We laughed for a minute, probably the last carefree moments we would enjoy until after the March, and maybe even beyond. A few reminders and trivial pointers preceded a hug and kiss that would cement our friendship forever.

*   *   *

My interview schedule was meticulously laid out; every last second was accounted for. In the two days preceding my coming out, reporters from the country's major newspapers and television stations clamored for the inside scoop about the star military man they had heard would be plunging himself into the crucible of the military debate. I answered the same twenty questions at least 50,000 times each, 95 percent of them platitudinously.

"Keep my family out of this as much as possible," I asked one reporter after he asked one personal question too many. As a journalist I knew better. Maybe it was the threat a writer might gain proximity to my loved ones, innocent victims in this impending action.

Howard Schnieder, an engaging bear of a man, was the *Washington Post* reporter assigned to cover this story. Our interview proceeded in much the same manner as the five previous interviews had, a brief glance at my three-page official biography followed by questions eliciting already-thought-out answers, delivered with as much spontaneity as I could muster. I had a knowledge of what reporters needed for a story, and so far that knowledge redounded to my benefit.

Schnieder leaned forward in the hotel-room chair and cleared his throat in preparation for his next question.

"Have you," he started hesitatingly, perhaps questioning the relevance of the question but asking it nonetheless, "ever had sex with a man?"

My mind raced in a million different directions. How to answer this question while maintaining my honor. Answering yes would ensure me time in the brig for sodomy charges. A nonanswer would cast doubt. A no would avert all additional questions. In the seconds between the moment he asked his question and I voiced my answer, I didn't stop long enough to realize that the implications of a false word uttered in an attempt at self-preservation could set off a chain reaction. In delivering my answer, I learned the harshest lesson about my profession, one I suppose my journalism professors glossed over or I slept through: always tell the truth.

"No," I answered angrily, "Now, would you have asked that of a straight man or woman?"

"You never slept with a man?" he asked again like a skeptical, prove-it-to-me journalist.

I refused to answer the question again. But it was too late, the chain reaction had been set in motion. As much as I wanted to put the issue of duty and sex asunder, I had to face the reality. Our interview ended with a firm handshake and a look on his face that confirmed his doubts. I would refuse to answer any such questions in the future.

Panic! What if he figured out my relationship to Dave and Laurie? There was no question that in a world of sound bites, where romantic entanglements make for juicy gossip-column fodder, our relationship would be torn to shreds. How could I explode the established notion of what constitutes family in a two-minute news segment? How could I explain the meaning of family by blood, love, friendship, and community to a jaded journalist allotted five inches of copy for his story?

Please, God, don't let our enemies pick up on this. Dave, Laurie and I redoubled our efforts to live as a family, work as a team, but appear to the world to be simply friends.

Dress blues, the most formal of the Army's uniforms, carry with them hundreds of years of honor and tradition. It was the uniform of the day or night for generals George Armstrong Custer and Ulysses S. Grant, from battlefield to banquet hall. I had requested a set of blues from the supply room, because this was to be my declaration of war and celebration of freedom rolled into one night. My dress blues had seen plenty of wear in the last forty-eight hours, with every major newspaper in the country demanding a photo of me in uniform—it would add "oomph" to the story value, one photographer explained.

Tonight I carried my uniform and its just as traditionally steeped accoutrements draped over my shoulder in the same travel bag I used to carry my uniform to the Sixth U.S. Army Soldier of the Year competition in Reno not more than six weeks earlier. There was no changing room, an organizer said apologetically.

"I never needed one in the Army," I answered tersely, walking to a bathroom behind the designated VIP room.

This will be the last time you wear this uniform with the same honor afforded a soldier in good standing: a random thought among the microcosm of syllables and half-thoughts cluttering my head, my hands shaking as I attempted to straighten a tie that was probably already perfect. Dave, a look of worry blanketing his usually serene face, rushed in after less than ten minutes. Without saying a word, he reached out and returned my tie to its original position. Dave had worked magic. I felt secure.

I did not witness the event itself, although I heard periodic reviews from people running in and out of the green room at the conclusion of each segment. I had arrived before any guests filled the cavernous hall of Old Postal Square. Having had the opportunity to revel in its majesty, I momentarily entertained the thought of seeing this refurbished expanse of emptiness filled with my new family.

A beyond-capacity attendance expected, Robert squealed with an ear-to-ear smile. What more could we hope for, as far as impact is concerned, than a full house, he asked rhetorically. Noticing my nervousness, he stopped himself. A repentant look swept over his face as he realized that his self-congratulatory comment, one that would normally muster a celebratory retort from me, had only increased my tension.

I was sequestered in the VIP room stage right until seconds before my scheduled appearance. Laurie and Dave stood nearby as I paced the room, cursing myself for not having memorized the speech. As my moment approached I slowly sat down, leaned back in the armchair, and shut my eyes. I was suddenly suffused with a feeling of imminent freedom, an oceanic swelling in the pit of my stomach.

"I think I'm ready," I told anyone who would listen.

Dave, Laurie, Robert, and James escorted me out of the room, parting the liquid crowd. James pressed against me like flotsam stuck to a bow. As I stood frozen in place a few feet from the stage, my mind suddenly went blank. Looking at pictures of that night now, the look of utter terror I wore as a mask does more justice to my feelings than words could ever do.

Why was I here? What was I going to prove? James's warnings of possible punishment . . . Sandra's words of caution about the disastrous effect my actions would have on my father: both echoed in my dazed mind. But General Mallory's venomous diatribe pre-empted them all, answering the why and making clear what I needed to do.

"Enough is enough," Margarethe Cammermeyer said emphatically while we were still in the VIP room, embracing me in arms that for twenty-eight years had consoled many spirits, including those of dying soldiers in Vietnam. Hers was the maternal hug I had desperately needed for more than three years.

"Good luck, Joe," Tracy Thorne said before his name was called to appear on stage. A random wish Alex were here now . . .

"When we met with President Clinton last week"—Torie's speech was interrupted by a roar filling every ounce of space in the cavernous hall—"the president said that the single best thing we could do for our cause was to bring out people in our community with whom the average American could identify." Torie was beginning a suspense-filled introduction of the night's surprise guest, known only as "Luke" to members of the media with whom I had yet to interview; outright whistles and cheers made clear the audience knew it.

"Groomed for the Pentagon. On the fast track for military success. In the words of U.S. Army General Glynn C. Mallory, 'You can be justifiably proud of this distinction and I know you will continue to serve with the same dedication which prompted your selection as Soldier of the Year.'

"Twenty-three years old. Until tonight he has never come out as a gay man. The Sixth U.S. Army's Soldier of the Year, Joe Zuniga!"

Torie's introduction concluded, the crowd in an uproar, I ran up the stairs, stumbling on the first step, which helped dissipate the nerves that would otherwise have transformed me into a stammering fool. I was lucky I didn't fall like a luger, crying out a Wagnerian tenor. I righted myself and, because my faux pas had occurred so low on the steps leading up to the platform, only those in the front row had seen it. They did not seem to care.

I approached the podium, where a warm bearhug awaited me. The image of a proud but nervous soldier in dress blues loomed overhead on a Jumbotron twenty-foot screen. Stage lights and the barrage of the cameras clicking off frame after frame temporarily blinded me. My mind screamed "Get the hell out of here!" No. I felt, as Winston Churchill once described, as if I were walking with destiny, that all my past life had been but a preparation for this hour. Do it for every gay man, lesbian, and bisexual who was ever kicked out of the military simply for being who they were. Do it to atone for every fag joke you've ever told. Do it for whatever reason you can think of, but for God's sake, don't stop now! Taking a deep breath, like a diver about to make a jump, I launched into my prepared speech and clicked into autopilot.

Two years ago 50,000 soldiers, sailors, airmen, and Marines converged on this city to receive a nation's homage for their victory in the Persian Gulf. I was among those soldiers who marched down Constitution Avenue past throngs of grateful American flag-wavers, prouder than ever before to be wearing the uniform of the world's greatest armed force. Proud to have answered the nation's call in a time of crisis, saddened only by the fact that not all of us had returned to this national victory celebration.

It is ironic that my return to our nation's capital will result in an end to a love affair between the U.S. Army and a proud soldier. The Army and I have been extraordinarily good for each other. I have served for three years with distinction, in peacetime and in war. It is an unmitigated shame that the same Army that entrusted me with the training of its troops and rewarded my many accomplishments is not mature enough to commit to this relationship for life, but rather, will likely choose to separate me from service for my action here tonight.

For three years, I have lived the life of a heterosexual soldier. I have told my share of jokes about homosexuals out of necessity. I have painfully witnessed the harassment of suspected gays and lesbians and not said a word to stop it. I have waged an emotional battle to combat what certain segments of society term deviant feelings, living a life of confusion, fearing to act on these emotions because the military's version of morality would force me to violate the very principles of honor and integrity it promotes.

I cannot continue to serve my country if I must choose between serving honorably and living a lie. Today I come out as a gay soldier to denounce wrongful discrimination in the guise of proper policy; to decry the literal theft of opportunity to excel in military service because of who I am.

I am proud to be a soldier and noncommissioned officer in the U.S. Army. I am also proud to be gay.

The Army would rather pretend that the thousands of gay, lesbian, and bisexual soldiers like me are figments of gay activists' imaginations. Those few of us whose existence the military does acknowledge are portrayed as activists set on destroying unit cohesion and esprit de corps. I am not an activist, nor am I looking to pin a pink triangle beside my medals. I am simply a soldier who wants to continue a distinguished career, but who happens to be gay.

Today, my military career will likely come to an abrupt and unnecessary halt. As emotionally wrecking as that undeniable conclusion is to me, I am inspired to persist in the hope that after July 15, gay, lesbian, and bisexual members of the armed forces will no longer face persecution because of status—a status that clearly makes no shred of difference in our performance, as proven by the exemplary records of those of us before you today. Our combined successes highlight all the more dramatically the irrationality of the Department of Defense directive: irrational discrimination, pure and simple.

My hope, that my coming out today will benefit our common cause, leaves me with only one concern: that July 15 could pass without the ban being lifted. To ensure that does not occur, I join my community in calling out to President Clinton and saying, "Sir, you have shown the will to end the institutionalized discrimination that forces thousands of dedicated soldiers to live in agonizing silence, and that ruins the careers of thousands more. I urge you, Mr. President, lead the way, show us the courage and the conviction to guide our country, and specifically the military, into a new era of understanding."

I thank the National Gay & Lesbian Task Force and the many friends who helped me gather the courage to be here today. I would be remiss if I did not salute the distinguished members of the U.S. Armed Forces with whom I now join ranks in this fight. The cumulative impact they have already made on America is enormous. Together, we shall continue the struggle for what is just and what is right. God willing we will be back here not too long from now to celebrate our victory. On that day, I will be as proud, if not prouder, to march shoulder-to-shoulder with you as I did two years ago with the heroes of Desert Storm. Thank you.

My "thank you" was inaudible over the electrifying excitement of the seamless crowd. Many of them, especially a large number of military veterans, were in tears. They knew the magnitude of the sacrifice I made here tonight. I stood on the stage for what seemed infinity, accepting the warm embrace of my new family. Seconds later Torie and the contingent of gay military heroes joined me on stage, hugging, kissing, raising my arm in the symbolic gesture of victory. Camera flashes went off like the blue and orange streaks of Allied missiles I had seen exploding over the Iraqi horizon. Reporters ambushed the stage, practically stepping over each other.

Dave and Laurie? James? Robert? I couldn't focus enough to spot them on the other side of this sea of journalists, reporters ravenous for an exclusive.

The remainder of that night remains a blur, like watching film credits on fast forward: By the time you understand who the characters are, they have moved on to the music credits. Outside of pondering the consequences of my action, there were no vacancies in the hotel space of my mind to accommodate any other memories. Snippets of dialogue, other people's accounts, and hundreds of photographs are all the memory I have to focus on the distorted canvas of a night that will forever symbolize my birth as a gay man. I was whisked off the stage and into the back room in a trance, a Bambi-stunned-by-headlights look veiling my face. The press ignored warnings not to follow me. The clatter of camera equipment hounded me. Photo ops abounded. Martina Navratilova, Melissa Etheridge . . . I remember the lump in my throat, tears beginning to form, the magnitude of it all soaking in by the second, a realization of just how desperately alone I was. No one here could feel my pain.

"Why did you do it? How do you feel?" A couple of reporters asked in stereo.

"What have you accomplished? And what do you think will happen now?" a "Day One" producer asked, his assistant almost jabbing a microphone in my mouth.

"How do you spell your last name?" another reporter asked. Did he expect me to dignify that question with an answer when he was writing notes on the back of a three-page biography Laurie and Robert had just passed out to him?

I was unable to construct a thought, much less a sentence. I suppose the Pentagon's public-affairs spokeswoman on duty that night had a bit of the same problem when she told a *Washington Post* reporter, "He is a very courageous young man and obviously he is committed to who he is and what he wants to do. [But] talented people leave every day for a variety of reasons." Funny, I never learned that response in public-affairs school.

"Better get out of here before they start asking tougher questions," Robert said, while shielding me from any more press, providing an escape route. Thank God, too, because even were I able to answer reporters' questions, I possessed little command of the politesse of the gay rights movement. We jumped in a cab and retreated to the safety of our hotel room.

The 5 A.M. wakeup call was about as welcome as reveille after a night of heavy debauchery. The buzz of the alarm clock seconds later was not any more welcome, a fragmentary flashback to a muezzin at 0500 calling the first hour of daily prayer in the port of ad Dammam, inciting the instinctive rolling over and hitting snooze. The alarm went off again, and Laurie and I jumped out of bed.

"Don't hate me if I sleep through this one," Dave said, his voice a syrupy, sleepy whisper. He had rolled over to the edge of the bed to watch us throw on our predesignated outfits. "Good luck."

We ran down to the lobby. A Lincoln Town Car sat waiting outside, ready to drive us to the Washington Monument for a live taping of "Good Morning America."

"Hi, Sergeant," the show's producer said, her voice as sweet as a cedar waxwing warbling outside a windowsill, as if it weren't 6 A.M. "We'll be about an hour, okay?"

It was an hour spent talking (schmoozing, some would say) with the show's other guests: Melissa Etheridge and her lover Julie; Phil Donahue; and Campaign for Military Service Director Tom Stoddard. It was also time for reflection, but one that could not possibly be resolved in an hour. To reach that plane would mean to completely submerge oneself into the soul, and that would require an extended leave of absence from the hindrances of everyday life that I could not then— and could not imagine ever—having time to do.

Perched on top of a teetering platform overlooking a mall abuzz with the flurry of pre-March activity, Tom and I were interviewed about the gay ban and the March on Washington, a celebration that would be attended by far more than the thirty thousand later estimated by the National Park Service.

"I'm nervous," I complained to Laurie as we cuddled by the Winnebago, waiting for the tape playback, shivering in the 45° morning chill.

"You'll be okay, honey," she said, placing her arms around me. I suddenly felt warmer.

A SIMPLE MATTER
OF JUSTICE

THE 1993 MARCH ON WASHINGTON FOR LESBIAN, GAY, AND Bi[sexual] Equal Rights and Liberation was a balm to the ravaged souls of gay America. This was a time to mourn for those who fought valiantly against the AIDS pandemic. A time to celebrate the fact that a powerful gay political coalition helped end twelve years of Republican reign in the White House; that Bill Clinton, president of the United States, not only recognized but embraced the gay community; and the real possibilities of an end to the military ban and passage of a federal civil rights bill. It was also time for a color snapshot of the state of queer liberation—a snapshot depicting a community poised on the brink of irrevocable change, a community no longer willing to endure the hatred of Bible-wielding bigots and homophobes propagating asinine prejudice.

More than one million gay, lesbian, bisexual, and transgendered bodies—humans one and all—made a pilgrimage to the nation's capital with a list of demands* among which was an unspoken demand for gay-shy America to take notice that, paradoxical as it is, we are all the same, only different. Homosexuals are as human as straight people, but we are different because we have historically been invisible, silent or outcast.

---

*Demands of the 1993 March on Washington platform are listed in Appendix C.

Unfortunately, even in the heart of our momentous gathering, we were being snubbed by the very man who inspired hope in our community, a man who assured gays, "I have a vision, and you are a part of it." The first sign his promises had been an attempt to curry favor with our community?

Critics lashed out against a perceived lack of focus or theme, but for the vast majority the March was a forum for collective euphoria and unified prayer for a better tomorrow. It was not about intimidating Clinton into fulfilling his campaign promises—that was a given. It most definitely was not a show of force against far-right extremists who suffered a childish myopia. And it was definitely not about pulling a federal gay civil rights bill out of Congress over a weekend that most of its members coincidentally decided to take vacations. To me it was more a gay Woodstock—a pivotal gathering with different meaning for each person in attendance, a historic event nonetheless. This was an opportunity to show our community's human face in a gathering of people running the human spectrum.

The March on Washington was about freedom to speak far beyond "We're here! We're queer! Get used to it!"

All gay views were represented here. For each militant activist, there was a corresponding first timer. Even if it required a mouthful, there was a need to express the excruciating pain of losing thousands of gay teens to suicide. The suffering of gay people of color who struggle on two fronts to secure their rights as racial and sexual minorities. The anguish felt when the struggle for acceptance chronicled in our pockmarked history returns to haunt us, when hatemongers with their lopsided sneers dismiss us as a segment of society something less than human.

Above all, this March was about justice, *A Simple Matter of Justice*, at the butt end of the twentieth century. In 1939 America closed its doors to the *St. Louis*, a ship carrying 939 German Jewish refugees. In World War II Japanese Americans were relocated to concentration camps in inland areas. Before the 1960s, when Jim Crow was the law of the land in the South, it was justified to treat African Americans as less than equal because of the color of their skin. Before the Civil Rights Act of 1964, discrimination on the basis of religion, national origin, and sex was, if not the American way, at least acceptable. And today, a formidable force was attempting to turn the gay struggle into an orgy of hate and bigotry unrestrained by any protection offered by the law. It has always taken strong people to swim against the current; dead fish will always float with it, my mother once told me. The strong shall shake the Nation to the marrow of its bones. . . .

Dave, Laurie, and I joined a group of about ten friends in the lobby of the Hyatt-Dupont Circle at around nine o'clock in the morning. Arm in arm, we followed the throngs of people heading toward the Washington Mall, chanting slogans, singing "We Are Family."

Wait! For the first time in my life I felt free to echo their words. I held Dave's and Laurie's hands as we traversed the city, no need to look over my shoulder anymore. I was truly free! This was my family, a family that, unlike the military family I had given some of the best years of my life, would not abandon me because of who I was.

I had promised the military contingent I would march with them for half the route. They were just forming when I arrived. Keith, Tracy, Tom, and other gay and lesbian veterans stood at the head of the contingent. The media swarming around them before my arrival wasn't about to ignore me.

What does it mean for you to march in the nation's capital again, Sergeant?

How do you feel this morning, Sergeant?

Heard from the Army yet?

As the reel of mental images of April 25, 1993, floods my mind, I remember that meeting murdered Navy Radioman Allen Schindler's mother, Dorothy Hajdys, was among the most powerful. Clutching an eight-by-ten portrait of her son, his lover and a friend standing at her side, Dorothy Hajdys expounded to members of the press that the real tragedy of having lost her son was losing him to the hatred nourished by military-sanctioned homophobia. Schindler, assigned to a Navy vessel docked in southwestern Japan, had been brutally murdered by twenty-one-year-old Airman Apprentice Terry Helvey in a public restroom. During court-martial proceedings,

219

Helvey claimed that ignorance and homophobia had fogged his judgment. He got life in prison instead of the death penalty.

Tanya Domi, who was commanding the Gay, Lesbian, and Bisexual Color Guard, introduced me to Dorothy minutes before the March kicked off. Dorothy acknowledged having read the story of my coming out the night before, which had been prominently displayed on the front page of *The New York Times*. We did not talk much. I praised her bravery in taking on the military establishment, in demanding justice be served, and in the mother-turned-activist's undertaking a personal crusade, using her suffering to show America the ultimate price exacted by homophobia. Fate had forced her to make a voyage from fear and intolerance to understanding and acceptance. The cost of that journey had, unfortunately, been Allen's life.

"God bless you, Joe," Dorothy whispered as we hugged. Within seconds we were each pulled away for interviews.

James and I would march alongside Keith and Tracy. In deference to Dorothy, we stepped back from our assigned position at the head of the contingent, marching closer to the main veterans' contingent formed in mass behind us. All of us, from the World War II infantryman to the Persian Gulf medic, had served our country with distinction and honor. Today, although vilified by some, we marched shoulder to shoulder, standing tall and proud, showing the world, not just the Pentagon, that we were more than worthy to wear the uniforms of our armed forces.

I stepped out of the veterans' contingent halfway through the parade to join Dave, Laurie, and our friends, all of whom waited patiently for me to deliver on my promise to join them. Standing on the sidelines, I saluted the Stars and Stripes, the rainbow flag by its side. How beautiful, how natural.

We stepped into the vanguard, eventually marching with the Kansas City contingent of Parents and Friends of Lesbians and Gays (P-FLAG). How overwhelming the feeling of pride was as I marched arm in arm with the two people I loved most in the world, lovers who, with their effulgence, were seeing me through my painful evolution.

"Happy birthday, Soldier of the Year!" a cute face topped with a crew-

cut shouted from the crowd. The twenty-one-year-old Marine would shake my hand later at the post-March rally.

"I know your pain," the Reverend Jesse Jackson said, hugging me carefully to avoid injuring the broken arm he kept wrapped tightly in a neck-to-arm bandage. "But this too shall pass."

"We are fortunate to have people like Sergeant Joe Zuniga, the Soldier of the Year, come out and destroy the stereotypes." Martina Navratilova told a crowd of thousands at the rally.

"We love you, Joe," Dave and Laurie whispered in my ear as we cuddled in bed that night. "Don't ever doubt that."

Robert drove me from his home to an Italian restaurant in Georgetown. I had spent the two days since the March either in an office provided me by the Task Force or on the Hill. I was spending my last days of freedom fielding media queries or lobbying congressmen* or legislative assistants to help reverse the Defense Department policy that would surely terminate my military career. The car ride was a time for mutual discovery. We were more alike than different, the media wizard blurted out. How? We seemed to disagree on everything political except gay rights.

"Oh, what do you know?" his words reflected a mischievous sense of humor and irony. "You're just experiencing radically self-conscious evolution via destruction of old, tired philosophies."

Huh?

"I mean, don't end up like *some people we know* who start out addressing the wrong and end up celebrating their anorexic selves," Robert sneered. "Don't become a marionette."

"I think you know I won't. I just want to tell my story."

"You want to be a Paul Revere, awakening the countryside to the Truth," he said sarcastically. This coming from someone who called himself Johnny Apple Queer?

He noted my hurt. "There's no thrill in easy sailing, girl. You're going to have to bear the whips and scorns because it's hard for America to even think about us."

---

*See Appendix D for a letter from Representative Steve Gunderson.

"But we made the word *AIDS* palatable, you admitted that Saturday. Why not crush the complexity and anguish of gay life into chewable tablets?" I asked rhetorically, not expecting or needing a response. There was none. He was throwing more attitude than the law should allow. Silence. Had I said something wrong?

Robert, constantly thumbing his nose at convention, ordered his meal, took a swig of his drink, and finally spoke: "You'll agree with me some day."

Maybe. I preferred not to think about what lay ahead. The future, aside from the reality of my impending discharge, was nebulous. I made myself a promise as we waited for the garlic bread that no one would ever own me. I would be no one's marionette. Enough of that. This was my last night in D.C., and Robert had promised to help me spend it "like one of the *gays*." P Street for some beers, dancing, pretending ... Pretending to be just another twenty-three-year-old gay white male for whom the future bears little consequence because the present is all that matters.

Later, I received this letter:

Joe,

What an amazing time this has been, no? A time filled with revelations, liberation, love, and the sublime power of the Truth. It has been my pleasure to help you arrive at your own Truth—to come out as a proud gay man, able to face the injustice and maybe even change the world. What you have done transcends merely the military policy. It shatters the myths that perpetuate the closet. It explodes the stereotypes that render gay people invisible and hated. It saves the lives of gay youth. It makes *all* of our lives more whole and complete.

Of course, don't let all of this fame go to your head, my friend. Stay close to your people, and remember the virtues and dignity of humbleness.

I may have "handled" numerous dramatic coming-out stories in the media. But something about you touched me deeply. Perhaps it's how we communicate on some similar unspoken wavelength. Maybe it was even when I witnessed your first-ever reflexive "snap" queen gesture. Maybe it's your wonderful and provocative family of Dave and Laurie. Maybe it's your eyes full of innocence, yet also the fire of conviction to right a moral wrong. Who knows? I do know, however, that this feels good and right and real and rare, and that I *live* for experiences like this. We kicked homophobic butt big time!

Everyone here misses you already. People come up to me on the street and ask about you. I truly look forward to seeing you, Dave, and Laurie soon in San Francisco. Then we'll reminisce, laugh, flirt, and plot new schemes to shame the institutions of intolerance. Until then, *con cariño*,

Robert Bray

PART 4

HONORABLE
DISCHARGE

═══════

GETTING OFF A LATE FLIGHT AT SAN FRANCISCO INTERNATIONAL
Airport, I did not expect the more than sixty reporters and cameramen awaiting my arrival. Anticipating that someone had tipped the
press off about my flight home, I had exchanged my flight this morning at Dulles for a later arrival time. I did not even bother shaving
this morning. Thank God I was over my hangover! My mind wandered to blurry scenes of a drunken Soldier of the Year.... An
airport security guard approached my seat and handed me a card.
Dave's warning was scribbled on the back of his business card: *Tons
of press!* This had to have been Robert's idea.

A two-minute impromptu press conference stretched into more
than ten; the reporters and cameramen followed me through the
airport to the baggage-claim area. James seemed to relish the
media attention. I tried to keep us moving toward baggage claim.
Dave and Laurie tried staying out of camera shots. Although I
craved a hug and kiss from each—it had been two long days since
they'd left D.C.—I needed to suppress the urge. The story must
remain simple, and that meant hiding my relationship with Dave
and Laurie.

"See you tomorrow, Sergeant!" a *Sacramento Bee* reporter announced. My fuzzy mind was mired in other thoughts. I could not
answer another question if it involved complete sentences.

"Okay," I mumbled, feeling like a baby.

Soldier Who Came Out Awaits Army Response

Sergeant José Zuniga, a highly honored Presidio soldier, returned home to San Francisco yesterday after creating a media firestorm by announcing his homosexuality during last weekend's gay rights activities in Washington, D.C. As he stepped off the plane at San Francisco International Airport, Zuniga appeared stunned as newspaper and television photographers crowded around him. The twenty-three-year-old soldier, a Persian Gulf War veteran recently named the Sixth Army's Soldier of the Year, said he assumes the Defense Department will start discharge proceedings against him when he returns to work this morning.

Zuniga rebutted suggestions that he was manipulated by gay rights activists.

—San Francisco Examiner
April 28, 1993

April 29 was a media circus well before my arrival at the Presidio to meet with my company commander. The sun must have just been rising as television camera crews perched themselves outside my Market Street doorstep. Laurie had negotiated an agreement with the cameramen that they would avoid filming the front of our house. Just in case, she had covered the address with silver duct tape and cardboard the night before.

A brief statement delivered while walking to my car was all they were getting this morning. They seemed to treasure every second of footage. The crews followed me in a caravan of satellite linkup trucks to the Burger King on post, where I was to meet James for breakfast. They taped footage as I got out of the car, got back in the car to retrieve some notes, got out of the car again, and walked into the restaurant. Not allowed inside the fast-food restaurant, the cameramen zoomed in through the glass doors to tape footage of soldiers and civilians shaking my hand.

Henrietta Stewart, a Family Advocacy Center volunteer, took my outstretched hand and pulled me toward her with a hug.

"I'm so proud of you . . . and scared at the same time," she said, her hazel doe eyes moist against her richly colored skin. "We went through the same thing, baby. Used to be I couldn't be served in a restaurant with white patrons. . . . But you've just got to move on."

Such warmth fortified my conviction.

Driving to company headquarters, James and I rushed past a throng of cameramen. We were already ten minutes late for our 0800 appointment. Lieutenant Colonel Fredericks and the provost marshal stood under the shade of a eucalyptus tree, coordinating via radio with the unseen ringmasters of today's charade. The cameramen tripped over cement parking blocks, each other, and ran into vehicles and trees as they herded us toward the Headquarters Company commander's office, then stopped dead in their tracks as James and I entered the building.

The drama ended and reality began just inside these doors.

"Close the door, Sergeant Zuniga," First Sergeant Richard Griego instructed.

"Yes, First Sergeant," I answered assertively, quietly closing the door behind me with a lingering hand. This would be a short meeting, James had advised me, with as few players as possible. Captain Tracey Sharpe looked uncomfortable in his chair, nervously eyeing us, as well as the packets of paperwork (red tape) pinned under his elbow. Formalities seemed over before they even started.

"We all know why we're here," Sharpe muttered. "Even if we are a *little* late."

"Sir, the press—"

A shift in his gaze and wave of his hand ended my attempt at an explanation. There was no excuse.

"This may seem like a frivolous question, but Army Regulation 675-1 requires I ask and you answer. Sergeant Zuniga, are you a homosexual?"

Was this really necessary? Had front-page articles in the *Washington Post*, *The New York Times*, *San Francisco Examiner* and *Chronicle*, and his hometown newspaper, the *Sacramento Bee*, left a shred of doubt? What of the coverage on CNN and every major network? Hadn't General Mallory shared the letter couriered directly to his home at the precise time I was delivering my speech in D.C.?

I looked at James, who nodded incredulously. He and I had decided in advance that this was not the time for a political statement or any conduct underscoring the absurdity of what was happening. Make it easy for them to follow the book, James advised. "Yes, sir," I said neutrally.

Within less than ten minutes Captain Sharpe had breezed through the required bureaucratic drill. He notified me of my proposed separation from the Army, "under Chapter 15, Paragraph 15-3B, Army Regulation 635-200." He further stated he was recommending my military service be characterized as honorable. A crisp salute, about-face, and fifteen paces to the front door began the official end of my military career, which had actually ended at the podium in Old Postal Square.

I was not allowed to return to duty at the public-affairs office. The rumor around post was that General Mallory's initial response to my letter had been rather . . . dramatic.

"They [the activists] know where I live!" the general was quoted as saying with the disdain of someone who would rush off to his doctor to make sure he hadn't contracted AIDS from the encounter.

The general had been blunt in pronouncing he didn't want me in the same building with him. My hope that he would understand the motivation behind my action was dashed. I came to realize that first week that sadness had developed after his initial anger. I thought he would not plan a retribution.

My first assignment in my new gig involved researching and writing the Letterman U.S. Army Hospital history. I would be working with hospital archives stored and never touched except for brief hauls from one empty space to another. This wasn't exactly journalism, I thought, but at least my skills and abilities would be used wisely in my last days of military service. I worked directly for the hospital commander, a colonel with whom I had worked in the past on medical feature stories ranging from stress to smoking to AIDS.

My first day back on duty my sagging spirits were bolstered as the hospital commander and I walked the hospital halls to the archive storage area. Civilians and soldiers alike smiled, mouthed words of encouragement, or stopped us dead in our tracks to shake my hand, the way people were starting to do in the Castro. The medical community is indeed more tolerant of diversity than other professional communities, I had known that since my training days at Fort Sam Houston. Even the colonel did not seem to mind.

Four days into the assignment, before I could even skim through the archives, I was unexplainably transferred to the Headquarters Company supply room. Someone in my chain of command had to know why this transfer was ordered. No one told me the reason. I suppose the Army didn't feel the need to give an explanation for inflicting clerical drudgery on its Soldier/Journalist of the Year.

My duties included supervising two specialists and answering, on average, three telephone calls daily, dealing with such matters as toilet-paper depletion in the barracks or a misplaced lawn mower. This new action was degrading but expected. Tracy Thorne, an A-6 Intruder aviator, had warned me during the March weekend about the lengths the military would go to punish nonconformists. After spending more than $2 million training him to fly, the Navy had assigned Tracy to an orderly room pending discharge. His mission: Making photocopies.

I was isolated from the barracks in which I had lived for months. I was assigned to live in the post's Gulag, an empty building with a private bathroom and shower. *My* privacy was cited as the reason for this move. The real *reason* was that the privacy of the soldiers with whom I'd shared a community shower for months was now compromised by Don't-Drop-the-Soap ignorance. Sharing a dormitory, shower, and foxhole with hundreds of fresh and pimple-faced soldiers through basic training and a war, I assiduously respected common decency and my comrades' boundaries. I kept my sexuality to myself. Prior history was discounted.

Most painfully of all, I was urged to wear a pager while on duty like a criminal under house arrest, so that the command could keep a tight rein on my activities.

Were it not for the hours of discussions Captain Sharpe and I shared during two weeks of administrative limbo, I would surely have gone crazy. Before coming out, I had been used to constant work and constant contact. Now my only contact was with a rotary telephone, a few friends, and those who called me "Sergeant" but whose eyes avoided me after my revelation.

Fortunately, in my commander I had a friend. Captain Sharpe considered himself an intellectual, along with being a soldier and a man of action.

Behind closed doors we dropped all pretenses. His questions did not start with "Sergeant Zuniga," and my answers did not end in "Sir." His seemed a genuine desire to understand; most people seem to live in a shallow blur. He asked general to complex questions about homosexuality, the movement, and the gay cause. His luminous face was a mirror reflecting my own new, rapt interest in the subject. Questions are better than obliviousness, I thought.

His first question was if I had risen the military ladder unaware of what I would someday become.

"Where destiny leads the willing," I shared, "it tends to drag the unwilling. I had to know that I could help destroy the vortex of innuendo and misrepresentation. Until then, I was one of the unwilling."

I sometimes wish I could take credit for the culmination of a master plan years in the making. But I cannot. I accomplished what I did because of who I was, although I never fully revealed my true character—even to myself.

Why didn't you turn yourself in? This discharge would have been a Top Secret affair, he speculated. Why the media fanfare?

In reviewing the genesis of my decision, I reminded him that before I came out, I had come to him and asked, however covertly, his advice in a matter that would change my life forever and impact many others. I saw in him a wise and compassionate officer who, of anyone in the command, would understand my dilemma.

Not more than two weeks before my announcement, I had waited in the hallway outside his office to talk to him. Contrary to company policy, I had made no appointment but simply announced my arrival. Captain Sharpe knew I was not the type to ignore protocol. I never dropped in for casual conversation. If I was waiting for him, especially after close of business, there was a powerful reason.

"Sergeant Zuniga, what's up?" he asked while straightening his desk.

"I need your help, sir."

I sat down and quickly came to the point, veiling my predicament in a Rosa Parks analogy about the power of one human being to affect change in the world.

"What's your question?" he asked, his question meant to search the fire with a poker.

I evaded the question and he gave me the best advice he could, Captain Sharpe now said defensively. He still did not seem to understand. There was a logical basis for my decision not to make a full disclosure that day, I assured him. I did not wish to place him in a position where he would have to compromise *his* loyalty to the Army. I needed to make a difference. I believed maximum exposure was needed to undo the harm done by homophobes. And I believed that to do that I had to reduce language and politics to a form that penetrates the masses. The key was to turn my personal sacrifice into a sound bite and ensure it was spread far and wide.

"I understand that. . . . But if you trusted me enough to ask my advice that day, why not trust me with the truth?" he asked.

At once I saw that his question was not only naive but an example of exactly what was wrong with the policy. By *The Book*, he had no discretion once my secret was disclosed to him. He had to run this information up the chain of command until I was either discharged or sent to Fort Leavenworth.

"I suspected for a long time," the career officer retorted, with a hint of resentment that he had not clued in two weeks ago.

"Did it make a difference?" I asked, making a final point.

A muscle in his face twitched and a pout became a sly smile. A peek behind the thin disguise. I knew he would ensnare me eventually. His kindness and sympathy were the bait.

"No, and it doesn't make a difference now, Zuniga. Don't get defensive on me," he pouted, his head looking askance at me. He wanted to convey more, but what? Insights, too difficult and taxing, evidently, for completely lucid formulation. It *did* make a difference! The world, not only the Army, now knew. The book would be followed to the letter of the law. Unfortunately, there would be a few unexpected twists as to which parts of the book were followed.

While most of the city slept under the fingers of fog that envelop San Francisco from dawn to dusk, a tightly knit formation of 120 soldiers, ARMY spelled out across the heaving chests of three squad leaders at the head of the formation, trudged up the steepest hill on the Presidio. Careful to avoid the potholes that could shatter a shin or sprain an ankle, they moved like a giant caterpillar, lifting and setting down each foot with every "left, right, left . . ." in the cadence. Picture slaves pushing and pulling oars on a great Roman vessel to the command and whip of the master, each oar move choreographed by his barked cadence.

There were actually 121 runners this morning; I no longer counted myself among them. Where I once led the group in five-mile runs, encouraging the few who lagged behind (usually because they neglected their physical upkeep), today I ran second from the last in the third rank.

My mind was swimming with trivial thoughts and worries. I will accept the honorable discharge, not because I am giving up but because it's the only way I can make a difference, I thought, managing to distract myself and keeping from instinctively uttering a word of the age-old cadences.

"When my granny was eighty-nine, she did PT just to stay alive! ... She growled, 'Son, who you talking to? ... I'm an instructor at the Airborne School!' "

No one seemed to mind my silence. No slap on the wrist for nervously checking my watch every ten minutes. I was impatient to finish the run, drive home, throw on my uniform, finish out processing, and hold a press conference, in that order.

I spent over an hour dissuading CNN and several local news outfits from ambushing the "Soldier of the Year's final run." I finally lied to them about the time and route of the run. I was hoping for as uneventful a day as possible, under the circumstances. If the Army was planning to separate me with a minimum of hassles to avoid bad press, as it seemed to be doing, I would let them. When free of their yoke and the possibility of reprisals, I would use my career as an indestructible weapon against them, telling my story to anyone who would listen.

An uneventful week had passed since my return. Sure the reporters and cameramen were enough to make my life chaotic, but thanks to their extensive coverage, the Army appeared to be handling my case with kid gloves.

"Don't go holding a press conference during duty hours, Zuniga!" Sharpe screamed as I walked out the door to do exactly that. Of course I understood the ramifications of doing so, especially now that I had been given a direct order prohibiting me from speaking to the press while on duty.

I was to meet James in the Letterman Hospital parking lot at 1625. Laurie said she would try to come, although a heavy case load buried her desk in paperwork. First-years get all the grunt work, she complained. Pulling into the lot, I glanced toward the Lombard Gate. Television satellite linkups lined the streets. Two military police vehicles whizzed by, stationing themselves alongside the gate.

Laurie watched patiently as I parked the car, grabbing my civvies from the trunk, and walked the twenty feet to where she sat on a concrete bench beside the hospital's automatic doors. I was in no hurry to do this, and she knew it.

"Looks like a huge turnout!" she announced after giving me a tender hug and warm kiss. My heart really needed that, I meant to say, but probably forgot. I wished I had the time and that my hands weren't full, so that I could wrap my arms around her and hold her. Unfortunately, these days had forced the three of us to shift the priority from our relationship to the exigencies of the movement.

Dave and Laurie were evolving into the eight-cylinder motive force behind my fight. But mistakenly, as the future grew bleaker, I sold my soul to The Fight, pushing away the need to restore balance to my conflicted emotional life. Although to what extent The Fight was to blame is questionable.

Her arm wrapped around my waist, Laurie explained she had spent all morning calling reporters, selling the news conference. "Not a tough sell, even to the 'CBS Evening News.' " I changed in the men's room, mentally rehearsing the speech I had written less than an hour before. How would it play? Would they consider me a quitter? Obviously I would prefer to continue serving, but that was not an option. At least if I was out of the Army, I thought, I could fight the thousands of discharges that would occur if the ban were not lifted.

As the television cameras focused on the Lombard Street Gate welcome sign, James and I quizzed each other. The press conference had been hastily called this morning after my battalion commander approved and signed the orders authorizing an honorable discharge. A two-second pause to muster some courage and then I read my statement:

This afternoon the approving authority for homosexuality discharges at the local level approved my honorable discharge from the Army effective midnight, May 20, 1993.

The military's willingness and determination to expel me from service despite my exemplary record makes today one of the saddest days of my life—a day when the military career I have cultivated for more than three years through combat and peacetime is over. It is also a day, however, that helps strengthen my resolve to fight against the formidable opposition to lifting the ban on gay men, lesbians, and bisexuals in the armed forces.

My choice not to contest discharge may appear to be a retreat from that fight. Nothing is further from the truth. My accepting this discharge and requesting deletion from the Standby Reserve is a way of ensuring that I am free to tell my story without the substantial restrictions of the Uniform Code of Military Justice.

It was never my intention to adjudicate this case in the media. It was and continues to be my intention to be a living example of the irrationality of a policy that would have the Army terminate my distinguished career solely because I am gay.

Please let me make clear that because I have severed my ties with the military, I will now be able to tell my story from Middle America to the Halls of Congress without the military imposing a gag order. This fight to ensure gay men, lesbians, and bisexuals are not forced to live in the agonizing silence I was forced to live in for so long will continue over the next few months.

My career is the weapon I have chosen to use in that fight—a fight I will devote myself entirely to in the months before President Clinton makes a decision on this issue.

I was happy to announce the Army's decision to grant me an honorable discharge. Now it seemed I was but a few days of paperwork away from freedom. Above all, I was relieved because I had come to the conclusion that an effective war against this directive could be fought only if I severed my ties with the military. Fighting the discharge in court would mean my story could not be spread to the hinterlands.

The concern that people would think I was quitting the fight rumbled in my mind. I rationalized that there was already a number of similar federal cases being adjudicated in the media and in our judicial system. Mine would make no immediate difference. Meinhold, Steffan, and Thorne all had cases winding their way through the judicial system. My case would be so far behind (considering Steffan's case, filed in 1987, did not reach a judge's bench until 1993), yet I'd be suffering the same daily indignations and extra scrutiny. By severing my ties I was free to travel, tell my story, and put a human face on the issue without the fear of retribution or censure many of them endured for the cause.

SLAP IN THE FACE

I BEGAN THE LENGTHY OUTPROCESSING RITUAL THAT PRECEDES ANY discharge on the rainy morning of May 11. If all went according to schedule, my company commander assured me, I would be out of the Army in three days.

But the Army was not through with me yet.

A mandatory interview with an Army Education Center counselor was interrupted when my first sergeant paged me. It was urgent I report to the battalion headquarters. Within ten minutes I was standing at attention before my battalion commander's oak-stained desk. Wayne Agness was a lieutenant colonel who believed in doing everything by the book. An infantry officer new to this command, he believed that anything less constituted disorder.

"Sergeant Zuniga, I am considering whether you should be punished under Article 15 for committing a violation of Article 134 of the Uniform Code of Military Justice, punishable under court-martial with up to a year in the brig, do you understand?" he said sternly.

I stared at him in disbelief. This man had signed my honorable discharge just forty-eight hours ago. What was going on here? And what the hell was Article 134? They'd been holding this in reserve, thinking that they might strategically damage my rear flank as I retreated. Since I'd announced my discharge, they calculated the media spotlight was now off and they could do their dirty work.

I clenched my teeth.

"You have forty-eight hours to decide whether you wish to face a military court-martial board or accept Article 15 proceedings. Do you understand the difference between the two?" he asked rhetorically.

"Yes, sir!" I was stunned.

I phoned James. He had been informed by the Army prosecutor just minutes before. The charge was that I had worn an unauthorized ribbon on my uniform at the Honoring Our Allies event. Apparently, James explained, the command had ordered an enlargement of a *San Francisco Examiner* full-color photograph of me under a 72-point banner headline, " '93 Soldier of the Year: I'm Gay," on its front page. The command's mission was to ensure that every award and decoration pinned on my uniform was legitimate. Their goal was to try to discredit me.

There was no reason for alarm, I told myself; my conscience was clear. I had been recommended for the award shortly before my coming out. Luck had been on my side; the March coincided with my transfer from the Presidio to South Korea. The award was an end-of-tour commendation for my accomplishments while at the Presidio. I had called the Military Personnel Office to ensure the award had been posted in my records and was told, in no uncertain terms, that it had been. Every soldier in the Army knows that once an award is posted in his personnel record they can wear the award— no official ceremony is required by any written U.S. Army regulation.

The drive down Divisadero Street to James's place should have been agonizing. I was going to court this morning. *Soft and easy music*, a warm spring sun, and a gentle breeze stroked my brush-cut hair. Every traffic light turned green as I approached—a good omen, I predicted, of things to come. There was no way Lieutenant Colonel Agness could find me guilty of such an offense. He knew me far better than that. Agness had signed my promotion orders, my battalion soldier of the month certificate, and with battalion Sergeant Major James McKay, he had recommended me for the Soldier of the Year competition. They knew my deeply imbued convictions and profound interest in achieving honor.

The Army's accusation was triggered by self-defense or a need for political propaganda. James and I knew it was driven by the top brass, the yes-men. Evidence of their effort to make an example of me was the absurd but strategically sound delegation of court-martial and Article 15 authority from Captain Sharpe, whom the command deemed as too lenient, to my battalion commander, a field-grade officer who could impose harsher punishment. His track record as a ball-breaker in these matters was well established. Their plan, I hoped, would fail because Agness was a fair and honorable man.

James shaved his now-signature beard off for this occasion. He wanted nothing to jeopardize what should be an airtight case. I gave him a copy of my written statement and he copied it, immediately placing the copy in his portfolio. We had also asked for Sergeant First Class Banks to testify on my behalf. After all, the crux of their argument seemed to question my supervisor's promise to push through my orders. Sergeant First Class Banks was resistant to attend the proceedings, and it had been unclear after we talked that afternoon whether he would appear or not. He had no choice in the matter, James explained. If Agness ordered him to testify, he would. I had worked through all the possible scenarios. There was no way the very people who at one time guided my career and praised me as a hero would scorn and disparage me.

My spirits were high. James and I confidently discussed battle plans for after my discharge. I opened the Acura's sunroof, turned up Mariah Carey's "Emotions," and relaxed.

James and I waited in the Headquarters Command Battalion anteroom for the battalion commander to arrive. At 0850, Agness and everyone in my chain of command—Sergeant Major McKay, Captain Sharpe, and First Sergeant Griego—barricaded themselves in Agness's office. Not less than a month ago, Agness and I had met in his office, a massive room attractive in a derivative way, its simple interior an expression of its occupant's simplicity. I had interviewed him for a personality feature.

Now how different the circumstances. That man would today play judge and jury in my case.

Sergeant First Class Banks and Sergeant McGarrah joined James and me. They were both ready to testify on my behalf if called to, they claimed. James suggested their involvement might not be necessary in these proceedings. The facts were in black and white and needed little support, he explained. Regardless, I was happy to have two more people in my corner.

The buzz of the intercom on the secretary's desk indicated the proceeding was about to start. "Good luck," the secretary said, a look of sympathy on a face usually stuck in a stalwart, inexpressive blank.

The almost-seven-foot-tall battalion adjutant (another name for an overpaid uniformed gofer) barged into Agness's office.

"Sir, a call from garrison. Colonel Renn." The message delivered, the lieutenant closed the door gently.

It was no secret to anyone on post that Sergeant Zuniga's trial by court-martial or Article 15 proceedings—whichever I chose, and I chose to waive the court-martial—would start at exactly 0900, May 14, 1993, in the Headquarters Command Battalion building. James and I glanced at each other but said nothing. We knew what the other was thinking. Garrison. Colonel Renn. Should we worry? I began to wonder if the word "Executioner" should be added to Agness's list of roles.

By 0910 Agness was ready to start. Following regulations, I knocked on the door and waited for permission to enter. That given, I marched to the center of the room, centered myself on Agness's desk, came to rigid attention, and delivered a crisp salute. "Sir, Sergeant Zuniga reporting as ordered!"

Agness returned the salute, ordered me to stand at ease, and asked James, who had been standing patiently at the door, to join "the party." My nervous hand signed a waiver for full court-martial proceedings. I had decided, with James's input, that I would do so because, although it would achieve much more press coverage and highlight the Army's vindictive spirit, a court-martial would not only distract attention from the irrationality of my discharge but could possibly delay it indefinitely. They would no doubt also dredge up other charges. James once said, "Every soldier is a walking UCMJ violation." I wanted no more digging, as knowledge of certain details could be devastating to me and might also harm the very cause I aimed to advance.

My eyes wandered from their disciplined dead-ahead stare. Trouble? The first possible sign had been the phone call from garrison. As I stood not more than three feet from Agness's desk, I saw a sure sign that something was very wrong. A set of specialist pin-on ranks (the rank below Sergeant) sat ominously on the corner of his desk. It was clear they had already decided to demote me. I didn't know whether James had seen them.

"Sergeant Zuniga," Agness read from the manual, his words delivered slowly and carefully. "I am considering punishment under Article 15 for the following misconduct: In that you did in the Washington, D.C., metropolitan area, on or about 24 April 1993, wrongfully and without authority, wear upon your uniform the ribbon representing the Meritorious Service Medal.

"As you know, we have a copy of the *Examiner*, and several other newspapers." He pulled them out of a desk drawer. A picaresque approach. "You will have an opportunity to address this charge. But first I want you to understand I have not yet made a decision. I will not impose any punishment unless I am convinced beyond a reasonable doubt that you committed the offense," he explained. "There is no predetermined outcome here."

What about the rank inches from his stubby fingers? Prior Planning Prevents Piss Poor Performance? Or was his statement that he had not yet made a decision true only because it had already been made for him by higher-ups? Agness was taking on more and more the aura of an executioner. Time to pray; it certainly couldn't hurt.

I respectfully declined to make any comment now. Instead I submitted a four-page written rebuttal to the charge. After the statement was read I would answer any questions. My requests were granted. Agness asked everyone to step outside while he read the statement. Before we made our exit, however, James began an impassioned plea for reason and a warning that should this proceeding fail to administer justice fairly, the backlash to the Army would be sensational. Whether the overt interjection of real world politics was appropriate or not, Agness's interest was piqued. A rap at the door forced an unexpected end to James's monologue.

"Phone call, sir. Colonel Renn, again."

Agness motioned for the room to clear.

Here is my memo:

13 May 1993

MEMORANDUM FOR Lieutenant Colonel Wayne C. Agness, Commander, Headquarters Command Battalion, Presidio of San Francisco, California
SUBJECT: Article 15 proceedings

1. Sir, I have elected Article 15 proceedings (instead of a court-martial) for two reasons. First, I have faith that you have not prejudged me. And second, to bring this matter to a closure expeditiously without creating a media circus and continuing to be an active-duty thorn in the Army's side. This memorandum addresses the allegation of wrongdoing leveled against me in the Article 15 reading before you two days ago.

2. During the week of 12 April, I was informed by Sergeant First Class Donald Banks, my public-affairs supervisor, that I had been recommended for a Meritorious Service Medal. My squad leader, Staff Sergeant Pleasant Lindsey III, was tasked with writing bullet comments for the award recommendation. I assisted him in drafting a list. An award recommendation form, Department of the Army Form 638-1, was then typed and, after I caught some misspellings, was retyped by the public-affairs secretary.

In a conversation at the end of that week, Sergeant First Class Banks advised me that the possibility of the award being approved before my permanent change of station [PCS] was slim. He said, however, that he would push the paperwork through the system while I was on temporary duty at the Defense Information School in Indianapolis. He added that the certificate, not the orders, would be forwarded to my new command, the 2nd Infantry Division in Korea. By so doing, the new command would be impressed with my work at the Presidio, to include the 1992 Forces Command Print Journalist of the Year honor.

I advised Sergeant First Class Banks that my last supervisor at the 1st Cavalry Division public-affairs office hand-carried my end-of-tour award recommendation form to get it approved before I left that command (a far larger command than the Presidio). The award was approved and posted in my official records while I was in transit to my assignment at the Presidio. I wore that ribbon upon hearing it was posted in my records. I believe this to be proper procedure. I was taught that this procedure was in compliance with applicable regulations. The former battalion commander formally presented the 1st Calvary Division's award certificate in an awards ceremony here. As Sergeant First Class Banks acknowledges, the presentation made a remarkable impression on the command.

I was conscious of the timing issues involved in wearing the MSM ribbon on 24 April. On 22 April, in preparation for my departure for Washington, D.C., and my last duty day on the Presidio, I phoned the Military Personnel Office to determine whether the MSM had been approved. In that telephone conversation, I was advised that the award had been approved. It is clear to me now that I should not have trusted a telephone conversation with people with whom I had dealt with in the past.

It is difficult to put into words the incredible stress I was under as I prepared to make a life-altering speech in Washington, D.C. But I would never have worn an award to which I was not entitled. I did not think twice when accepting a fellow soldier's word at face value. The soldier I spoke to told me that my award had been posted. Whether that soldier made an error or there was a miscommunication is irrelevant. There should be no doubt, however, that I made the telephone call. And it should come as no surprise that I trusted and assumed the answer I received was more than sufficient for me to pin the MSM ribbon on my uniform.

Additionally, I had no reason to doubt that the medal would have been approved and awarded. Based on my conversation with Sergeant First Class Banks, my accomplishments during my tour of duty here, and my good standing with the command, it was logical for me to believe that the recommendation would be approved in record time, despite the bureaucratic politics involved in awarding a sergeant a Meritorious Service Medal. It is a shame that, in hindsight, I now regret not having walked across the street to the Military Personnel Office and requested to see proof of their work.

3. Sir, I ask that you to take into consideration my service record when deciding my fate. I wore each and every commenda-

tion I had earned in my brief career on 24 April 1993. I needed to dispel pernicious rumors about gay service members by using my career as an example of the accomplishments a gay soldier can garner with honor and distinction in our armed forces. The last thing I needed was unnecessary Army or media scrutiny. Indeed, the absence of the MSM ribbon would not have detracted from the reality that I wear five Army Commendation Medals, an Army Achievement Medal, the Southwest Asia Medal, the Good Conduct Medal, the Kuwaiti Liberation Medal, and a host of other ribbons and decorations on my uniform. One less ribbon would not have detracted from the irrefutable fact that I am the 1992 Sixth U.S. Army Soldier of the Year. I had no motive to lie about the Meritorious Service Medal, because by so doing I would cast doubts on my record as a whole and risk diminishing the impact of my actions.

Finally, I point to the very nature of my actions on 24 April 1993. Sir, a major factor in my decision to "come out" was to live honorably. I could not live with the fact that duplicity is a requirement for continued service to my country. My sense of honor and integrity, as reflected in this and other actions in my past, makes it inconsistent for me to wear an award to which I am not entitled. I believe that my action regarding the Meritorious Service Medal was not in violation of the Uniform Code of Military Justice. Insofar as my conduct regarding the medal may have caused even the appearance of impropriety, I apologize. But I must plead Not Guilty to any charge I violated any article of the Uniform Code of Military Justice.

José M. Zuniga
Sergeant, U.S. Army

Less than ten minutes later, Agness's coven of courtesans was called back into the office.

James looked nervous. For an instant, my mind wandered from this plane to another. Callie Vassar's interpretation of *Antigone* began to percolate in my already jumbled mind. The struggle between Creon and Antigone dramatizes the conflict between private conscious and public duty, sacred obligation and arbitrary punishment by a State.

I was as mute as a dream and focused on something elsewhere when a whisper brought me back to reality. "Joe?"

James tugged at my arm. We had been asked back in.

"Your statement was very well written," Agness began in editorial sophism. "But I just can't accept it on face value. The facts as I know them are that you *never* called MILPO and that you wore an MSM ribbon *without* authorization."

James tried to discredit the sworn statements produced by an Army prosecutor who interviewed the personnel-office staff. Before addressing individual testimonies, James pointed out the striking similarity in each statement. With the exception of personal data, each was verbatim, to include misplaced commas. As if that wasn't enough, many of them had denied knowing a Sergeant Zuniga at all, James added.

"Apparently, since his coming out," James quipped, "six out of fourteen people in that office, some of whom had been his acquaintances if not friends, suddenly developed selective amnesia."

The judge, jury, and executioner in theoretical conflict within this lieutenant colonel's mind could not, or would not, process this new evidence. Why? Because, Agness countered, according to standard operating procedure, had I called the personnel office no one would have discussed personal information over the phone. In Agness's mind, my claim to have heard official word about my award from anyone at MILPO, doppelgänger or otherwise, was neither credible nor even plausible.

"Privacy Act of 1974, Public Law 93-579," he quickly added. "You of all people should know that shortcuts are never taken here. Everything in the Army is run by the book, at least in my battalion they are."

I had been listening and waiting to engage him. But gradually, with every furrow of his brow, my reticence increased.

"Frankly, I think your actions were despicable. You violated our trust in you, and simultaneously sacrificed, if not destroyed, your honor and integrity. Your actions were simply those of an opportunist looking for some type of earthly immortality." Agness nodded his grizzled head indignantly. He grabbed the stack of newspapers from on top of his desk and threw them in the trashcan. This act gave a tinny ring to the deepest chords struck by his campaign. He should have scripted a loud "thud" to punctuate the point. No. This was farce, not drama.

Agness had failed completely to understand the emotions that had

swayed me and thousands like me to abandon the closet that is tanta-
mount to rejecting one's own identity. Control your rage, I chanted
to myself, worried I might fail and worsen what I knew to be my
predetermined fate. I was strangled with rage, though, unable to speak
even if I wanted to.

James glared at the lieutenant colonel with scornful eyes, a dull glit-
ter of mingled anger and frustration. "How much of this zeal is your
judgment of my client's homosexuality, the morality issue? Did you
even listen to his words? And did you cut through the obscurity of the
facts presented by the prosecution?"

With a wave of his hand, Agness cut short James's comments. Agness
did not care for rationalizations, repeating earlier statements ad nauseam. The following ear-chafing military what-for became an unending curse.

Agness finally turned to his advisers.

"Captain Sharpe, your recommendation?"

"His lack of loyalty reflects poorly upon him as a soldier . . ."
Betrayal.

The lieutenant colonel pounded his fist on his desk. "That's a different matter! I want your recommendation on the MSM issue."

"He is guilty of an opprobrious UCMJ violation and should be punished accordingly." Captain Sharpe's words were cutting to shreds any
last vestige of hope.

"First sergeant?"

First Sergeant Griego grew pale. He clearly did not want to answer
the plug-pulling question, but knew he must. "If found guilty, Sergeant
Zuniga should be punished like any other soldier. But I feel his outstanding record to date should be considered before making any decision," he said, adding a wry poignancy to the kangaroo court
proceedings.

An abbreviated pause. Agness's deadly contemptuous eyes, though
used to seeing me, were battling something nearly inviolate within
him—moral strictures, forcing him to look beyond rather than at me,
assigning invisibility, anonymity, namelessness.

The first sergeant looked at me from across the office, and when
our eyes met, his face changed in degree from stoic to sorrowful to
vaguely sad. Surely he was not practiced in which face to present to
the Soldier of the Year. I fixed my eyes on his so relentlessly that he

soon turned away and slowly bowed his head, stopping when his eyes reached his combat boots.

Agness dismissed my argument, through his lopsided sneer, with a screed from the UCMJ Manual. Interesting how the law keeps some from the arduous and often unpleasant task of thinking.

"All matters presented in defense, mitigation, and consideration having been considered, I find you guilty as charged of violating Article 134 of the Uniform Code of Military Justice."

My face became a cubist rendering, planar and unassimilated.

"A letter of reprimand* will be placed in your Military Personnel Record. Additionally, because you have shown an inability to serve as a noncommissioned officer, you will be reduced in rank and grade to that of Specialist (E-4), effective immediately."

My chin, lips, and nostrils quivered, the sadness that one feels during the closing measure of a song smothering me like gospel blues.

The specialist pin-on ranks still sat on the corner of Agness's desk. They had been pre-ordained. This was not justice, this was a morality play dealt like a three-card-monte game.

I was stripped of my rank minutes after Agness's verdict. The first sergeant led me to the conference room. We both knew how wrong the outcome had been. Yet as I stood at attention before him, he tore the sergeant stripes off my collar and replaced the emptiness with specialist ranks. For a faint minute we each bordered on the brink of sentimentality, eyes temporarily glazed, but ashamed of being lachrymose.

James fought valiantly. The first sergeant had put his neck out on the line for me by asking for clemency or a reduction in punishment. The typical punishment for such a first offense was a letter of reprimand, James later told me. The command had obviously gone for my jugular with a draconian punishment.

I shivered with concentration as I drove up Divisadero on my way home. Something in the plan had gone wrong. The proof of the terrible mistake was pinned on my collar. That afternoon, for the

---

*Article 15 Letter of Reprimand is contained in Appendix E.

first time since my decision, my confidence, energy, and will to fight deserted me. A bitter taste invaded my mouth. This day exemplified the emptiness that stands in the place of patriotism when our government takes on the role of an engine cranking out discrimination rather than protection and inspiration for its people. Agness admitted in his statement that, in the normal course, the Meritorious Service Medal would have been awarded. Nothing was normal now and I bore the brunt of that change.

Franz Kafka's brief "Before the Law" is the story of a man who seeks the Law but is prevented from doing so by a doorkeeper who warns him that it is useless to try to get past him, for there is seemingly an unending number of doorkeepers who will also block his way. The man has not expected such difficulties: the Law, he thinks, should surely be accessible always, to everyone. Despite the doorkeeper's warning, he decides to stay and wait. Finally, at the edge of death, he asks the doorkeeper, "Everyone strives to reach the Law. . . . So how does it happen that for all these years no one but myself has ever begged for admittance?" In response, the doorkeeper shouts into the dying man's ear, "No one else could ever be admitted here, since this gate was made only for you. I am now going to shut it."

I took a deep breath as I parked the car in front of the house. Not bothering to announce my arrival, I ran up the stairs into the den and sat at my desk. I laid a tormented head on my arm and sobbed for the first time in years. I was not in the rage of hair-pulling and blasphemies the Army wished I'd be in. Mine was more a contemplative, angry trance, a feeling of resignation toward the perpetual abuse I was being dealt at the hands of the Army. Maybe they expected a fag to cry. In the solitude of my own home, at least, my tears would not disappoint them. Thank God I held myself together while facing them. They would derive no pleasure from my torment if I could manage to hide it.

Music? Dave must be home. His strong hand squeezing my knotted shoulder served as confirmation.

"They demoted me," I said.

Silence. He squeezed my shoulder again, harder.

The bankruptcy of my soul could not understand his silence.

"My life as a soldier has been wrapped, labeled, and stored away," I joked, succumbing to an intense consciousness of failure. Couldn't he hear my heart break with every sigh?

By way of reply, he pulled a clipping from his pocket and handed it to me. It was a poem, an elixir to salve the wounds of a love affair's decline and fall. My love affair with the Army?

"What does this mean?" I asked resentfully. Here I had forsaken everything, and he wasn't comforting me in my time of grief. But was it really resentment or a deflection of the wallowing confusion and loss I was feeling inside but chose to project on him? I had faulted him as insensitive before, but he revealed himself to be the opposite.

Dave didn't respond. He was obviously disappointed with my reaction, but he made one more attempt, appealing to the child that lingers inside every adult.

"I know you're hurt. . . . The question is, how does it heal, or will it *ever* heal. I know you're strong enough." Dave had said in a number of contexts that I was too good for the military. Rank, like pomp and circumstance, was not something he gave much thought. He could see how much it meant to me and offered sympathy, but there was no empathy. Right now I needed a double scoop of empathy and a pint of Ben & Jerry's.

Scrunching up my shoulders, I wiped away a lingering tear.

"And when you're not at your strongest, I'll be here for you," Dave said, kissing the nape of my neck. "Besides, you'll always be Private Pepé to me."

"Fuck off! It's *specialist* to you!" I was starting to cheer up.

He smirked, "It's a good thing to the media it will always be Soldier of the Year."

In my despondency, I drew myself a warm bath, but I couldn't make the water the temperature I wanted. Several times I dipped my foot into the bathwater water and each time it returned unsatisfied. I abandoned the bath, watching the water as it was sucked down the drain and with it, I hoped, my sorrow and self-pity.

"You've lost it all, Specialist Zuniga," Agness crowed in my

249

dreams that night, an outstretched arm pointing an accusing finger in my face. The rest of his coven followed suit, forming a semicircle of jabbing fingers.

We knew the Army's retaliatory attempt to discredit me backfired by eyeing the *Examiner*'s evening edition through the window of the newspaper rack. Having covered my story since the March, both the local and national press quickly jumped on the scoop. Reporters, through their fair and honest coverage, lambasted the Army morning, noon, and night—not to mention the hours in between, when "CNN Headline News" helped fill the news void. This was no liberal press knee-jerk reflex. The press offered the Army numerous opportunities to justify its action. In blunder after blunder, the Army could not deliver an answer worthy of credibility.

The *Examiner*'s 48-point banner headline that evening summed up the country's feeling: "SLAP IN THE FACE: Gay G.I. Demoted: Army's Parting Shot?" The *Denver Post* editorialized, "U.S. Army Demotes Soldier of the Year." But it was a story in *The New York Times*, "Military Demotes a Gay Sergeant: Contends Soldier Wore Medal He Hadn't Received," that became the Army's worst public-relations nightmare. An unnamed Presidio spokesman confirmed the existence of the award nomination packet—"Sergeant Zuniga had been recommended to receive the commendation"—a fact that until now was vehemently denied.

Presidio phone lines, a post operator told reporters, were tied up for the next two days as incredulous and heated calls were fielded from around the country. Hundreds of letters of support from members of the gay and straight community poured into the company mailroom daily, boosting my morale and providing the encouragement to help me carry on the fight. The Army's strategy had, in the end, failed miserably. In their bungled attempt to destroy my credibility, they had inadvertently elevated me to the status of martyr for the cause. But martyrdom exacted a personal toll that continues to be collected to this day.

I had expected the discharge. I was prepared for that, as much as one can prepare for such a devastating act. But the demotion still stirs anger. Luckily, the press continued to refer to me as "Sergeant Zuniga." Soon I became "former Sergeant Zuniga." The Army's paperwork said otherwise, but the press had learned not to put too much stock in military recordkeeping.

The public had another lesson [of the military's witch-hunt mentality] when Sergeant José Zuniga was demoted for appearing at the recent gay rights March "wearing a decoration which he had not yet been formally awarded." Mr. Zuniga had been named Soldier of the Year by the Sixth U.S. Army in 1992 [sic] but is about to be discharged from the army because he revealed his homosexuality during the March. An Army spokesman was quoted as saying, "The one thing we have in the Army is integrity. . . . When you misrepresent yourself, we take that very seriously." Which was precisely Mr. Zuniga's point. We should not be asking people to compromise their honor and integrity, to misrepresent themselves, as a condition of serving their country. Sergeant Zuniga took his integrity so seriously that he was prepared to sacrifice a brilliant military career for the sake of it.

Representative Gerry E. Studds (D-Mass.)
Washington, D.C., May 18, 1993

BIRTH OF A
GAY ACTIVIST

THE EMBERS WERE STILL BURNING A WEEK AFTER I DROVE OFF THE Presidio for the last time, a bittersweet taste in my mouth as I viewed the historic post through my rearview mirror. The *Chronicle* and *Examiner* printed updates daily, the angle changing from "unemployed twenty-four-year-old" to "gay activist with a multimillion dollar movie deal." The latter, of course, was not true. Had it not been for Dave and Laurie's financial support, my role as activist would have ended as soon as it began. Robert Bray was right—there is little glory or financial gain to be had as an activist.

National news magazine and talk-show hosts from Oprah Winfrey to Morton Downey Jr. vied for my story. But I avoided sensationalism to keep the message simple. Every gay and lesbian group in the country seemed to want my presence at their rally, fundraiser, or anniversary bash. I gladly obliged, as long as I was provided an opportunity to tell my story. If I was surprised at the political impact my action made, I was dumbfounded by the amount of media coverage. Like ripples in water, the Soldier of the Year's coming out had touched off even more debate in what Clinton had chosen to be the national homosexual issue of the year. It was now fueled by choruses of journalists across the country. It was probably for this reason that I landed on the Army's express-line train through discharge proceedings, slowing down only long enough for some retaliatory punishment. A bit of time to lick my wounds and then on to the next battle.

The media furor receded shortly after my honorable discharge. My role was not over, however. Instead of job-hunting, I embarked on a five-month speaking tour—and a serious course of debt accumulation—that would take me around the country, telling my story to anyone who would listen. The concept was abstract until my first speaking engagement on May 20 in San Francisco—a quick change in job description on the very day I was discharged from the Army. That very afternoon I had held a press conference at the San Francisco War Memorial to announce my discharge.

"Today the U.S. Army honorably discharged me for my public announcement April 24 that I was gay," I started my statement before a mass gathering of press. "Five generations of Zunigas have sacrificed their lives for the principles of loyalty to country. Today, a policy of bigotry has denied me the right to do the same because I am a gay man."

Later that evening, standing before a group of more than six hundred gay and lesbian members of the Bay Area NonPartisan Alliance, Zoe Dunning and I each accepted a 1992 Proud Gay American award. Of all the awards the Army had heaped on me, none meant as much to me now as this piece of glass on which the words *Proud Gay American: SGT José Zuniga, May 20, 1993* were etched. The ceremony ended, and a two-hour impromptu question-and-answer session began. Zoe and I were both new to the politics of gay activism and fundraising that require a degree in schmoozing neither of us sought, much less accepted. With the mass of people thinning, Zoe and I saw our chance to make an exit. Are you hungry too? we asked each other.

Just as my life began turning upside down in the military, Senator Nunn's high-profile hearings seemed aimed more at finding the needles that might support his position in the haystack of contrary facts. The senator's opposition was made clear daily in hearings where eliciting information was nowhere on the agenda. Nunn swore his hearings were fair and represented all points of view. His ploy was transparent, however. As I toured the hinterlands, America's teeth-gnashing, hand-wringing public discourse reached a crescendo. Deep in the bowels of a nuclear submarine, with the assistance of more than a hundred reporters and cameramen, six senators and television-watching America *inspected* close quarters, latrines, and showers. Sailors were asked, while standing in formation, how they would feel if they were *forced* to bunk not more than six inches from an openly gay sailor. How about taking showers with openly gay sailors? The senators' trip here was not in vain. The sought-after sound bites, usually examples of the basest bigotry, were delivered straight into America's living rooms. In a Machiavellian way, Nunn managed to make Americans squirm, shifting debate to a subject this prudish country tried to avoid: sex. A highly publicized fact-finding mission to Norfolk Naval Base revealed "the truth" about shipboard toilets, showers, and berthing facilities.

One statement made the banality of the hearings clearer than any other: Senator John Kerry, a Democrat from Massachusetts, observed that despite military antisodomy laws, heterosexuals were not punished for engaging in oral sex in the privacy of their bedrooms. "Heterosexuals don't practice sodomy," Republican Senator Strom Thurmond responded archly.

Senator Nunn's pledge to pursue the Truth seemed hollow. Plato wrote, "We can easily forgive a child who is afraid of the dark; the real tragedy of life is when men are afraid of the light." No one seemed more afraid than those impervious to a changing American philosophy. It was almost as if the military, supposedly an accurate reflection of American values, was choosing to disassociate itself from society's corrosive influence.

By early May the debate was fast approaching a compromise position: "don't ask, don't tell." The military would no longer ask recruits whether they "have homosexual tendencies," and, in return, lesbians and gay men would be allowed to serve so long as they didn't announce their sexuality. This proposal, gay activists pointed out, could work were society dealing with automatons. For human beings, however, not announcing one's sexual orientation is not the simple request that proponents of this compromise were having the public believe. There is no on-off switch when dealing with human identity. This proposed policy affected gays at the core of who we are as a people. In essence, it forced us on an ongoing basis not to accept ourselves, to constantly live a lie.

Having lived in the military closet and dealt with the many emotions that come into play, I believed it important that as many people as I was able to reach understood the central problem with Nunn's compromise: In asking service members to live a lie, he was compromising the very principles of dignity, honor, and integrity on which the military institution was based.

It is important to note the concessions that had been made in arriving at "don't ask, don't tell." The issue was no longer whether there were homosexuals in the military—suddenly, all conceded that there always had been and always would be. Moreover, because so many service members had dared come out of the closet, it was now conceded that there was no correlation between a service member's sexual orientation and his ability to perform. It was now common knowledge that homosexuality did not mean bad soldier—rather, like straights, gay people come in all varieties, from soldier of the year to the mediocre sailor simply wanting to complete a two-year enlistment.

These acknowledgments sounded a bitter defeat for those who even a year before had buried their heads in the sand over this issue. Unfortunately, it also forced a shift in the rhetorical focus to *unit cohesion*. "Don't ask, don't tell" purported to solve this problem by avoiding it; if a gay or lesbian soldier simply doesn't tell, the Rubicon will never be crossed and unit cohesion will not be compromised. This solution may have sounded credible in the halls of Congress, but it had no plausibility at any battle site.

While the order that lesbians and gay men "don't tell" anyone about their sexual orientation sounded simple, it simply was not. It was true that the military explicitly asked recruits twice if they were gay upon recruitment, and could indeed stop asking. But lesbian and gay service members could not be expected to make such a black-and-white, one-time decision not to tell as they went about their everyday lives. A closeted homosexual adhering to "don't ask, don't tell" would constantly have to negotiate a minefield to securely hide his sexual orientation; he must be on twenty-four-hour alert.

Heterosexuals, on the other hand, display their sexual orientation a hundred times each day, from discussing Saturday night events to simply commenting on the babysitter. If announcing one's homosexuality was to bring nondiscretionary discharge, all conversation could become a trap for the reckless. A gay G.I. would be forced to either withdraw from all social interaction with his peers or live an endless string of half truths, avoided answers, and downright lies.

Former Navy midshipman Joseph Steffan explained when asked why he told Naval Academy officials that he was gay: "Personal honor is an absolute—you either have honor or you do not." In short, good soldiers don't lie. Politicians debating this issue were arriving at political solutions that would force soldiers to make a choice between living honorably or continuing to serve their country.

The most obvious objection to this compromise was its discriminatory nature. It was acceptable to ask and to tell about sexual orientation so long as it was heterosexuality. In military life, as in civilian life, public discourse about heterosexuality is omnipresent: dates, weddings, divorces.

Lesbians and gay men do not seek special rights; nor do we flaunt our sexual orientation. Indeed, the gay and lesbian soldiers I knew during my three years of service were hardly the radical activists portrayed as reflective of the gay community. They were generally conservative individuals, sworn to defend their country, who only wanted to do their jobs without facing the risk of losing their livelihoods based on the discovery of an irrelevant characteristic. All we ever asked was the opportunity to be honest about our lives in the same manner as everyone else.

"I served my country selflessly and valiantly as a soldier and should be entitled to do so honestly and honorably as well," I told more than five hundred attendees of a fundraising dinner in San Jose, California. "Allowing gays and lesbians to be open about their sexuality will not wreck military cohesiveness if strong leadership works to ensure it does not. Forcing the military to abandon truth and fairness as central concepts, however, has the potential to do real damage to military honor itself."

The "don't ask, don't tell" train needed to be derailed before it got too far out of the Beltway—much worse, before President Clinton endorsed it as the law of the land.

*   *   *

Once the media sank its jowls into the issue, to Clinton's mortification, it refused to let go. When there wasn't a front-page news story reporting on the travails of an openly gay or lesbian service member, rumor- and speculation-chocked stories citing unnamed sources made the inside pages almost daily. By May 11, the debate had reached a crescendo following the testimony of Marine Colonel Fred Peck and Desert Storm hero, retired Army General H. Norman Schwarzkopf. Their testimony sent tongues wagging as both the tone and content of their pro-ban arguments were analyzed by the press.

"I love him as much as any of my sons," Peck said of his gay son, Scott, visibly struggling to balance his devotion to family and his loyalty to the military, "but I don't think there's any place for him in the military."

Nothing made their combined words of wisdom on the subject sound more hollow than, when on the heels of the Tailhook scandal and its fumbled cover-up investigation, General Schwarzkopf, speaking of war with an erotic attachment, testified that soldiers learn early in the induction phase that if they are racist they must get over it. Ditto when it comes to sexual harassment, he added either in self-delusion or in self-congratulation for a feat not yet accomplished. Yet heterosexuals could not be *persuaded* to live and work around open homosexuals, Schwarzkopf concluded without much more of an explanation. This from a man who in a speech to West Point cadets referred to Army personnel who never saw combat as "military fairies."

Senator Kennedy explained to the retired general that it is the military's responsibility to eradicate, or at least attempt to curb, prejudices recruits bring with them as excess baggage. The military, which has always denied its role in social experimentation, had successfully integrated blacks and women, not because their integration improved morale or unit cohesion, but because every government institution must reflect certain basic American ideals.

Colonel Peck and General Schwarzkopf, two all-American heroes, chose to cater to the basest of prejudices even when such prejudices affected loved ones, as was the case with Scott Peck. They wouldn't admit there was anything the least bit odd with their positions on the issue.

After a delayed and haphazard start, the progress made on the issue in a little less than four months was phenomenal. Openly gay and lesbian service members toured the nation, putting an all-important face on the issue. C-SPAN provided live coverage of the committee hearings. Newspaper editorials across the country, the strongest of which were in *The New York Times* and *Washington Post*, strongly urged President Clinton to proceed with his plan to lift the ban. The Mixners and Osborns of the gay movement kept weekly tallies of the number of congressional votes crossing over to our favor. Public-opinion polls and man-on-the-street reporting showed the country's support for lifting the ban increasing almost daily. The caveat was that any support relied on strong executive leadership, which the gay community believed it had secured.

Even Nelson Mandela weighed in on the issue when discussing the role South African gays would play in any future defense force: "The ANC rejects all forms of discrimination. This equally applies to discrimination on the basis of sexual orientation. . . . Promotion within the ranks shall be on the basis of merit." With such encouraging news pouring in from literally all fronts, the ban's repeal seemed a reality.

Cementing our defeat was Barney Frank, a Democratic representative from Massachusetts. In a move mistaken as our community's willingness to wave a white flag on the issue, Frank advanced the ambiguous "don't ask, don't shout, don't investigate." One of two openly gay congressmen, Frank was providing Clinton political cover by endorsing something not much unlike Senator Nunn's "don't ask, don't tell." No need to call the Psychic Friends Hotline to predict the outcome now, political analysts joked.

Representative Frank, already under fire for wishy-washy stands on other issues, delivered a vague plan allowing homosexuals to serve in the armed forces on one condition: that they express their sexuality only when off-duty, never on-duty. He touted his proposal as an improved version of "don't ask, don't tell."

His idea was worthless, considering the military makes no concrete distinction between on- and off-duty time. Whoops! Someone neglected to inform the congressman that service members are either on-duty or on-call in their off-duty hours every day of their enlistment.

In defending his stance, Frank predicted that without a compromise, Congress would overturn Clinton's expected July 15 executive order lifting the fifty-year-old ban.

"My sense was that many members of Congress had already made up their minds on this," Frank insisted in a May 13 *USA Today* article. "The choice seemed to be whether we would get zero or offer some kind of a compromise that was more permissive than Nunn's. I think my proposal reopens the battle for us."

The community vented its collective anger and frustration on a fellow gay man who was bartering away our rights just as we were beginning to secure them. By misunderstanding the community's wrath, the media helped propagate the notion that the gay congressman was our official spokesman and that his proposal met with widespread support.

The senator from Georgia must have been chortling to his buddies about how a *faggot* had screwed his own community by proposing something so fundamentally similar to his more conservative "don't ask, don't tell." In a sound-bite society, the differences between the two plans would evaporate and the appearance remain that a gay spokesman had endorsed the perpetuation of the closet.

Urvashi Vaid, former executive director of the NGLTF, most accurately described the gay community's frustration with Frank's pandering in a June 29 commentary in *The Advocate:* "Four decades of fighting for gay rights has brought us to where the hallmark of our oppression, the closet, is offered as the precondition for our progress. We are asked to stay in the closet (don't tell) in exchange for nondiscrimination (don't ask). They would allow us to be gay off-base, but not allow us to be open participants in the service. And they would leave the current policy intact."

Whether or not the votes were there, Barney Frank should have offered a proposal, if any at all this early in the game, that had a basis in the moral notion of equality. Frank's foolish proposal boiled down to maintaining the status quo, while attaching a new but untenable off-duty clause. The government stamp of second-class citizenship would remain firmly affixed. To hell with equality, he seemed to be saying. It's okay to agree to remain in the closet of our oppression, to continue catering to prejudice, so long as we can come out under the cover of darkness.

"This is not the time to raise the white flag," Representative Studds said on May 18 about Congressman Frank's solution. Studds continued:

> Several proposals have been put forward in recent days that would allow gay men and lesbians to serve in the military so long as they not reveal their sexual orientation. I cannot endorse such a compromise at this time.
>
> This battle has demonstrated that we have a long way to go in our struggle for dignity and equal rights, but also that we have come a long, long way. For the first time in our history, a national debate is taking place on what it means to be a gay or lesbian— that in itself represents enormous progress. Even our opponents have been forced to acknowledge what we have always known: that gay men and lesbians have served honorably and are not unfit for military service.
>
> Our adversaries have done their worst—after week upon week of distortion and innuendo, they are reduced to tedious repetition. The country is only beginning to hear from our side in this debate, and I do not believe the American people have concluded that the debate is over.
>
> The issue raised in the debate is of fundamental civil rights. On this, there can be no compromise. Rosa Parks did not fight for the right to sit in the middle of the bus, and we cannot accept a compromise that continues to require us to live a lie.
>
> I realize that the time may come when we will have to decide whether to accept half a loaf. Nevertheless, I have faith that the American people will ultimately perceive the fundamental justice of our cause. Our country is only now beginning to understand what is really at stake here. This is not the time to raise the white flag. The debate is just beginning. Let us not lose hope.

The battle to allow gays, lesbians, and bisexuals to serve openly in the military began well before Clinton had raised the issue and demanded debate. Before now, Americans had been permitted to bury their collective heads in the sand for far too long. Much of the media attention spawned by those who felt passionately about the issue had come from rabid bigots whose mouths overflowed with purported biblical hellfire and brimstone. Ironically, at this point in the debate, the very ranting of these religious zealots (of which the Reverend Lou Sheldon was only the most notorious example) was awakening many Americans to the irrationality and hatred and bigotry gays faced all along.

The headway we had made owed much to the ludicrous and indefensible arguments originated by fundamentalists and enshrined in Department of Defense policy: that the very closet imposed by the policy makes us security risks, that we are unfit to serve, that we are predators who cannot be trusted under "conditions affording minimal privacy."

While months before the issue was made prominent in the national consciousness, Americans did not even believe that gay, lesbian, and bisexual service members could serve honorably—the military had long denied we had ever done so—by this point it was common knowledge that thousands had and would continue to serve valiantly and with distinction. How Barney Frank could have witnessed such progress and concluded that the battle was lost is a mystery. Even if, as Frank believed, the issue was doomed to congressional defeat, a moral stand on one's convictions to make a point is of immense value, even if the issue is eventually lost.

In the guise of aiding our struggle, Frank was gradually backing away from his promise never to surrender this moral issue to political expediency. I remember how he ambled backstage at the post-March rally to assure every openly gay and lesbian service member risking both career and livelihood that he would help lead the fight to a well-deserved victory. Listening to him read a prepared statement months later, I could only feel the cold of his betrayal. He had lobbed a grenade into the debate on top of which a few had jumped to save the rest from the shrapnel. It was now time to salvage what was left of our fight.

A high-school political science course taught me that we elect representatives to serve as our voices in the halls of government. When the rhetoric of politics muffles our united voices and the issue of basic human rights becomes fogged, it is every gay, lesbian, and bisexual person's obligation to rise to the occasion and scream over the din of battle, "We will not give in!" Our community knew that the goal was nearer than it seemed to a faltering man.

The Clinton administration mistook intense public debate, scrutiny, skepticism, and political turmoil for an actual fight. Clinton would never truly fight. The son of an alcoholic, he had compromise in his bone marrow. Regardless of Clinton's waffling, we continued to fight as more Americans began to side with our community. Octogenarian hawk Barry Goldwater, who once chaired Nunn's committee, staked out a position to lift the ban unconditionally. "It doesn't matter if you're not straight, so long as you can shoot straight," he said. Pro-gay politicians on both sides of the aisle, most risking their constituents' wrath, sought swift presidential action to put a halt to the military's wrangling on the issue. Senator Bob Kerry from Nebraska, Vietnam veteran and recipient of the Medal of Honor, simply noted that it was time for the military to change. "Only by completely lifting the ban can we assure homosexuals that they can continue to serve honorably if they are forced out of the closet," he said on the Senate floor.

Clinton had made a promise, and he erred by not lifting the ban with the stroke of a pen. Now, bloodied by anti-gay attacks, he painfully retreated, finding political cover behind the thoughtless pondering of an openly gay man whose slanted view had been wrongly interpreted as communitywide acceptance of a compromise so blatantly coddling bigotry. Clinton was slowly shrinking to the sidelines, where eventually he would stand and shake his head in mock disbelief.

The inequality and discrimination represented by "don't ask, don't tell" was much more covert and insidious. Because most of straight America did not understand the self-hate and duplicity bred by the closet, Senator Nunn's proposal did not seem nearly as pernicious as it really was. "Just be quiet and don't wave it in our faces" pandered to America's general discomfort with sexual differences.

I said then, and continue to say today, that Representative Frank's solution to a perceived logjam was essentially responsible for ending the fierce but productive debate through which we were educating America. Smarting from Frank's response to my public denouncement of his proposal—"What's his alternative?"—I focused my attention on derailing not only Senator Nunn's but now a gay brother's sellout masquerading as a compromise. Ultimate responsibility, however, falls

squarely on the shoulders of the man who, when attacked on his lacka-
daisical approach to the issue, claimed to be the first chief executive
"to have raised the issue . . . and thus done more than any other president." True, the door had been kicked open—but who would ensure
it would never close again?

Meanwhile, the Senate debated Clinton's nomination of openly lesbian San Francisco supervisor Roberta Achtenberg, one of my earliest
supporters, to the position of assistant secretary of fair housing and
equal opportunity in the Department of Housing and Urban
Development.

"I am not going to put a lesbian in a position like that," Republican
Senator Jesse Helms barked during the confirmation hearing. "If you
want to call me a bigot, fine!" Too late; many already considered him
a demagogical bigot to the point of lunacy. Calling Achtenberg "a
damn lesbian" in a subsequent outburst only confirmed the notion.

Achtenberg's nomination was approved 58–31 May 17 after three
months of bitter debate. A victory for the cause clouded by the continuing saga of the struggle to overturn the ban.

FRIENDLY FIRE

The Advocate: "Do you find it difficult to reconcile those [political] values with what you find in the gay community?"
Zuniga: "A little. ACT UP and Queer Nation—I don't endorse their way of doing things, but I realize there's room for all people in our community. I guess that's conservative in a way, not wanting to rock the boat in the way that I felt Queer Nation would, but seeking to resolve things peacefully and through dialogue.... I'm not knocking them at all, because I do think they've been instrumental in change. But my conservatism doesn't go much with what they try to accomplish. I don't have anything against those who are part of the fringe element, but I don't think I'm alone in my feelings about them."

—The Advocate, July 27, 1993

AT NOON THE PORTABLE PHONE RANG IN THE ROOM I HAD commandeered as my office. Dave and Laurie's house was beginning to feel like home, and without really analyzing all the ramifications, we were integrating into a functioning family unit. One of Laurie's three daily phone calls, I surmised, checking up on and briefing me on the progress of her day. I had not anticipated, as I pressed the talk button and said hello, that this call would be out of the ordinary. Our routine gave me a little of the stability that I surely lacked since my separation from the service.

"Nothing happening here," I said matter of factly, going on to describe how Teardrop was splayed out on his bed in my office. He kept me company in his peaceful daylong slumber, except when a fire engine raced down Market Street, sirens blaring, causing my usually quiet companion to let out an eardrum-piercing howl.

Laurie's day had been mediocre at best, she said. The usual

big-firm legal crap, I assumed. Her tone of voice hinted that there was something she wanted to say but was afraid to disclose. You can't keep it from me forever, I said, telling her not to put caution for my sensitivities over the need to convey relevant information.

In Laurie's typical by-the-way manner, she described a phone call she had made to Michael Petrelis in Boston. I knew only the briefest biographical sketch of this man. He identified himself as a queer activist, he was known for unapologetic incendiary remarks and sound bites, but he was, although condemned by some in the community, an icon of in-your-face diplomacy. His activism was not my style, but I had great respect for his zeal and ardor.

Laurie had called Petrelis after reading his opinion piece in a local newspaper about the terrible miscarriage of justice in the Schindler murder case. She had been moved by the piece, so she sought out his telephone number and called to thank him for his conviction to seeing justice served. He had singlehandedly raised money, flown to Japan, and pressed Schindler's case in the media, where it had been largely ignored. Seaman Allen Schindler, Petrelis swore, would become "the gay Rodney King."

Their conversation soured, however, when Petrelis discovered Laurie's activities and efforts on my behalf specifically, and on the gays in the military issue in general. I was incensed as she detailed his twenty-minute tirade. He was upset that I was vilifying ACT UP and Queer Nation (organizations for which he had been a backbone and was now revered) as a "fringe element" of the gay community. In an *Advocate* cover story, I had mistakenly used that term while attempting to explain my conservatism as a new activist. More than that, however, in the phone call he had labeled as "opportunists" the gay and lesbian service members who had come out publicly to oppose the ban. Because I had given up so much, and was reaping no rewards for my sacrifice, this single swipe cut like a knife.

Almost immediately after the *Advocate* article was published, I had been flooded with letters of support from around the country. Mixed in were a few scorning me for referring to certain elements in our community as the "fringe element." Although those letters accomplished little because they attacked rather than educated, I learned my lesson quickly. My teacher was an unexpected one. While on my first road trip to Texas, I made a stop in Austin to address a group of Human Rights Campaign Fund members at a rally held in the unlikely venue of a parking structure. After the rally, my voice all but gone from three days of nonstop talking, one of the rally sponsors drove me to a piano bar on Austin's popular Sixth Street for a hot rum toddy. I looked forward to the medicinal value of the drink, and a chance to wind down from my constant storytelling and pontificating.

A tall, stocky, corseted queen, whose swanlike neck was choked in a black feather boa, held court on stage, vamping, mocking, and hologramming Judy Garland as she entertained the motley crowd with a campy rendition of "Somewhere Over the Rainbow." Sassy was a versatile female impersonator (he preferred that title to drag queen), who looked as coddled and protected in his thigh-high boots as I had been in my chemical protective mask and gear during Scud alerts in Saudi Arabia. He was on friendlier territory, though, and the crowd actively appreciated his efforts. After the performance, my host invited Sassy to our table.

No introduction was necessary. His eyebrows swirling like trelliswork acknowledged my existence, and showed clearly that I was not on his A-list. Nothing made the fact that he recognized me clearer than when in a voice as damp and swollen as a rain cloud, he said, "Glad you're not afraid of us *drag queens*, Joe." I took this as a clear reference to my incomplete and misleading comments in *The Advocate*. I desperately hoped this would not become an ugly scene. If I had been less tired, I would probably have switched, autopilot style, into defense mode and tried to explain what I'd really meant and how my words did not do justice to my respect for all types of activism.

It didn't turn ugly. Sassy and I had much in common, and he started telling me about himself before I became reflexively defensive. He too had been a military brat. He too had been afraid early in his coming out. Now at age thirty-five, he professed to have seen the world and learned life's lessons in the school of hard knocks—"not the ideal way for you to learn them, sweety," he said, pinching my cheek with a gloved hand twice as large as mine. A rapport had been established, and he could see I not only liked him, I admired him.

Half an hour had passed as he and I shared experiences I never knew I had in common with someone so seemingly different from me yet, in so many ways, so fundamentally similar. The bar owner, an Archie Bunker lookalike without Archie's politics, ran to our table to try to get Sassy to perform again. Sassy responded with a wave of his hand and a snippy quip, cigarette smoke unfurling from his slit-red mouth like skeins of wasted silk.

Having established rapport, Sassy moved in for the kill. He was going to make his agenda known, and I would have no choice but to listen. So I did, intently.

"I know you don't need a *drag queen* to give you advice," he said, leaning against me, positioning his legs evenly to distribute the weight of his burly male body on a pair of five-inch spike heels, "but if you remember anything I say tonight, remember this: We're all one big family. Drag queens, leather daddies, military boys, college boys ... When one of us gets screwed, we all get screwed. ... Remember *that* and you'll do okay, honey."

I had never really understood certain of the fetishes and subcultures in our community. I saw that I didn't need to understand them, but that it was incumbent on me to respect them. Otherwise I was guilty of the same moralistic evaluations of others that I so abhorred from the right wing, a group of people who felt an intense desire to be the yardstick by which American standards were measured. My comfort level and personal tastes cannot be used to define the inherent value of people. I may choose not to wear pumps, leather, and nipple clamps, but that is no reason to devalue others who wish to.

As Sassy wrapped his massive arms around me and planted carmine-red lipstick-glossed lips on my cheek, I felt more comfortable than I thought I ever would. I translated his words into one of the most valuable lessons of my neophyte career as a gay public spokesman: Do not cast aspersions on any part of our community.

Going back and looking at articles covering my many speeches around the country, I saw the radical changes in my thinking through my accumulation of knowledge and experience. So much had changed since the day I stood up on a podium and promised to fight against the politics of hatred and discrimination. The tour had taught me about the birth, problems, solutions, team chemistry, and extraordinary growth of the movement. Sassy, in his own peculiar way, had taught me that we are a multiracial, multicultural, multi-social conglomeration of tribes—a complex community facing a plethora of vexing issues. Although I would never become a Sister of Perpetual Indulgence (a San Francisco-based drag-nun organization), I now valued their contributions and considered them an asset to our community.

It is a shame that the media is enamored with the footage of these colorful elements of our community without mentioning that their values are the same as those of most Americans, gay or straight. Even the Sisters are made up of people who, when out of costume, look, talk, and feel a lot like America. The shame is that we cannot parade our gay doctors, lesbian lawyers, and bisexual architects before Middle America because their nontitillating images would not sell newspapers or add color to a television broadcast.

"Michael, I admit the phrase 'fringe element' was a bad choice of words. . . . I don't want to feed into people's fears or misconceptions, and I can see where my words may have contributed to that," I now said apologetically. "But most people will read not just that phrase or sentence, they will read the whole article and should understand the context of what I said."

My apology was declined as he continued to flog me verbally, rather like my childhood nun teachers, for that unfortunate part of the quote.

"I wasn't born an activist, I was born gay!" I screamed into the receiver, my voice quavering with emotion. Perhaps this statement would start him thinking that, just as newborns make mistakes, so I had made a few in my childhood days of activism.

My frustration grew over the next several months, as some members of the gay community questioned the amount of time, energy, and money spent on the campaign to lift the ban when thousands were dying of AIDS. Anything distracting the community from dealing with the pandemic was unacceptable.

I had come out for a reason, and it was not personal gain. Jail time in Fort Leavenworth on sodomy charges was a real possibility. I risked facing that jail time because I believed my actions could help move our community forward; I risked it not to become a Nelson Mandela– or Andrei Sakharov–type figure in gay history, but because Silence truly does equal Death.

Some people are temperamentally inclined to be street fighters, while others' efforts are best spent in formal lobbying. So many people do nothing, so many chant and scream at the prejudice, hatred, and homophobia, yet few even volunteer to wage battle against the ignorance and apathy within our own community. Despite arguments to the contrary, there is a correlation between the fight for gay rights and the fight to eradicate the blight of this pandemic.

"Yes, AIDS remains a serious problem, but that is not to say that it ought to be the monomaniacal focus of our energy," I responded to a group of AIDS activists protesting at a gay rights rally in Dallas a few months later.

As I sat in my office, calming my mind after slamming down the receiver, tears started welling up in my eyes. Right-wing assaults had been easily dismissed. If they had not been, I predict I would have started taking Valium in preparation for the pricks and arrows of the coming months. Each prick hurt, but I'd have been a fool to expect to go unchallenged by the rabid right. Today, though, my soul had been denigrated by one of my gay brothers.

This was my first clue that gay infighting had probably caused as many derailments in our progress as assaults from the outside. Leaders and spokesmen don't need to go unquestionably revered, but so much more could be achieved by holding back our friendly fire. A hateful letter delivered to my doorstep in the afternoon mail served as proof of the near futility of this proposal among a population of self-hating, repressed "members" of our community.

José,
  I am a gay, conservative, Republican, Christian San Francisco native who disagrees with you and your way of doing things.
  First, nobody goes into the military to be gay or straight. You go into the military to train and defend your country. That's all.

I'm very surprised that you would fall for the *liberal experiment* that you did.

I have never hung around with other gays or lesbos because they do not know how to behave in public. *All my friends* are either straight or bisexual. They accept my lover & myself.

I'm fifty-one years old and my lover is sixty-five years old. We have been together for almost ten years. He served in the Marines during Korea and all his commanders knew he was gay, but he had no trouble at all. He served eight years and did his duty. No need to advertise his gayness.

Here is some more you need to know about our lifestyle:

1) We are involved in political Republican things.
2) We are pro-life, pro-babies, and pro-birth. If your mother had had an abortion you and every gay person or straight person would not be here today. *Abortion is Nazi genocide.*
3) We go to church every day and to Mass on Sundays.
4) We will not change our views ever.
5) We both never do interracial sex—it's disgraceful.
6) No trouble in jobs, housing or banking.
7) There are millions of us who are gay conservatives.
8) We don't support gay bars. We go to straight bars. People are more real.
9) We don't support porno book stores. They should be closed down.
10) We don't support the ACLU. *They're stupid.*
11) We do support strict border closings.
12) We do support strict gun control and, if necessary, all guns must be turned in.
13) We don't support radical Left Wing commie groups.
14) We support prayer and Bibles in schools.
15) We believe in our God, country, and flag.
16) We do not support people with AIDS getting taxpayer help. It's not our fault people get AIDS. Most get it from what they do as far as sex. If you have sex with every Tom, Dick, and Harry *you deserve it.*
17) In short, get real, get a life, and stop bitching like a little baby. You made your bed, now lie in it. Goodbye!

Two blows in one day—ouch!

THE CRUSADE

A FOUR-DAY TRIP THROUGH TEXAS WAS ONLY THE BEGINNING OF A whirlwind speaking and media tour, much like one of those if-it's-Friday-we-must-be-in-Paris excursions through Europe, that would take me from coast to coast, telling and listening to a litany of pain suffered by gay brothers and sisters, only in different voices.

Well before the Southwest Airlines plane touched ground in San Antonio, as we circled the city, waiting for traffic control's clearance to land, my heart jumped to my throat as I looked out the window and identified landmarks. Two years had passed since I had last set foot in San Antonio. Then I had been just another guy on the street. Today, I was coming home as a media darling and gay rights activist. But I was also a son hoping to reconcile with an estranged father, hoping in some way to convince him, if he didn't already know, that I was still the José Zuniga he said he was proud of before I left for war.

A crowd of sixty or so well-wishers surged forward. There would be an impromptu press conference in the airport, followed by a rally for Bob Kreuger, the doomed interim senator from Texas who stood little if no chance to defeat Kay Bailey Hutchinson, a female clone of Senator Phil Gramm. My nervousness was obvious to even the most aloof observer. I hesitated. If you're blessed enough (or damned) to climb up on a platform and say, "Over here! Everybody look at me!" then you damn well better have something to say.

"We're going to blow the doors off the closet forever," I said.

A question-and-answer session followed my brief statement. At first, questions related exclusively to the fifty-year ban. Gradually

271

they began to shift to broader issues, like Texas's sodomy statute, Colorado's Amendment 2, and a federal gay civil rights bill. I had used my career as a deliberate bullet aimed at the heart of the offensive against lifting the ban, but that was not enough now. This should have come as no surprise. Robert Bray had predicted that a gay sergeant baptized by fire would become a gay activist.

Reporters took tremendous latitude with accuracy; any story that tries to squeeze too much into 10-point type tends to gloss over the details or be a little too loose with the facts. In San Antonio, a copy of the *San Antonio Express-News* was delivered to my hotel room. The front-page story quoted my father as saying, "I have no son named Joe." Although I had not talked to my father for almost three months, the "news" caught me off-guard. Calling home seconds after reading the article, Sandra informed me my father did not wish to see me.

He doesn't want to see me.... My thoughts were muted by the torrential rain I focused on as I gazed out the window of my San Antonio hotel room. I recalled the torrential rains from the diluvian days and nights of Noah I had learned about in Sunday catechism classes, the deep blue of the floodwaters illustrated in my book of Bible stories making me thirsty or inviting me to do the dead man's float, even if it meant doing so among the corpses of the unheeding or the sacrificed who never heard the warning.

After a Texas-style kick-off in four major cities, my schedule called for more than twenty-five lectures, speeches, or appearances in cities ranging from Oklahoma City to my birthplace, Cincinnati. It was heartwarming to travel the country and meet people, whether or not they agreed with my views. All the more reason to maintain a fast and furious pace.

The fight made me impervious to bodily needs, devoid of any desire that wasn't gay rights–related, deaf to the chaos swirling around me. Ignoring the emotional and physical pleas, the pleas of a body that was often on the verge of complete shutdown. "Carry on, troop," my father would say.

"Self-love is not so vile a sin as self-neglecting," Shakespeare would counter.

But the pleas had become so wrenching that after each engagement I would have to wander around the hotel or around the block to get my concentration back long enough that I could sit down and construct another thought about the next day's speech. Many were the nights when I just crawled into my hotel room to welcome slumber.

The priorities of the fight, my well-being, and my relationship with Dave and Laurie frequently became scattered and filled with conflict as I tried to juggle the world's affairs all at once. Loneliness now tore at me. Although Dave accompanied me on many engagements and Laurie was able to join me for a few, it was in my hours alone and away from home that I opened my portfolio and laid out the pictures of my father and mother, Dave and Laurie, even Teardrop, as if the physical trace on the emulsion could temporarily replace the yearning in my heart.

Returning home to San Francisco between engagements helped to cure my emotional strife. But eventually my mind would begin replaying memories like a videotape of distorted and obsolete guilts and fears, squeezing the joy out of the present. My soul screamed, "Don't lose faith!" I felt like Michelangelo's sculpture "The Captive," in an unfinished struggle to emerge whole from a block of marble, beset by interpretations, admonitions, forewarnings, and descriptions of "my kind" by the self-appointed prophets, priests, judges, and prefabricators of my travail. I thank God today that I had the safety net of Dave and Laurie's love to see me through my dark moments of self-torment and despair as I struggled to define my new identity. Where Sergeant Zuniga had stood yesterday, a hollow form awaited structure. Who am I now?

"We're not asking for pity—and I use that word against my better judgment. There's a vast difference between us wanting pity and us wanting Americans of good faith to realize the contempt in which bashers and bigots should be held—because according to the Pat Robertsons of the world, God loves *fags*, just not the Sin," I rounded out a speech at Florida Atlantic University. He'll just send us to hell afterward, I muttered to myself.

"Note the irony," I pointed out to a rapt audience of college students. "In one breath religious zealots suggest, rightly, that there is meaning to being gay without sex, and in the next, they character-ize queers as one-dimensional caricatures *driven* by sex."

An eighteen-year-old stood up and apologized for interrupting my speech. He announced he was heterosexual and began to express his religious convictions. The crowd, a little more than three quarters of which was gay, went into an uproar, forcing the young man to his seat.

"Wait!" I boomed into a microphone that my resonant voice did not need. "The gay and lesbian community, should not quiet those whose views disagree with ours. It's just as wrong to judge our de-tractors as it is to be judged by our foes in *The Gay Agenda*."

The labels often slapped on those with faith—*religious fanatic, won't listen to reason*—do a terrible injustice to a large number of people who, although differing in religious beliefs, listen to our words and spot the glaring wrong in the treatment of gays before agnostics all but run over it. Saying "the Methodists are against us" is like saying "all queers have limp wrists." An example was Dallas Affirmation, a Methodist denomination congregation that invited me to lecture in their church. More than a hundred and fifty congrega-tion members, more than half professing to be straight as they shook my hand and introduced themselves at the end of my lecture, were in attendance this warm night in June. We joined hands in song and faith before my lecture. A standing ovation (which I sometimes thought my lecture agent intentionally placed in my contract) could not stir me more than the communion of spirits under one roof, their music, their joined hands in stark contrast to a speaking en-gagement in Denver where hatred was palpable and plastered on placards and fliers.

DEATH PENALTY FOR HOMOSEXUALS IS PRESCRIBED IN THE BIBLE, a not too pleasant thought, greeted me in a McDonald's bathroom on the same morning I read conservative icon Barry Goldwater's editorial opposing the military ban in the *Denver Post*. The flyer belonged to a Colorado-based group called STRAIGHT (Society to Remove All Immoral Gross Homosexual Trash), whose motto was "Working for a Fag-Free America." How I wished generals Powell and Waller could see this take-off on the Ku Klux Klan motto. In the Jim Crow years our country saw the most lurid embodiment of evil—ironically, they cast oblique light on our times because of the countless possibilities.

Maybe Professor Lani Guinier, one of Clinton's briefly considered nominees for the post of assistant attorney general for civil rights, was right when she said, "Too many of our leaders have concluded that the way to remedy racism is to simply stop talking about race."

The morning after my speech to Dallas Affirmation, I was invited as a guest on a popular conservative Dallas radio talk show. This was my first time on radio, so the host of the show was cordial enough to excuse my performance as I macheted my way through the perplexities and dolorosities of the rather bigoted questions we were fielding. I stopped answering questions, allowing some very hateful callers to self-destruct as they delivered stock rhetoric. What better way to demonstrate the internal inconsistencies in their argument without wasting one's breath? A scene from *Inherit the Wind*, a dramatic portrayal of the 1920s Scopes Monkey trial, came to mind. Attorney Clarence Darrow standing silent as Populist presidential candidate turned religious fanatic William Jennings Bryant defended the firing (on moral grounds) of Tennessee teacher William Scopes for violating a ban against prohibited curriculum: Evolution. Soon defiance became self-preservation. I was no Clarence Darrow. In an attempt to deflect further attacks, I delivered a mini-speech combining Guinier's racism theory with a simple analogy summarizing the human struggle with diversity.

"As things stand now, it's rather like children who dislike each other but who are forced to play nicely together while their parents watch. As long as the parents are present, playing is nice; but no one even pretends that the kids like each other."

Get to the point, the host seemed to be saying as he stared at me quizzically.

"Until those children are allowed to discover that they're all the same—which they won't as long as someone is ordering them to behave in a way they don't want to—no attitudes will change. One will continue to be selfish and the other will feel he can only get what those in charge give him. Result: insecurity for the underdog and resentment for the kid with the toys who isn't allowed to discover for himself that perhaps sharing the toys makes more sense in the long run."

Okay, so it needed a little fine-tuning. The bottom line was that I needed to help position the gay issue and frame its context in the eyes of the rest of America. To do so properly, "don't ask, don't tell" needed to be described as the segregationist policy it was, the gross violation of fundamental rights that it implemented. I knew I had succeeded in my mission when, at the end of the Florida lecture, the young man whom I had protected from a jeering crowd came backstage and expressed that, although he disagreed with some of my views, he was grateful someone had challenged him to search his beliefs for any trace of bigotry.

As Holocaust survivors know, people with no historical perception of or connection to the culture or theories of hatred are being unsuspectingly indoctrinated. Demonizing public pronouncements are back in vogue in the form of nonsensical but potent fabrications like the phrase "special rights" woven in with visual deceptions and trickery. *The Gay Agenda*, a right-wing propaganda video that comes complete with a viewer warning label (*Sexually Explicit Material*), was distributed at no cost to churches, Rotary Clubs, in some cases in supermarket parking lots, and hand-delivered to the Joint Chiefs of Staff. The video shares infamy with such visual deceptions as *The Eternal Jew*, which claims, "The Jew is the demon behind the corruption of mankind. . . . These pictures prove it"; the narrative is followed by black-and-white stills of Jewish people strolling down a street. Similar, too, is the Ku Klux Klan's *Blood in the Face*, which features David Duke expounding about how "white people in this country have got to unite." Today the message pumped out by a million-dollar propaganda machine, known affectionately as the Vatican West, is "to the victor go our children."

Holocaust survivor Primo Levi warned, "It happened that an entire civilized people . . . followed a buffoon whose figure today inspires laughter, and yet Adolf Hitler was obeyed and his praises were sung right up to the catastrophe. It happened, therefore it can happen again."

The more I witnessed the religious right's machinations in my stops around the country, I began to see how easy it really was to tear down a campaign of lies headlined with the infamous "special rights" canard. As put so precisely by Humpty-Dumpty in *Alice Through the Looking-Glass*, "When I use a word ... it means just what I choose it to mean—neither more, nor less."

When I stood before a mixed crowd of supporters and protesters in Colorado Springs and exhorted my gay brothers and sisters to continue fighting for equality—*equal* protection under the law, gay *equal* rights—I meant nothing more and nothing less than what Webster's dictionary defines as *equal:* "of the same measure, quantity, amount, or number as another." Staring at my detractors after making that observation, I saw a look of shock in their faces that debunked the concept that their twisted campaign cannot be dismantled brick by brick. Their deceitful tactics are double-edged, and therein lies our victory.

A new McCarthyism waits in the wings, a powerful force that, like the Ku Klux Klan, yearns for an American *Gemeinschaft* that would exclude blacks, Jews, Catholics, and gays. Their power is intimidating. More so when for more than a century Americans have learned to depend on the camera lens to bear witness to civil rights marchers in Selma, to burning hooches in Vietnam, and to starving babies in Somalia.

For years we have trusted images more than words. Americans decided that the government's optimistic reports about the Vietnam War had to be lies after seeing the images of carnage in Vietnam. The videotape of Los Angeles police officers beating motorist Rodney King was so brutal people refused to believe explanations and could not reconcile the verdict in the first trial with the incontestable visual evidence. The real dangers of fuzzy media and blurred standards lie in their effects on immature Americans, who may be unsure of anything beyond a vague desire to be a part of the mainstream.

A prime example of the right wing's vigorous efforts to bamboozle Americans is a continued emphasis, especially in *The Gay Agenda*, to class homosexuality with behavior disorders easily reversed with reparative therapy. The truth is that in 1973 the American Psychiatric Association dropped homosexuality from its manual of mental disorders, stating that "homosexuality per se implies no impairment in judgment, stability, reliability, or general social or vocational capabilities." After twenty years of additional research, the association published findings in 1993 that "there is no evidence that any treatment can change a homosexual person's deep-seated sexual feelings for others of the same sex."

The truth alone is capable of countering the perception that we are a highly promiscuous community of lisping, effeminate men and threatening bull dykes displayed through the distorted lens of propagandist newsreels and "educational" clips. A veteran gay activist attending one of my lectures captured in one sentence the dilemma our community faces in disseminating the truth. "If a man wants to walk with a thorn in his foot and will not allow another to remove it," he said, "there is nothing we can do but let him walk with that thorn in his foot." Once the thorn is out, people get past the picture of two men embracing, two women holding hands. They see human tenderness and love.

My experience, during my long lecture circuit, was that Americans wanted to hear the truth.

I held the sheet of fire-engine-red paper long enough to read it and then crumpled it into a tiny ball. Was I insulted or glad I had another example of the bigotry pervading in our society? The letter, written in response to "My Life in the Military Closet," an article I penned that was published in *The New York Times Magazine* the Sunday before Clinton's expected announcement, was forwarded to me unopened.

Dear Sir,

The New York Times Magazine section recently contained an article by José Zuniga, a pedophile who was recently dismissed from the U. S. Army. Zuniga is not an attractive looking individual. His face resembles a lizard.

As a teenager, Zuniga was a sneak thief and a shoplifter. On one occasion Zuniga broke into the poor box of a local Catholic church to obtain money for alcohol. In the Army, Zuniga was a known coward and spent most of this time as a "REMF," a rear-echelon mother f——. Zuniga never saw one day of actual combat.

In the United States, Zuniga would spend time on weekends lurking around elementary schools. Zuniga is a "chicken hawk," attracted to young male boys as small as seven or eight years old. Zuniga's locker was inspected and found to contain hundreds of photographs of young male children between six and seven years old apparently taken by Zuniga at a local pool during the summertime. Zuniga has bragged of obtaining cocaine and providing it to fifteen- and sixteen-year-old boys in return for having them pose for pornographic videos. Zuniga is currently under investigation for the rape and sodomization of a twelve-year-old boy he picked up in a Greyhound bus station in San Francisco.

It is clear that Zuniga is a disgrace to the U.S. Army, a disgrace to his nation, and a disgrace to the human race. Zuniga defends his lust for children as "normal." Everyone knows better.

—Unsigned

A gaggle of ten to twelve college students huddled around me after my speech, inviting me out to coffee and a night of dancing in Cleveland's hottest dance club.

"You deserve it," explained a twenty-year-old microbiology major with whom I'd carried on a conversation before the lecture. The kid's freckled face looked cherubic, emphasized by a shaved head topped by a curly wisp.

They were right, of course, but it was not the ideal activity for someone on the verge of zombiehood.

Yet escape called me. I was expected in Cincinnati tomorrow for three television interviews, a meeting with the editorial board of the *Cincinnati Post*, and two fundraising events. Should I indulge that part of me that yearned for some semblance of a normal life? I danced until two in the morning with no regrets.

"DON'T ASK, DON'T TELL. BILL CLINTON, GO TO HELL"

NEWS OF CLINTON'S IMPENDING DECISION REACHED ME WHILE I waited for Dave and Laurie's flight to arrive at the San Diego airport on July 15. They were flying in to join me for what had originally been thought to be a celebratory weekend. It had started with an interview on the "Charlie Rose Show," a talk show too hip for public television but with too much brain for commercial television. It would culminate with my stint as co-grand marshal, with Tanya Domi, of the San Diego Gay Pride Parade.

From a pay phone by the terminal I checked my voicemail messages. Two requests for interviews and a good luck message; the standard lot. There was also a message from Jeffrey Gibson, a San Francisco activist. Each of his well-weighed words knocked the wind out of me as I committed his message to memory. President announcing endorsement of the policy ... Unbelievable ... Press conference scheduled ... Civil disobedience planned ... Sorry ...

Much to the gay community's chagrin, President Clinton endorsed the "don't ask, don't tell" policy in a benighted retreat from principle driven by politics. He announced his retreat in a speech on July 19 before the National Defense University at Fort McNair, Virginia. Adding the phrase "don't pursue" in an attempt to make his compromise more palatable to those whom he was betraying, Clinton claimed that the new policy represented "a real step forward." The announcement made no one happy. Even after much publicized debate and a grandly announced compromise by the President, Senator Nunn stood on the Senate floor and threatened to codify the former policy, claiming Clinton's order was untenable. Senator Thurmond summed up the anti-gay sentiment of victory when offering his reason for writing the policy into law: "So some future president won't be tempted to lift the ban."

Don't ask. Don't tell. Bill Clinton, go to hell!

Gays angrily rallied in the streets of America, protesting Clinton's sellout to homophobes and bigots. A united community asked the question—why? Our votes had helped make the difference between winning and losing an election. Our financial support in the campaign's early weeks provided crucial credibility. We'd stuffed envelopes and made phone calls. It was the first time some of us had given money to a candidate or volunteered to help out in a campaign. Why betray us?

I was one of a series of speakers in the San Francisco "Darkness at Noon" demonstration on July 20. What had begun as a group of ten was massed into eight hundred angry gays and lesbians holding signs, holding hands, all in protest of the man who had promised the community a place at the American table but had instead stood on the sidelines as the two sides duked it out, finally offering us a raincheck. His was a pervasive confusion between conviction and political expediency.

"My name is Joe Zuniga and I am the Sixth U.S. Army Soldier of the Year!"

The crowd roared in recognition. I crumbled up a prepared speech and threw it to my side.

> A few months ago I sacrificed my military career because of one man's promise to make amends for the suffering of thousands of my gay, lesbian, and bisexual brothers and sisters in arms.

281

Today I am an angry gay activist. I am angry at the lackeys who argued with the foolish consistency of hobgoblins with small minds. . . . I am angry at a man who promised us basic civil rights, knowing full well all would not be champagne and roses, and delivered instead an "honorable" setback. . . . I am angry at the betrayal draped under the mantle of an "honorable" compromise. . . . And I am angry at some of our own who lobbed grenades in our direction and sat back as we salvaged what was left after losing those who jumped atop the grenades to save us from the shrapnel. . . .

Keep your mouth shut, our president says, and you can go to Somalia and lose your life defending your country's interests. Open your mouth and you're no longer considered worthy to die for your country. Let's join together as a community and send a united message to those who would have us boxed up in railroad cars and shipped away into nonexistence: Bill Clinton, Sam Nunn, Strom Thurmond, Colin Powell, Barney Frank, the religious "wrong" . . . History will note your grave lapse in judgment. Far worse, God will condemn your inhumanity!

"On [the] grounds of both principle and practicality, this is a major step forward," Clinton said, contesting the allegation that he had abandoned his campaign pledge to lift the ban. Spoken like the "Bureaucratic Man" sociologist Max Weber defined as a half-man who slavishly worships rules, never asserts his will, or acts out of the dictates of his conscience. Standing before a mass audience of military officers, including the joint chairmen, in a Fort McNair auditorium, a weak-kneed Clinton touted "don't ask, don't tell, don't pursue" as an honorable compromise. A *USA Today* poll published two days later found that the Clinton compromise was deemed acceptable by 58 percent of respondents.

The issue was never exposed as a dishonorable attempt to ignore the plight of the thousands of gay men, lesbians, and bisexuals to whom the president of the United States had given a glimmer of hope through his promise. He had sanctimoniously duped the American public and some ingenuous members of our community by spinning his immoral compromise to the religious right as noble. There can be no honor in a compromise that ignores that most sacred of American values: equality.

Our would-be savior, in essence, gave a homosexual wanting to serve his country two options: remain in the closet, or swear to an oath of celibacy. Neither option meant equality by any stretch of the imagination and he knew it, no matter how he chose to spin his policy. Was Clinton prepared to order General Powell to deny his spouse's gender if someone casually asked about his wedding ring? Or require him to swear on a stack of Bibles that he would not engage in heterosexual conduct for the remainder of his time in service? Was such conduct even relevant to the chairman's performance as a soldier? Clearly not. But the Clinton policy, a clone of Nunn's original "don't ask, don't tell" policy, assumed that any such equivalent conduct by gay, lesbian, or bisexual service members would somehow hamper the accomplishment of military missions. By the letter of this policy, gays were presumed to be predators, unless they swore otherwise. Gays were assumed guilty, as if love were a crime. Clinton's policy, intentionally or unintentionally, furthered the notion that homosexuals are defined by their sexual acts. Just when we were beginning to hear three cheers rise up from the national media for the gay soldier, the gay FBI agent, the gay Republican ... It had become patently clear to most informed Americans that what a person does in the privacy of his own home should not determine how he should be treated as a human being or the extent of civil rights he should be afforded. Humanity transcends sexual orientation, I told a crowd of college students in Texas; therefore, so must equality.

Even credible comparisons to the militaries of seventeen other nations who already followed nondiscriminatory policies could not support the policy. It could only find basis in homophobia and ignorance.

True leadership would have seen our forty-second president stand his ground rather than pander to the hatreds sown of ignorance and religious fanaticism. Even had an executive order been overturned by Congress, as political talking heads predicted, each legislator would then have been forced to make a decision. The political process then, and not the president now, would have yielded what was a purely political compromise.

History has shown that majority-driven representative democracy sometimes has difficulty protecting the rights of its minorities. But the president should not tolerate, much less propagate, such lapses from American ideals because of public-opinion polls. Unfortunately, in the 1990s civil rights are mandated by popular opinion.

By October, the "don't ask, don't tell, don't pursue" compromise had undergone a dramatic transformation. The Senate diluted even this watered-down policy. The promise of evenhanded punishment of homosexual or heterosexual misconduct fell by the wayside. Clinton's "don't pursue" clause was erased, winding up the personal relic of a defeated commander in chief who still clung to the illusion of victory. While supporters of the former Defense Department directive were disappointed with Clinton's compromise, legislation codifying the Nunn proposal was passed by both the Senate and House Armed Services committees. Whether it was Nunn's imprimatur or Clinton's token signature that made the bill a law on November 30, 1993, became irrelevant. The media had already moved on to the other news of the day, so the vast difference between Clinton's honorable compromise and the new law was lost in the shuffle.

No Queers
Allowed!

My voicemail was activated at 11:30 p.m. A stranger called me from Boston, thanking me in a weepy voice for what I had done, consoling me on our loss. Roger left his telephone number but added that he expected never to hear from me. On any other day he may have been correct. Not tonight, though. Dave and Laurie were asleep. Two sleeping pills and three hundred sheep later, I still could not close my eyes and rest. Worse, I could not shut off the echo of my voice scoffingly reading my horoscope in the *San Francisco Bay Times* this morning.

"Taurus: You may experience a crisis of faith or an opportunity to grasp radical new ideas. This may first take form as hostility to old dogmas, but those old notions, however outdated, probably contain the seed of the new truth you are looking for."

I dialed Roger's number. His voice registered shock when I announced my name. I don't remember the beginning, middle, or even the end of our conversation; most of the time we were reduced to sobbing infants. I do remember the illusory peace that settled over me before dozing off to sleep.

July 19, 1993, left me feeling like an opera diva having lost her voice. Since May I had been touring the country, explaining how simple both the bigotry in this matter and the justice required to reverse it were. So many demands, so little time to meet them. My experience had always been that the people who actually achieve in life don't waste a lot of time fretting about the boulders they see in their way. They figure out a way to go around, tunnel underneath, or just plain climb over. Sergeant Zuniga had done just that. But what more could Joe Zuniga have done? Was I going insane?

I felt there were two of us: a relentless public figure and a worn-out private citizen. I blamed myself. Failure. "But it's not your fault," Roger said sympathetically. "Clinton would have signed his name to Nunn's policy months ago to get this all over with."

It was no use trying to cheer me up. Like thousands of my gay brothers and sisters, I had been sold out, and the price was exacted emotionally. We had been told we had a place set at the great American dinner table; but evidently, only our money and ballots were to be seated.

One of the major factors on my mind when deciding whether or not to make my announcement had been the ludicrous arguments of senators Sam Nunn, Strom Thurmond, and Dan Coates reverberating in the Senate Hart Building chambers. In the middle of my discharge proceedings, and at the urging of the Senate Armed Services Committee's own general counsel, with whom I'd met while lobbying on the Hill, I had mailed Nunn a letter requesting inclusion in his kangaroo court hearings. My letter was delivered by certified mail on May 13, 1993. His response:

> June 30, 1993
>
> Dear Sergeant Zuniga:
>
> Thank you for your recent letter requesting to testify before the Senate Armed Services Committee during our hearings on the Defense Department's policy concerning homosexuals in the armed forces. I appreciate your willingness to share your views with the Committee on this important matter.
>
> The Committee's hearings on this issue will be thorough, fair, and comprehensive. . . . The Committee will also make every effort to hear from individuals and organizations who want to change the current policy excluding homosexuals from serving in the armed forces, as well as those who support the current policy.
>
> I am sure that you can understand that we have received far

more requests to testify in person before the Committee than we will be able to accommodate. . . . I would like to invite you to submit your views on this issue in writing to the Committee. Your written testimony will be carefully reviewed by the Committee and will become part of the permanent record of our consideration on this issue.

Thank you again for your willingness to share your views.

Sam Nunn

What was Nunn afraid of if his position was as solid as he claimed? Why stack the cards against us if he stood on sound moral ground? And why was he allowed to get away with chicanery in such a blatant way?

I wrote him another letter. Two months later, I received a three-page form letter in response to my many queries.

August 6, 1993

Dear Friend:

Thank you for contacting me concerning the Defense Department's policy with respect to gay men and lesbians in the armed forces.

During the 1992 campaign, presidential candidate Bill Clinton stated that, if elected, he would change the Defense Department's policy prohibiting gay men and lesbians from serving in the armed forces. Shortly after President Clinton took office in January, an amendment was offered in the Senate to prevent the President (from) making any change in policy in this area.

I opposed that amendment because I believed that a comprehensive review was needed before the Executive Branch or the Congress took any action on this issue. . . . Over the past six months the Armed Services Committee has held a total of nine hearings as a part of our review of this issue. We heard from experts in law, military history, and military sociology; from members of the Senate; and from current and former military personnel here in Washington and in the field. . . .

Our hearings have shown that this is an issue on which people have strongly held views. For many people, it is a moral issue touching upon deeply held religious and ethical beliefs. For many others, it is a matter of individual rights, involving the fair and

287

equitable treatment of individuals with a particular sexual orientation who want to serve their country in uniform. . . .

We have heard clear and convincing testimony that military service is a unique calling. For service members in training or on operational deployments, their ship, their tent, or their barracks is their home. Military men and women do not have the right to choose with whom they will share this home. . . .

The Committee received compelling testimony that in the unique conditions of forced intimacy and minimal privacy that characterize much of military life, the presence of persons who engage in homosexual acts, or who demonstrate propensity to do so, would have an extremely negative effect on unit cohesion and combat capability. . . .

This has been a very difficult and emotional issue. Every man and woman in this country has a right to be respected. Our military services cannot and must not allow or tolerate mistreatment of any individual. Our Constitution enshrines individual rights and liberties. Our Constitution also underscores the essential role of government in providing for the common defense. The constitutional rights of military personnel reflect the longstanding principle that in the U.S. Armed Forces, the mission is the first priority, the unit is the second priority, and the individual is the third priority.

In my view, the legislation in our Committee bill, which I now hope will be enacted into law by the Congress, recognizes the unique nature of military service and ensures that our military leaders will be able to maintain the high standards of morale, good order and discipline, and unit cohesion that are the essence of our military capability.

I appreciate your taking the time to share your views with me on this important issue.

Sam Nunn

Comprehensive review? What had they learned in that review? Or were they so busy pontificating and taking advantage of photo ops aboard submarines that they'd completely missed the point millions of Americans had gotten during the debate? Who could forget the dyed-orange-haired Senator Thurmond, his line of questioning the type that epitomized the buffoonery of these hearings? "If we can find a way to change ya'll, would ya' seek out such help?" he asked the distinguished Colonel Cammermeyer. Would that we could change him!

How could anyone on that committee look a gay or lesbian combat veteran in the face and tell that veteran that he or she was incapable of military service? It was done all the time, though. Hey, buddy, thanks for dodging bullets in Vietnam or risking your life to defend your country's interests in the Persian Gulf, but you know we've had a "no queers allowed" policy in place for fifty years and, yep, we aim to keep it.

LOSS

UNTIL SHORTLY BEFORE MY COMING OUT I HAD BEEN IN CLOSE contact with my father. Our relationship had been revived by our shared grief and was blossoming in a fashion that ten years earlier would have been wishful thinking. Every telephone call was chock-full of advice.

Our communication ceased on April 22, 1993. The colonel had not received my letter in time and unfortunately heard the news first on "CNN Headline News." Through the discharge proceedings, I spoke with my sister a few times, checking up on my father's health, gauging whether or not I should fly to San Antonio to confront him, always being told that now was not a good time. I stopped calling home because the sense of loss was more than I could bear. More precisely, because I feared confirmation of the "news" as reported in the article.

Inundating myself in work, I accepted every speaking engagement, channeling my anger, sadness, and frustration into the cause. Maybe I could convince the colonel that my actions were honorable by continuing to place my face on the gay issue. I was wrong not only about him, but about the only living family member I thought supported me in my fight: Sandra. She sent me this letter:

August 8, 1993

Joe,

It has been several months, as you stated in your letter to Dad, since we last talked. It has not been easy for us either to deal with people staring at us as if we were from another world. One thing has become apparent, who our real friends are.

I don't appreciate that "reporter" saying things that are not true. She had no right to make things up about us. Dad has *never* said he doesn't have a son because he never talked to her. I talked to her and said we had no comment when she tried interviewing Dad. She in turn prints that horrible, false statement as if it were fact. Don't believe her.

Dad doesn't hate you. He will just never understand your change. He (we) don't believe in that widely used phrase that you are "born that way." That is a bunch of nonsense that only you (and others like you) want to believe.

Now, tell me what you have accomplished with your "coming out"? NOTHING!!!! Clinton endorsed "don't ask, don't tell." It's the same way it was before. That goes to show you that you and your friends are back to square one. I know what you are thinking, that you have made a difference. I don't see how, but that's beside the point.

Well, now that you know some of the things that have happened to us these past months you know it hasn't been a bed of roses for us, either. It won't be easy for us to adjust to the changes because we can't change each other, but we'll just have to make the best of what we still have of each other. I know this letter hasn't been very nice, but people like your "friends" are responsible for making kind people say evil things. Hope you are okay. Take care.

Your sister,
Sandra

I read and reread her letter, checking for any word or phrase I could attribute to my father. There was none. Had the entire world turned against me? Were they all laughing at what they perceived as my failure? That is what it felt like over and over, no matter what anyone said: my failure. I had not said enough, done enough, traveled to enough places, made myself understood. . . .

Dave and Laurie continued to stand by me. Why? Did they feel sorry for me? I did not understand their patience and compassion because I had banished, or temporarily switched off, all emotion but anger and despair. Love? Could it withstand the lashes I was taking at them both? I was using them as human punching bags because I had flogged myself until I bled. The frightening reality was that there was a Pandora's box full of destructive energy inside me. It was as if every slur, every insult, every arrow I endured in the name of the Fight was festering inside me.

Depression, a psychiatrist diagnosed immediately. He tossed in a twist of identity crisis—now you know why you've been asking yourself "Who am I?" he said. No. Depression was for the weak. I was still a highly functioning human being, counted on to deliver extemporaneous speeches on any gay subject. But wait, my insides were vacuous on good days and full of detritus on bad ones. In locking the door to my heart, burying my pain, and denying myself any time to heal, I had lost myself.

I was no longer Sergeant José Zuniga. I no longer had a family. My lovers would soon abandon me, if they knew any better. And I had no idea what lay ahead in my future, except the host of questions plaguing my grieving mind: Who am I? Who do I want to be? Who does the world want me to be? And which is most important? Maybe a little Prozac will help, then maybe some time . . .

TRIBAL MOSAIC

Let us weave these sturdy threads into a new American community
that once more stands strong against the forces of despair and evil because
everybody has a chance to walk into a better tomorrow....
                                                    —*President Bill Clinton*

PERHAPS IT WAS WHAT *GENERATION X* AUTHOR DOUGLAS COUP-
land aptly described as "historical overdosing: to live in a period of
time when too much seems to happen" that afflicted me, but I became physically ill at the sound of Bill Clinton's voice expounding
on a New American Community. What better tomorrow was he
promising us now? Was it as stilted and leaden as the heroic statuary
in the nation's capital, whitewashed with pigeon droppings? The
audacity of a man who sold my community poison in a new bottle.
The pain and disillusionment of seeing our elected messiah sign his
name to a parchment negotiating away our freedom had taught us
a valuable lesson: the need to entrust ourselves with our own destiny
instead of joyfully, naively placing our fate in the hands of one man.

Ever since the Stone Age, and in all parts of the world, humans
have expressed their solidarity with other forms of life by incarnating
experiences and aspirations. But our community lacks collectively
what has historically pulled other tribal melanges together—religion,
culture, language. Despite the amount of hatred, prejudice, and bigotry of which we are victims, we scatter like leaves before a wind of
focused malice. Because no saber is as lethal as that which we point
at ourselves, conflicts among us not only tear at the delicate fabric
of our community, but they disrupt and fracture our conviction to
secure the justice we deserve.

Unlike John Keats, who said that knowing about the rainbow

shatters its beauty, I've come to understand that knowledge can only enrich. Our country is in desperate need of the very real knowledge that a campaign to destroy specific segments of society is underway. But we, as a fractious community, cannot provide that knowledge without first denouncing the bigotry that exists within our own community, bigotry threatening to destroy us even faster than our enemies could ever do.

In Dallas someone argued with me that we can discriminate against "old flaming drag queens." But how is that any different from the discrimination we suffer at the hands of our enemies?

The truth is that we have all suffered from a partial or complete lack of social, economic, or political acceptance. The obvious path would be one leading to the acceptance of each other, movement away from the intolerance plaguing our community.

We have not forgotten nor will we forget our brothers and sisters with AIDS. We have not swept the issue under the carpet, as some would allege, because we share in our family's pain. We must not minimize the enormous strides made by groups like ACT UP and Queer Nation who, through in-your-face diplomacy, kept the issue alive through twelve years of Republican denial and thus helped raise the level of AIDS awareness beyond the homosexual community, but we must realize that we are a complex community with a plethora of concerns, causes, and motivations, and that they are *all* intertwined.

In my abbreviated coming-out process, I learned that lesson almost immediately as I was confronted by transsexuals, leathermen, and others who, along with conservative gay America, form the nucleus of our community. It took their testimonies, wisdom, and patience to steer me away from unintentionally vilifying their existence in our community. They showed me that, in the bigger picture, we are all in this together and that we can ill afford to assault each other when the right wing is doing a fine job of doing that without our help. We have all shared the pain society has mercilessly inflicted in our community. Only by uniting as a tribal mosaic can we share with them in our overall human commonality. As valuable a lesson as that was to me, it is a lesson we need to remember as a community.

Although it is true that we may have temporarily lost the military battle, along with the wisdom we have gained as a political force, we must have developed a better understanding of ourselves as a family.

A parable my father once told me when I was a teenager has come to my mind a number of times. While traveling through an apple-growing area, a young man stopped to watch a farmer spraying his apple trees to prevent moth damage to his apples. The man asked the farmer, "How come you're so dead sat against them?"

The farmer replied, "I'm not really against them, but I sure am for my apples."

Like the farmer in the story, we should direct our actions and energy toward what we are all *for*. By doing so, we automatically let others know what we are *against*.

If we're not going to be for each other, how can we expect others to be for us?

EPILOGUE

DRESSED IN ZEUSLIKE VESTIGES, WORSHIPED AND SCRUTINIZED, then asked to explain myself, having packed at least two full lifetimes into my twenty-four years on earth—that has been my life since April 24, 1993. I have survived a life change that I have not regretted despite the heavy emotional toll it has exacted.

"You're going to be all right," said a paramedic who, I couldn't help noting, even as I lay doubled over in pain, looked like Kevin Costner. He tried calming me before straightening out my right leg to apply traction, making it possible to transport me to Davies Medical Center's emergency room.

"No word yet on the morphine. . . . This is going to hurt."

Translation: I'm going to inflict some major pain on you without giving you any painkillers. I started shaking. Shock? My mind wandered elsewhere, to the days in basic training when nineteen squad members and I jumped off cliffs and over obstacles with the grace of acrobats or stunt men. Not once had I gotten hurt. Tonight I lay in the middle of a street in San Francisco, my femur broken at midshaft, my leg bent grossly under me—and I was late for dinner. All for jumping (and falling) off a ledge I had managed to take successfully a dozen times in the past.

The paramedic's violent jerk on my leg was by far the most physical pain I had felt in my life. Despite the ensuing pain—relieved seconds later by a traction splint—I would look back at my little fall from grace as a welcome cost for the physical and mental time off I was awarded to relieve me of the out-of-control emotions festering inside.

With my life in disarray, I had feared the unavoidable end of my relationship. My moods were emotional poison, inflicted on me and anyone within striking distance, human or canine. The anger of failure and self-hatred securely manacled to a twenty-four-year-old wall during the Fight had not subsided since its escape.

Friends coping with depression or just on Vitamin P (Prozac) explained that anger was good as long as it was harnessed and focused. Prozac and a plethora of anti-anxiety drugs weren't the solution. I needed to acknowledge and embrace my fears and demons, my psychiatrist diagnosed. He added a visit to the Self-Identity Warehouse to his prescription.

You need to have the activist uniform dry-cleaned and grow into your new self, my psychiatrist said. When? How? You have no idea. I'm a busy gay activist now, I countered. College lectures . . . fundraising events . . . political rallies . . . spokesman duties . . . A push from Above on the emergency brake of my life forced me to a complete stop. Answer the who, the what, and the why behind your new life, Joe, and then deal.

Uh-huh, a pessimistic voice mumbled somewhere in my head. There is no set of chains strong enough to shackle the child within me who wants to cry and kill, laugh and swear, be held and flee. Happy is he who lives life an unknown and dies tranquilly in his deathbed—a random thought that was no longer an option.

"Looks like we'll have to operate," an on-call orthopedic surgeon said tersely less than an hour after my fall. The surgeon looked at X-rays of my shattered femur as if they were his patient. "No cast. We'll insert a fourteen-inch stainless steel rod from hip to knee through the femur."

I'd be in the hospital two days, it was predicted. Complications would prolong the stay to six. The message was loud and clear: No speaking engagements, no telephone calls, nothing but time, something of a luxury since I plunged off the end of the earth a year and a month shy of my present reality. By April 24, 1994, the exact anniversary of my queer conception, I hoped to have my life in some semblance of order.

Even in my darkest hours, in my few crises of faith, the warrior spirit I'd inherited from progeny helped me survive. I never regretted then or now the sacrifice I made in coming out. Regret tinged me when I acknowledged the bitter toll my self-imposed immersion in the movement was exacting on my life with Dave and Laurie. We had all been dealt difficult hands since coming together as a family. Our individual problems filled a Pandora's box we kept locked, hoping they would resolve themselves. The problem seemed to be that one problem led to another, unleashing the worst in us. Dave's post–law firm depression ebbed and flowed with the change in San Francisco's famed microclimates. Laurie's almost manic pace took on the semblance of escape. Collectively, the bad times often outweighed the good ones. Sanity would have demanded we walk away from a relationship we seemed to have forgotten to leave. Love is not enough, we tried to convince ourselves.

But love was enough. Our love alone allowed us to survive the emotional roller coaster of life together, my mind rationalized as I sought to find the José Zuniga who was cowering within, a sobbing, dejected adolescent who was told that, "men don't kiss, hug, or love each other" by the only man he loved.

Although not fully recovered from the emotional blows dealt me in twenty-four years of life, although I have not yet healed, I am confident my emergence from the cocoon that was the Soldier of the Year will hasten my healing and set me free. Torie Osborn warned me to avoid living the schizophrenic life of José Zuniga, the myth. No one warned me—I doubt they knew—that the amorphous broken soul residing within my fully functioning shell would have to re-create José Zuniga the man while bolstering his sagging resolve. Reality struck as I sat with Elizabeth Birch on the patio of a home tucked unobtrusively into picturesque middle-of-nowhere northern California.

"It would be great to have you on the board," the co-chair of the

Task Force's board of directors answered my response to her query about my goals and aspirations. "What else?"

I couldn't answer that question. Oh, my God! Depression clouded my thoughts and introduced lethargy and hopelessness. Away from the safe oasis of the cause, there was no haven. The Fight was a prison to which I willingly returned to bury my emotional burdens. I had been so blind—blinded by the obsession to conquer, protected from the swift kick that could crumble my purpose and render me a pathetic fool.

"Any regrets?" Elizabeth asked me not too long ago.

Elizabeth, I can honestly answer that no regrets blemish my heart. Unlike those who live their lives in blinding denial, I am no longer blind; nor am I bound by the paralysis of guilt that takes away the hope and color in life.

I have become what I should have been allowed to become years before—my own person. I have learned what it means to have my life, allow Dave to have his, allow Laurie to have hers, and enjoy the incredible overlap of our lives together. Perhaps the hardest lesson learned, and one that applies to our community, was to accept responsibility for my life and stop trying to assign it to my lovers.

More than a year after the Soldier of the Year's demise, I feel I can put to rest that tormented past, reap the rewards of my evolving existence, and fight for what I still believe to be just and right. I hope I'm right.

Romeo's days were full of dreaming, flowers, and poetry. Before I was a warrior, all my joy came out of the quest for love. How ironic to disavow the metaphoric parallels I forged in my youth to explain a love forbidden, literary devices buttressing my lonely life and rendering everyday life an unwelcome intrusion. Nothing, the young lover convinced himself, was worth letting Juliet's love slip through his fingers; death was not too much to have to pay.

I believe that if the most beautiful love story I have ever lived should ever end, I will never love again with such intensity nor be loved with equal devotion. I have learned that death—whether by means of poison or trying to be for each other what we aren't for ourselves—is too high a price to pay. That final lesson, mastered with tears of both pain and rapture, sanctions my belief that like the hundreds of storms the three of us have weathered together over the last year, this too shall pass.

Self-delusion? Denial? No, I assured my psychiatrist and in turn myself. Hope. Faith. Love. Bear with me . . .

APPENDICES

APPENDIX A

Petty Officer Keith Meinhold is a Navy sonar instructor discharged after announcing his homosexuality on "ABC's World News Tonight" in May 1992. He filed suit in federal court, resulting in a historic decision reinstating him to active duty in January 1993.

Navy Lieutenant Junior Grade Tracy Thorne is a Navy A-6 Intruder aviator. In May 1992, he came out on "ABC News' Nightline." The Navy immediately began discharge proceedings. Thorne remains on active duty pending discharge.

The Reverend Dusty Carolyn Pruitt is a former Army captain who admitted her lesbianism in a 1983 *Los Angeles Times* interview. She was discharged and then filed a legal complaint which resulted in a landmark decision directing the Army to substantiate the basis for her incompatibility for military service.

Joseph Steffan is a former U.S. Naval Academy midshipman who had advanced to the position of battalion commander, making him one of the academy's ten highest-ranking cadets in 1987. When confronted by academy officials questioning his sexuality, Steffan told the truth and was not allowed to graduate. Steffan's case awaits a rehearing by the U.S. Court of Appeals for the District of Columbia. He wrote the book *Honor Bound*.

Army Colonel Margarethe Cammermeyer was chief nurse of the Washington National Guard in 1987 when she was tapped to become the chief nurse for the National Guard of the United States. A highly decorated

303

officer, Cammermeyer's twenty-eight-year military career included a tour of duty in Vietnam, for which she was awarded the Bronze Star Medal. Asked by a Defense Investigative Service agent whether she was homosexual, Cammermeyer answered affirmatively. The Department of the Army moved against Cammermeyer and began proceedings to withdraw recognition of her rank and her military retirement benefits.

Army Staff Sergeant Perry J. Watkins was drafted into service in 1968 despite acknowledging his homosexuality. He reacknowledged it again when he reenlisted in 1971 and again during a hearing in 1975 that concluded he could stay in the Army despite being gay. It wasn't until February 1981 that the Army reacted to his homosexuality by revoking his security clearance. The Army eventually discharged him under the Defense Department's new regulation banning homosexuals from service, DoD Directive 1332.14. In the case of *Sergeant Perry J. Watkins* v. *United States Army et al.*, a three-member panel of judges from the U.S. Court of Appeals in San Francisco ruled in February 1988 not only that Watkins should be reinstated, but that the government had failed to show how their anti-gay regulation served any "compelling government interest." The Defense Department appealed to the Supreme Court, which ruled in November 1990 that the appeals court decision would stand.

APPENDIX B

Excerpts from the main sections of the Pentagon inspector general's report about sexual misconduct at the 1991 Tailhook Association convention in Reno, Nevada:

—**Executive Summary.** Many attendees viewed the annual conference as a type of "free-fire zone" wherein they could act indiscriminately and without fear of censure or retribution in matters of sexual conduct and drunkenness. Some of the Navy's most senior officers were knowledgeable as to the excess practiced at Tailhook '91 and, by their inaction, those officers served to condone and even encourage the type of behavior that occurred there.

Our investigation disclosed that 83 women and 7 men were assaulted during the three days of the convention.... In total, 117 officers were implicated in one or more incidents of indecent assault, indecent exposure, conduct unbecoming an officer or failure to act in a proper leadership capacity while at Tailhook '91. Further, 51 individuals were found to have made false statements to us during our investigation.... It should also be noted that the number of individuals in all types of misconduct or inappropriate behavior was more widespread than these figures would suggest. Furthermore, several hundred other officers were aware of the misconduct and chose to ignore it.

—**Witnesses and Navy Cooperation.** Most of the officers interviewed responded in a serious and cooperative fashion. Other officers were far less cooperative and attempted to limit their responses so as to reveal only minimal information....

The evidence revealed that other officers deliberately provided false information to us. Some squadron members appeared to maintain unified responses that were often contradicted by the testimony of witnesses not assigned to those squadrons. Similarly, individual officers specifically lied to us about their activities unless directly confronted with conflicting evidence.

—Indecent Assaults. By most accounts, there were few women in attendance at earlier conventions. According to most descriptions, Tailhook conventions in earlier year were largely "stag" affairs. Reportedly, "unwritten" rules prohibited officers from bringing spouses or cameras to Tailhook. There are also reports that during earlier years, a large proportion of the women attending Tailhook conventions could be described as prostitutes or "groupies."

The nature of the gauntlet activities apparently changed some time in the mid- to late-1980s when the gauntlet started to involve males touching women who walked through the hallway. Some witnesses suggested this was a progression from the cheering, catcalls, and ratings of women typical of earlier Tailhook conventions, to more physical contact in which officers would pinch and grab women's breasts, buttocks, and crotch areas as the women attempted to traverse the hallway.

A male Navy lieutenant described one unsuspecting woman's passage through the gauntlet. He states that . . . while standing in the third-floor hallway in the area of the elevators, he heard people chanting and pounding on something in a rhythmic drumming manner. He observed approximately 200 men lined up along the hallway walls.

He compared the activity to a high school football practice type of gauntlet. He saw a woman enter and it seemed to him that "she did not understand it was a gauntlet." As she attempted to walk through, he observed her being "groped and molested." She was obviously "not enjoying it" and "was pushing hands away from places she did not want them." As she approached the gauntlet, he "saw a look of fear in her eyes. She fought her way through the gauntlet and then busted out the side through a suite." He said the look of fear in the woman's eyes caused him to realize the gauntlet was not just a playful situation and he became concerned for other women in the hallway and vicinity of the gauntlet.

Another female civilian victim told us that, as she walked up the hallway, at least seven men suddenly attacked her. They pulled down her "tube top" and grabbed at her exposed breasts while she attempted to cover herself with her arms. She fell to the ground and the assault continued.

She bit several of her attackers in an attempt to stop their assault. After a few moments, they stopped their attack and she was allowed to get up from the floor. She turned and looked back down the hallway and observed another woman screaming and fighting her way down the hallway as she too was attacked.

—**Indecent Exposure.** One form of indecent exposure that occurred at Tailhook '91 involved "streaking," a term used by most witnesses to describe the actions of males who removed their clothing and walked or ran nude past onlookers. . . .

Another form of indecent exposure, referred to as "mooning," involved individuals baring their buttocks within view of other attendees. . . .

The third form of indecent exposure engaged in by naval aviators . . . involved publicly exposing their testicles, commonly referred to in the naval aviation community as "ballwalking." Eighty individuals reported to us that they witnessed ballwalking at Tailhook '91. . . . We identified 14 military officers who ballwalked during the convention. . . .

The terms "belly shots" and "navel shots" describe the practice of drinking alcohol (typically tequila) out of people's navels. . . .

Witnesses and participants reported that three male officers drank belly shots from the navel of a female officer. This occurred in the VAW-110 suite on the same night the female officer had her legs shaved by two of the male officers. The female officer reported that a few of the women who participated in belly shots wore short dresses and no undergarment and exposed themselves while doing belly shots. . . .

Another type of assaultive behavior that occurred on the third floor of the Hilton Hotel during Tailhook '91 involved individuals biting attendees on the buttocks. That activity was commonly referred to by witnesses as "butt biting" or "sharking." The origin of butt biting is unknown, but one Mariner major reported that, in his squadron, "sharking" was a common activity between males and females dating back about 20 years.

—**Other Improper Activity.** Over 200 witnesses told us they observed leg shaving at the 1991 symposium. This activity . . . involved the shaving of women's legs and pubic areas by male aviators. Our investigation disclosed that leg shaving has been an element of unit parties in the Navy for years. . . .

—**Officer Attitudes and Leadership Issues.** Tailhook '91 is the culmination of a long-term failure of leadership in naval aviation. What happened at Tailhook '91 was destined to happen sooner or later in the "can you top this" atmosphere that appeared to increase with each succeeding convention. Senior aviation leadership seemed to ignore the deteriorating standards of behavior and failed to deal with the increasing disorderly, improper, and promiscuous behavior.

APPENDIX C

Demands of the 1993 March on Washington for Lesbian, Gay & Bi[sexual] Equal Rights and Liberation:

1. We demand passage of a Lesbian, Gay, Bisexual and Transgender civil rights bill and an end to discrimination by state and federal governments including the military; repeal of all sodomy laws and other laws that criminalize private sexual expression between consenting adults.

2. We demand massive increase in funding for AIDS education, research, and patient care; universal access to health care including alternative therapies; and an end to sexism in medical research and health care.

3. We demand legislation to prevent discrimination against lesbians, gays, bisexuals, and transgendered people in the areas of family diversity, custody, adoption, and foster care and that the definition of family includes the full diversity of all family structures.

4. We demand full and equal inclusion of lesbians, gays, bisexuals, and transgendered people in the educational system, and inclusion of lesbian, gay, bisexual, and transgender studies in multicultural curricula.

5. We demand the right to reproductive freedom and choice, to control our own bodies, and an end to sexist discrimination.

6. We demand an end to racial and ethnic discrimination in all forms.

7. We demand an end to discrimination and violent oppression based on actual or perceived sexual orientation/identification, race, religion, identity, sex and gender expression, disability, age, class, or AIDS/HIV infection.

APPENDIX D

Dear Joe,

Let me begin by taking the time to thank you for your visit to my office last week. What a pleasure and inspiration it was to meet you. Joe, you have brought great credit to the concept that one can be both professional and gay. More than anyone I know, your conduct will assure a number of young people and their parents that people who happen to be gay are normal, professionally motivated, and excelling young people.

There is so much I want to say to you. I suspect that since we have talked, things have not been all that easy. Certainly, the Army must be troubled by taking such action against a young man of your status and performance. While we hope that most of your friends and colleagues will be supportive of your actions, I know you have been forced to see the real, and yes the ugly side of some.

As a Republican member of Congress, I too have shared many of the struggles you have faced. The big difference is that I was "outed" two years ago. That means you have simply no chance to choose how or what people say about you. Those who seek to embarrass you can make life quite difficult.

For me, the entire process of accepting who I am was a long and difficult one. As you know from our discussions, I come from a large, middle-class, Midwestern family. Religion and Republican politics have both played a large part in my family. So for most of them, accepting me for who I am took time. . . . It is certainly an evolutionary process. Being in politics, I think they were most afraid of the witch-hunts and personal defamation that my opponents could throw against me.

311

When I was outed, I sought to carefully project my words, not to help me, but to protect the thousands like me who seek to separate their personal and professional lives. It is exactly like I told the Human Rights Campaign Fund in a speech, and as you exemplified in your actions last week regarding the military. Our goal is to judge people by their conduct professionally, not their personal status.

All of this has caused me to consider long and hard my professional and religious tenets. First, you should know, I have found most of my colleagues to be very supportive of me based upon my professional conduct. Second, I have been lucky enough to have an unbelievably supportive pastor, who is an ex-Marine Corps chaplain, make it clear to me that the Bible does not condemn gays. And he has spoken from the pulpit that on the issue of gays in the military, the Bible is clear on two accounts only: We are instructed to love thy neighbor, and we are instructed to do justice.

On the issue of Republican politics, I told you about the book I have been reading, *Lincoln on Democracy*. Having read this book there is no doubt in my mind that if Abraham Lincoln were alive today, he would certainly be supporting the rights of everyone, including gays, to be judged only on their conduct and performance, and not their sexual orientation. When people suggest to you that it is not in the military's interest to allow gays in the military, that the government has a legitimate purpose in limiting the personal lives of soldiers, refer them to Lincoln's comments in the book. Finally, throughout the book, you will find that Lincoln's total political philosophy was based upon the Declaration of Independence, *"We hold these truths to be self-evident, that all men are created equal. And they are endowed by their Creator with the unalienable rights of life, liberty, and the pursuit of happiness."* [In an August 24, 1855, letter defending his antislavery position] Lincoln summarizes the implications of this phrase for all of us by saying: "As a nation, we began by declaring that '*all men were created equal.*' We now practically read it 'all men are created equal, *except negroes.*' When the Know-Nothings get control, it will read 'all men are created equal except negroes, *and foreigners, and Catholics.*' When it comes to this I should prefer emigrating to some country where they make no pretense of loving liberty; to Russia, for instance, where despotism can be taken pure, and without the base alloy of hypocrisy."

In that paragraph, I believe, he answers the question you asked so eloquently in your statements at the March. Do we mean to give the American dream only to white heterosexual men? Can we exclude blacks, foreigners, Catholics, or even gays? I don't think so.

Joe, you have become a hero to me through your quiet courage and distinguished personal action. Hopefully, I can work with you to professionally correct this legal wrong before us. Likewise, however, remember I offer my personal friendship based on similar challenges on both a personal and professional basis.

Representative Steve Gunderson (R-Wisc.)
Member of Congress

APPENDIX E

Department of the Army, Written Reprimand, Re: Specialist Zuniga, José M., Headquarters Company, Headquarters Command Battalion, Presidio of San Francisco, California.

1. On the weekend of 24 and 25 April you allowed yourself to be photographed in the Army Dress Blue Uniform. You made yourself available for these photographs as part of a public announcement on your part wherein you clearly represented yourself to the public and the media as a highly decorated soldier. Among the awards and decorations you wore while being photographed was the ribbon for the Meritorious Service Medal. You have never been awarded that decoration. By wearing that ribbon, you knowingly and wrongfully misled the people we serve, dishonored yourself, and subjected the integrity and honor of your fellow soldiers to question. That you wore the ribbon under circumstances clearly demonstrating your desire to further your personal goals and to inflate your military stature in the eyes of the American public and the media is particularly despicable. Such an action constitutes nothing more than lying to those who have placed their trust in the Armed Forces, and is completely unworthy of one who aspired to serve the United States as a soldier.

2. In deciding this matter, I have considered everything you presented to me at the hearing and your memorandum of 13 May 1993. I find your claim that you innocently believed yourself to be entitled to the award to be so inherently improbable and completely unsupported by the evidence as to be impossible of belief.

While you were told that you had been nominated for a Meritorious Service Medal, you were also told, by the individual who submitted your nomination, that it was unlikely that you would officially be presented the award before you arrived at your new duty assignment in Korea.... In the statement you presented to me at the hearing, you indicate you were conscious of the timing issue involved in wearing the award on 24 April 1993. This shows a knowledge on your part of the seriousness of wearing an award to which you are not entitled. In light of this, I find it extremely curious that you did not make inquiry about the status of the award to the noncommissioned officer who submitted you for the award, whom you indicate had told you he would expedite it. Further, I am convinced that you, as a noncommissioned officer and Sixth U.S. Army Soldier of the Year, were aware that, until an authorization order is prepared and executed, no award is approved, and you have never received an authorization order for this award. Given the number of awards you have previously received, it is clear to me that you understood how the awards system functions. Based on these facts, the unavoidable conclusion must be that you knowingly wore an award to which you were not entitled. I must further conclude that you did so with the desire to mislead those who would see you in uniform.

3. You are, hereby, reprimanded for failing to meet the standards of integrity and honesty expected of soldier of the U.S. Army. Through dishonesty and placing your own personal objectives above the truth and the duties of a noncommissioned officer, you have demonstrated that you are unfit to continue as a leader of soldiers. This reprimand is imposed as part of the nonjudicial punishment action taken on 13 May 1993 under the provisions of Article 15 of the Uniform Code of Military Justice. This reprimand will be appended to and filed with that document.

Wayne C. Agness
Lieutenant Colonel, Infantry

APPENDIX F

March 15, 1994

The Honorable Bill Clinton
President of the United States
The White House
1600 Pennsylvania Avenue
Washington, D.C. 20500

Mr. President:

I am writing you on behalf of thousands of gay, lesbian, and bisexual service members who have either lost faith in your administration or lost hope that our community will recover from a "defeating" blow to our unfinished struggle for equality.

Mr. President, I was the 1992 Sixth U.S. Army Soldier of the Year you referred to in a speech delivered in Cleveland, Ohio, while people like Senator Sam Nunn were applying hot pincers to a raw nerve in America. On the night of April 24, 1993, before thousands of my brothers and sisters gathered in Old Postal Square on the eve of the March on Washington, I publicly announced I was gay. Two major factors contributed to my decision. Foremost was the need to put an end to the hypocritical lie I was living as a "straight" service member. Contributing was the glimmer of hope you sparked in my community . . . the oft-repeated "vision" of gay men, lesbians, and bisexuals in your tableaux of America.

The press immediately propelled the story of a decorated Persian Gulf veteran using his career as a weapon against an irrational, destructive fifty-year-old ban to the front pages of national and international newspapers. I was honorably discharged at midnight May 20, 1993. The following day I began a four-month national speaking tour in which I told my story, one not much unlike that of thousands others, to anyone who would listen. Mr. President, Americans were listening . . . in Colorado, Florida, Michigan, Ohio, Texas, and every other state I visited, they listened, asked questions, and I'm proud to say some stalwart opponents of lifting the ban announced a change of heart.

Your announcement July 19 was a bitter disappointment for reasons that have been expressed ad nauseam by the leadership in my community. For me, though, your announcement before an auditorium full of military brass boiled down to a split-the-difference compromise the commander in chief of the U.S. Armed Forces was forced to accept by Mr. Nunn.

Should you be inclined to stop reading this letter for fear it is one whose sole purpose is to harangue you, I urge you to continue reading because that is not my goal. I have learned in my crash course on politics that the rhetoric of rancor and bitterness does nothing to advance gay rights. We stand a better chance attacking the strategy or the issue or the verbiage . . . never losing sight of who the real enemy is. Mr. President, I have not lost hope that you stand with us in this fight. Just as the concentric rings of California's redwoods reveal years of drought and rainfall through the ages, so the pages of history will record that bigotry and hatred failed to cripple your presidency. . . . They will also record, however, that those legions succeeded, if only temporarily, to coerce our government to sanction discrimination against its own citizens.

Mr. President, allow me to share a thought that I feel vividly captures the pivotal moment in history we are living. Annals tell us that the most visible symbol of the Renaissance of the Roman Catholic Church during the sixteenth and early seventeenth centuries was the destruction of Old Saint Peter's and the erection in its place, in a more classical idiom, of the famous basilica now standing in Saint Peter's Square. This was an act of colossal self-assurance that could only, perhaps, have been initiated by a man who displayed a willingness to dispense with medieval traditions. Pope Julius II, against the tired and corrupt usages of the time, committed himself to shedding light, instead of casting darkness. Centuries later a ray of that light still catches a visitor's eye as Bernini's seventeenth-century "art" penetrates darkness. In your State of the Union address, you again expressed your vision of a new American community. Forgive me for quoting from your speech, "Let us weave these sturdy threads into a new American community that once more stands strong against the forces of despair and evil because everybody has a chance to walk into a better tomorrow." Mr. President, we have not all lost faith in you. Out of our commitment to a vision larger than ourselves we can achieve victory. . . . America begs for a leader to pull it out of the darkness of despair and evil.

José M. Zuniga

Appendix G

THE WHITE HOUSE

WASHINGTON

May 11, 1994

Mr. José M. Zuniga
3029 Market Street
San Francisco, California   94114

Dear José:

Thank you for your letter and your comments about my Administration's efforts to secure equal rights for all Americans. I appreciate your candor.

Few issues in recent times have spurred the kind of debate that has occurred since the time I undertook an examination of our nation's policy toward homosexuals serving in the military. My responsibilities as President and Commander in Chief oblige me to protect and preserve our individual constitutional liberties while maintaining Armed Forces that are prepared to defend our national interests and promote our security. In adopting the present policy, I believe I have done my best to meet both objectives.

I welcome your constructive criticism, and I hope that I can count on your support as I continue moving forward in my work on behalf of all Americans.

Sincerely,

Bill Clinton